WHAT MAKES

WHAT MAKES US HUMAN?

Edited by
Charles Pasternak

ONEWORLD

OXFORD

A Oneworld Book

Published by Oneworld Publications, 2007
Copyright © this edition Charles Pasternak, 2007
Reprinted, 2009

ISBN 978–1–85168–519–6

Typeset by Jayvee, Trivandrum, India
Cover design by Mungo Designs
Printed and bound in Great Britain by T.J. International Ltd, Padstow, Cornwall

Oneworld Publications
185 Banbury Road
Oxford OX2 7AR
England
www.oneworld-publications.com

Mixed Sources
Product group from well-managed
forests and other controlled sources
www.fsc.org   Cert no. SGS-COC-2482
© 1996 Forest Stewardship Council

Learn more about Oneworld. Join our mailing list to
find out about our latest titles and special offers at:

www.oneworld-publications.com

Contents

Summary

W*hat makes us human?* is based on the talks presented at a symposium with that title, organised by the Oxford International Biomedical Centre in conjunction with the Royal Institution, in Oxford in March 2006. The five distinguished speakers on that occasion have now been joined by a further ten experts, giving the subject the broadest coverage possible. The background of the contributors, from Italy and New Zealand, from UK and USA, ranges across anthropology, biochemistry, medicine, neuroscience, philosophy, psychology, and religion. It is not often that you get writers of the calibre of Susan Blackmore, Walter Bodmer, Michael Corballis, Robin Dunbar, Maurizio Gentilucci, Richard Harries, David Hulme, Stephen Oppenheimer, Charles Pasternak, Thomas Suddendorf, Ian Tattersall, Andrew Whiten, Lewis Wolpert, and Richard Wrangham under one cover. Click on any of these names on the internet and the breadth of their erudition will be obvious. Several of the articles present new scientific data, yet each is written at a level that will appeal to a lay readership as much as to an academic one. Is it our cognitive abilities, our use of tools, our story-telling, our beliefs, our curiosity, our ability to cook, our culture, that make us human? Are we half ape or half angel? *What makes us human?* will not disappoint.

Foreword

What Makes Us Human? – An Introduction

Walter Bodmer

There are at least as many answers to this provocative and searching question as there are authors of this compendium. In the various articles you will find suggestions that include the 'spirit of man', referring particularly to religion, speech and not just language, imitation and 'mimetics', cooking, high levels of cognitive ability, causal belief, that humans are symbolic creatures, innate curiosity and the desire to know, mental time travel, and the ability to read other's minds. These all have cognitive ability as a common thread and, deriving from this, high-level development of language and cultural transmission.

Genetic differences

For a biologist, who is a geneticist interested in evolution, the obvious explanation for what makes us human must lie within the genetic differences that distinguish *Homo sapiens* from other species, especially chimpanzees. The data now available on DNA sequences of many species, including the complete DNA sequences of humans, chimpanzees, and several other mammalian species, already are enough to place *Homo sapiens* in the "chimpanzee family", and separated even from the other great apes. Though the human and chimpanzee sequences are very similar, sharing perhaps as much as 99 per cent of their sequence, that still leaves plenty of room for a large number of functionally significant differences. Even if only 1 per cent of protein coding genes show such a difference, that still means there are as many as 250 genes whose difference may contribute to the greater cognitive ability of humans. In addition, the new knowledge that there may be at least an equal amount of DNA sequence that codes for functionally active RNA that is not directly involved in protein production, would at least double the number of potential functionally relevant differences between humans and their nearest great ape relatives. Of course, many of these differences may be in genes which are most unlikely to contribute to brain function in a way that could influence cognitive ability such as, for example, those controlling household cellular functions, aspects of immune response to infections, or basic metabolic processes. Nevertheless, I believe that there is plenty of scope within the DNA sequence differences we can now see between humans and chimpanzees, to account for those features that we might consider distinctive to humans as compared to chimpanzees.

Every species has, more or less by definition, a unique DNA sequence signature that distinguishes it from every other species. Our challenge, however, is to discern those human features which make *Homo sapiens* qualitatively distinct from all other species, especially with respect to its cognitive and related abilities.

There is no such thing as 'a gene for' any particular characteristic. What must be sought is the variation in the sequences of those genes, or the versions of the genes, that determine, or contribute to determining the particular characteristic differences we see between humans and their nearest relatives. So the challenge is to find those genetic variations that are unique to humans and which really matter for establishing the key features that make us human and in some way qualitatively different from all other animals.

There is no consensus as to the existence of any anatomically defined area of the brain that is clearly and uniquely associated with human attributes. However, recent work by Pollard and colleagues (Pollard et al., 2006) on the analysis of human, chimpanzee and other mammalian DNA sequences has shown how it may be possible to identify those DNA sequences that may be most relevant to human uniqueness. From a comprehensive analysis of a large amount of DNA sequence data, they identified those sequences which had hardly changed over hundreds of millions of years, until the split between *Homo sapiens* and chimpanzees. This led to the definition of a set of 49 regions of DNA sequence that were very similar in a wide range of mammalian species, but which had evolved extraordinarily rapidly in the separation of humans from the great apes, including especially the chimpanzees. One of these was shown to be an RNA determining gene that was highly expressed in the developing neo-cortex. This, and the other newly defined DNA sequences, are obvious candidates for contributing to the unique cognitive abilities of humans, but the challenge remains of establishing their true functions.

Until we have answers from such biologically oriented studies, we must continue to seek the answers as to what makes us human from more general observations on human and animal behaviour, in the most general sense. Furthermore, we cannot assume that the whole answer lies simply in the genes, though it surely must be the evolved genetic differences that contain the potential for human cognitive uniqueness and other associated distinctive human features. I think it is important to emphasise that, at least in my view, only a subset of genes, perhaps mainly those not involved directly in significant cellular and organismal functions, are really selfish in the Richard Dawkins sense. Natural selection operates on the whole organism, and we therefore see its effects on a particular gene as a 'marginal effect', in the language of experimental design, as introduced by the great statistician and co-founder of the field of population genetics R. A. Fisher, namely averaging over all other genetic differences. We must ultimately seek the explanation for the evolution of the differences that led to an enormously increased cognitive ability in the conventional actions of natural selection. However, there is clearly a huge number of attributes that are a by-product of this increase, such as musical and mathematical ability, which cannot all be the direct result of natural selection.

Cognitive abilities

As I have already pointed out, a huge increase in cognitive ability is the most obvious underlying common feature to almost all the attributes that have been suggested to make us human. These include, in particular, language and speech which have enabled a considerable increase in the rate and efficiency of cultural evolution. Paleontological data clearly suggest that increasing brain size has been a major feature of the evolution of the human brain. However, it is clear that while an increase in brain size may be a necessary requirement for increase in cognitive abilities, it is not sufficient. There must be many increases in the complexity of brain function, at the level of cellular changes and interconnections, that have made the ultimate increase in cognitive abilities possible.

A persuasive argument, that cooking is unique to humans, is made by Richard Wrangham. I have no doubt, however, that he would not claim that this is the unique feature of humanness. It is just one of the many consequences of increased cognitive ability. The ability to cook follows from the discovery of how to make fire. Darwin argued that "The art of making fire ... is probably the greatest discovery, excepting language, ever made by man" (Darwin 1871). While fire may well have been a unique discovery, language surely must have evolved over a period of time and speech required the evolution of changes in the anatomy of the larynx, probably dependent on the evolution of bi-pedalism. The ability to make fire probably also depended on the evolution of bi-pedalism and subsequently, as a consequence of freeing the hands, on the evolution of the flexible thumb. As Wrangham points out, cooking improves food and reduces the energy expenditure involved in digestion, and allows a broadening of the diet. The evolutionary response to the dietary changes is probably seen, for example, in the smaller stomach of humans. It appears that "even wild chimpanzees take advantage of natural fires to eat foods that have been cooked by chance" (Brewer 1978). The current evidence suggests that Neanderthals had fire and so are likely to have cooked. This is one of many examples where Neanderthals had human attributes not found in chimpanzees. I should have thought that, in addition to benefiting the diet, cooking plays an important role in killing potential pathogens in raw food, especially parasites that are not bacteria or viruses which may have been the most important pathogens in early human societies. Infectious diseases are of comparable importance as components of natural selection, as are diet and predation.

Robin Dunbar suggests that there are different levels of cognitive ability, and that humans, uniquely amongst animals, have achieved a 'fifth order' of cognitive ability. By this he means an ability to follow through a five-fold sequence of causes and effects. He proposes that Neanderthals may have had a fourth order of cognitive ability, and that this would be enough for the evolution of some sort of religion. This, then, would be another remarkable ability common to

Neanderthals and *Homo sapiens*, but presumably not present in any of the great apes. Lewis Wolpert's claim that "Humans unlike other primates have a belief in physical cause and effect which enables the acquisition of new interactions and led to technology" just seems to me to be another facet of this higher level of cognitive ability in humans as compared to chimpanzees. There can surely be no doubt, even from causal observation of pets at home and in the field, that animals do have the ability, at least to some extent, of assessing physical causes and their effects. The difference between them and humans is a matter of degree.

A matter of degree and combinations

'Innate curiosity' is Charles Pasternak's choice for a unique human attribute. But, as he himself admits, there is innate curiosity in animals, but not to the same extent. He suggests a combination of four inherited attributes that makes humans unique:

1. Bipedalism – freeing the hands for other uses
2. Flexible thumb – a corollary of bi-pedalism
3. Voice box for speech
4. Increased brain size

All of these I have already mentioned, and in each case it is, again, a matter of degree.

For each of these features, and possibly many others, if they are measured on some quantitative scale, humans on average lie at the upper extremes. Thus, if all such variables were plotted in a multidimensional space, humans would 'cluster' in a region of the space widely separated from all other animals, even though in individual features there might be some overlap between certain species and humans.

The appeal to an unknown phenomenon: religion and reductionism

The complexity of the human organism and its cognitive ability, reflected in the gap between the understanding of the mind as compared to the brain, leads to a natural tendency to appeal to unknown phenomena as a form of explanation. For some, this is expressed in the form of spiritualism and religious beliefs, and the mind-brain distinction is paralleled by that between soul and body. Others may argue that some as yet unknown, but perhaps eventually knowable, phenomenon will provide the nexus between mind and brain, and so explain the nature of consciousness.

As Richard Harries asserts, there can be no scientific proof of the existence or non-existence of God. So long as religious beliefs remain consistent with prevailing scientific understanding, there can be no claim of an inconsistency between religious beliefs and the existence of God on the one hand, and science and its discoveries and methods on the other.

However, this requirement for consistency between science and religion is clearly very demanding. Thus Richard Harries argues against what he calls extreme reductionism, interpreted as "we are nothing but our genes" and "the whole is greater than the sum of the parts". I can hardly imagine that any self-respecting biologist or geneticist would ever have such an extreme view of the role of genes, nor would they contradict the view that the whole is more than the sum of the parts. The more we learn about fundamental molecular mechanisms, the clearer it becomes that almost all genetic functions interact with many, many other functions, and hardly any, if any at all, function on their own. In addition, it is clear that the environment, however assessed, has a huge impact on development. The environment involves a large element of chance that is essentially unpredictable, but that can be modelled using stochastic approaches. This element of chance plays a major role not only in an individual's development, but also in evolution, as evidenced, for example, by the enormous influence of major climatic changes and of meteorite impacts with the earth. Thus, reductionism has a much broader potential than appears to be envisaged by Richard Harries. There are many phenomena which we understand today in scientific and reductionist terms, including the whole mechanism of inheritance, which were simply mysteries well into the nineteenth century. There is, therefore, an obvious risk in assuming that the human mysteries of today will not be solved by the scientific method tomorrow.

Were Neanderthals human?

It is clear from archeological evidence that Neanderthals shared many features with *Homo sapiens* that are not found in any other species. They may well have had language, they had stone tools, they probably cooked their food at least to some extent, and, following Robin Dunbar, they may well have had a level of cognitive ability that allowed them to develop some form of religion. In our quantitative multidimensional plot, they would surely cluster well away from any extant mammalian species, though it is, I think, impossible to say whether they would be well separated from modern humans. Were they still extant today, would we consider them human? Would that decision be affected if they were distinctly less developed cognitively than modern humans? Would we grant them the same rights and privileges that are granted to all people, whatever their disabilities, in a modern civilised society? Would it be possible to educate Neanderthals to be acceptable members of present-day human societies, or would we need to give them special care and attention, as we do for many of those with severe mental impairment. Such individuals may often have cognitive impairments that take them below the level of Neanderthals, or even perhaps chimpanzees, but we nevertheless, in a modern civilised society, treat them as human. If Neanderthals are considered as human, when in hominid evolution was the threshold to humanity crossed? Perhaps it is fortunate that we do not have to face such decisions, though the issue of how we treat higher primates, the attitude to which has changed enormously even over the last fifty years, comes very close to that problem.

Altruism, group selection and cultural evolution

The late and remarkable naturalist and evolutionist, William Hamilton, expanded on the evolution of altruism, following the initial ideas put forward by R. A. Fisher and J. B. S. Haldane in the 1930s. Hamilton showed how altruism would, in general, work if it operated amongst genetically related individuals. Even casual field observations show remarkable examples of cooperation, for example within a related pack of African wild dogs. Outside humans, it seems that altruism amongst unrelated individuals is rare but not absent, as it is evident in Meerkats. However, it does seem that altruism amongst, at least not closely related individuals, may be quite common in human societies. Cooperation between individuals in small groups is certainly seen in modern hunter-gatherer societies, and may be presumed to have been quite common in early hominids, even before the evolution of *Homo sapiens*.

It has generally been assumed that group selection is a weak force in evolution, as compared to the effects of natural section on the individual. However, I believe that the wide-spread existence of cooperation and altruism between unrelated individuals in human societies may mean that group selection has played a much larger role in hominid evolution than is generally assumed. Robin Dunbar comments that religion "is a particularly effective way in which one can try to create a sense of belonging, 'groupishness'". That sense may be very important for the survival and success of groups in competition with other groups, and so could naturally be a basis for the evolution of religion. This evolution would be cultural, and not biological, though it is the preceding evolution of cognitive ability that makes this cultural evolution possible. Even in modern historical times, the relative world-wide dominance of a technology and many aspects of culture based on European society, and indeed the widespread use of the English language, could be interpreted as examples of group selection based largely on British colonisation over the last few hundred years.

Cultural transmission is not unique to humans. It was seen, for example, in the remarkably rapid spread in the UK of the practice of certain birds to pierce the aluminium tops of milk bottles (in the days when such things were delivered to the door step) to suck out the cream from the top of the bottle. However, cultural evolution, which depends both on transmission and innovation just as biological evolution depends on Mendelian inheritance and genetic variability, is hugely more developed in humans than in any other animals. It seems doubtful that the brain has evolved significantly, in biological or genetical terms, since the development of the potential for sophisticated language, which must have been a major factor in enabling the possibility of comparatively rapid cultural evolution.

The evolution of the use of clothing, after nakedness had evolved to help avoid parasite infections (an idea put forward by Pagel and Bodmer, 2003), is another example of significant cultural evolution. This development must have been essential for survival in the colder, mainly northern, climates to which *Homo sapiens* migrated after the end of the last ice age.

Pivotal changes, whether in biological or cultural evolution, such as the enlargement of the brain or the discovery of fire, allow subsequent rapid evolutionary changes to take place. That seems to me to be the reason why the pace of both biological and cultural evolution is not uniform. Pivotal changes will be uncommon and their occurrence largely determined by chance.

The key feature of cultural evolution is horizontal transmission within generations, rather than just vertical transmission from generation to generation. The horizontal cultural transmission process in humans, which is largely dependent on their superior cognitive abilities, is enormously more rapid than conventional biological evolution. This undoubtedly is the major determinant of the extraordinarily rapid development of human society over the last few thousand years, which are hardly a tick in the usual time frame of the clock of biological evolution. It is especially during this process that I believe that group selection has played a much more important role than is usually assumed.

Much of the extreme development of human culture, such as music, science, mathematics, and literature, may simply be a by-product of our superior cognitive abilities, which were selected, not to make music or solve complex mathematical problems, but for our better survival and adaptation to rapidly changing environmental conditions. Culture is nowadays largely passed on from generation to generation through education, and language, in one form or another, remains the main vehicle for cultural transmission.

Let us consider as an interesting example of cultural divergence, extant so-called primitive or hunter-gathering tribes, such as are still found in the Amazon basin. They must be presumed to have the same potential for cognitive ability that an educated person, say, in Europe or America has. Yet they will have a totally different culture and associated way of thinking. Nevertheless, it seems almost certain that if a newborn baby from such a tribe were brought up in, say, a typical British family, they would have ways of thinking that were just like other people brought up in that same culture. That surely emphasises the overriding importance of culture in determining our ways of thinking. Widely different human cultures have been superimposed upon the presumed unique cognitive features of humans.

Conclusion

The various chapters of this book contain many suggested attributes that contribute to human uniqueness which raise intriguing questions about the comparisons between human and animal behaviour. Do only humans have humour? Is the parrot that seems to be making fun of you not just doing it for the fun of it? And what about its extraordinary ability to imitate the human voice?

Is the capacity to show remorse specifically human? Is it only humans that can create an imagined world for themselves? How do we know that other species cannot explore imagined worlds? We have no means of adequate communication, even with chimpanzees, to be able to assess that. Small movements that, for example, dogs make when they are asleep, certainly suggest, as does the existence of REM sleep, that animals can dream. Does this not imply a certain level of imagined world? It is all a matter of degree, as already emphasised.

Sound transmission is the key to a spoken language, and Gentilucci and Corballis suggest that this followed visual communication and is peculiar to humans. But many, if not most animals communicate by sounds. Surely it is more likely that the transition was from sound to visual communication. That is what is suggested in the origin of flexible written languages from pictorial symbols, and, as already emphasised, it is the written language that has been key to the rapidity and fidelity of human cultural transmission.

Is language essential for symbolic thought? Is a chimpanzee really like a 4–5 year old child? How can this be reconciled with the fact that many children at that age have a much more sophisticated development of linguistic ability than any chimpanzee has ever had?

Is the ultimate function of the brain to control movement? While that is clearly a major function of the brain, what about the senses of seeing and hearing and, indeed, quite generally thought processes, even in animals?

And what about Susan Blackmore's memes, which she maintains are now driving evolution? Perhaps that is just another way of emphasising the importance of cultural evolution. Do memes have a selfish life of their own? Is that how the English language has spread throughout the world? It is, however, easy to see how the European-based technology has been advantageous, at least economically, and so ultimately even in terms of survival and perceived quality of life, if not reproductive performance. English, having become the lingua franca of science and technology is bound, therefore, to have had a selective advantage over other languages and has itself evolved to a simpler form for non-native English speakers. These sorts of arguments parallel closely the types of analyses that population geneticists have classically applied to the evolution of genetics differences.

It has been an interesting challenge for me to have had the opportunity to write this introduction and to try and organise my thoughts on human uniqueness, stimulated by the various contributions that follow. There can be no doubt that this book will make you think about the basic question of what makes us human in a new light. You will also, no doubt, make your own choices of what it takes.

Walter Bodmer
January 2007

References

Brewer, S. (1978) *The Forest Dwellers*. Collins, London.

Darwin, C. (1871) The Descent of Man and Selection in Relation to Sex. *Encyclopaedia Britannica*, Chicago.

Pagel, M. and Bodmer, W. (2003) A naked ape would have fewer parasites. *Proc. R. Soc. Lond. B* (Suppl.) 270, S117–S119.

Pollard, K. S., et al. (2006) An RNA gene expressed during cortical development evolved rapidly in humans. *Nature* 443, 167–172.

Contributors

Susan Blackmore

Sue Blackmore is a freelance writer, lecturer and broadcaster, and a Visiting Lecturer at the University of the West of England, Bristol (UK). She has a PhD in parapsychology from the University of Surrey. Her research interests include consciousness, drugs, meditation, and mimetics. Her books include *Beyond the Body* (1982); *Dying to Live* (on near-death experiences, 1993); *In Search of the Light* (autobiography, 1996); and *Test Your Psychic Powers* (with Adam Hart-Davis, 1997). *The Meme Machine* (1999) has been translated into 13 other languages. Her textbook *Consciousness: An Introduction* was published in June 2003 (Hodder UK, OUP New York); and *A Very Short Introduction to Consciousness* in 2005 (OUP). Her latest book is *Conversations on Consciousness* (November 2005, OUP Oxford).

susan.blackmore@blueyonder.co.uk

Walter Bodmer

Sir Walter Bodmer, FRS, FRCPath, is at the Cancer and Immuno-genetics Laboratory, Weatherall Institute of Molecular Medicine, University of Oxford (UK). His interests include an understanding of the genetic pathway leading to colorectal cancer, and the analysis and interpretation of HLA and other markers of diversity in human populations. He obtained his PhD at Cambridge University, and has been Professor of Genetics at Stanford University and at Oxford University. He was Director of Research, later Director General, at the Imperial Cancer Research Fund (now Cancer Research UK) between 1979 and 1996, and Principal of Hertford College, Oxford, from 1996 to 2005. His books include *Our Future Inheritance: Choice or Chance?* (with Alun Jones; Oxford University Press, 1974); and *The Book of*

Man: The Human Genome Project and the Quest to Discover Our Genetic Heritage (with Robin McKie; Prentice Hall, 1995).

walter.bodmer@hertford.ox.ac.uk

Michael Corballis

Michael Corballis, FAPA, FRSNZ, FAAAS, is at the Research Centre for Cognitive Neuroscience, University of Auckland (New Zealand). He obtained his PhD at McGill University. His interests are language, brain function and evolution. He is the author of *Psychology of Left and Right* (with Ivan L. Beale; John Wiley, 1976); *Human Laterality* (Academic Press Inc., 1984); *The Lopsided Ape: Evolution of the Generative Mind* (Oxford University Press, USA, 1991); paperback 1994); *The Descent of Mind: Psychological Perspectives on Hominid Evolution* (with Stephen E. G. Lea, eds.; Oxford University Press, 2000); and *From Hand to Mouth: The Origins of Language* (Princeton University Press, 2002; paperback 2003).

m.corballis@auckland.ac.nz

Robin Dunbar

Robin Dunbar, FBA, heads the Evolutionary Psychology and Behavioural Ecology Research Group at the University of Liverpool (UK). His interests focus on the behavioural ecology of primates and ungulates, the behavioural ecology of humans, and cognitive mechanisms and brain evolution. His books include *Grooming, Gossip and the Evolution of Language* (Faber & Faber and Harvard University Press, 1996); *Primate Conservation Biology* (with Guy Cowlishaw; University of Chicago Press, 2000); *Cousins* (with Louise Barrett; BBC Worldwide, London, 2000); *Human Evolutionary Psychology* (with Louise Barrett and John Lycett; Palgrave/Macmillan, London and Princeton University Press, 2002); and *The Human Story* (Faber & Faber, London, 2004).

rimd@liverpool.ac.uk

Maurizio Gentilucci

Maurizio Gentilucci is Professor of Physiology in the Department of Neuroscience at the Medical Faculty of the University of Parma (Italy). His current research focuses on brain mechanisms involved in visuomotor behaviour and in controlling spoken language and arm gestures.

maurizio.gentilucci@unipr.it

Richard Harries

The Rt Rev Richard Harries retired in 2006 after nineteen years as Bishop of Oxford. He is a Fellow and Honorary Professor of Theology at King's College, London University (UK) and sits on the crossbenches in the House of Lords as Lord Harries of Pentregarth. He chairs the Nuffield Council of Bioethics and is a member of the Human Fertilisation and Embryology Authority (HFEA). He chaired the House of Bishops' Working Party on *Issues of Human Sexuality* and was a member of the Royal Commission on the Reform of the House of Lords. His books include *Christianity and War in a Nuclear Age* (Continuum International Publishing, 1986); *Questioning Belief* (SPCK, 1995); *God Outside the Box: Why Spiritual People Reject Christianity* (SPCK, 2002); and *The Passion in Art* (Ashgate Publishing, 2004). *Public Life and the Place of the Church: Reflections to Honour the Bishop of Oxford* (edited by Michael Brierly; Ashgate Publishing) appeared in 2006. His biography by John Peart-Binns, *Heart in My Head*, is due to be published by Continuum in 2007.

richard.d.harries@googlemail.com

David Hulme

David Hulme has studied Psychology and Philosophy (University of Edinburgh), Theology (Ambassador College, UK) and International Relations (University of Southern California). He holds a doctorate from USC in International Relations, with an emphasis on Foreign Policy and the Middle East. A prolific article writer, his *Identity, Ideology and the Future of Jerusalem*, published by Palgrave-Macmillan in September 2006, speculates on the role that current findings in neuroscience may contribute to social change in that troubled region.

Hulme is currently publisher of the quarterly *Vision* and president of *Vision Media Productions* (VMP), based in Pasadena, California. VMP specializes in documentaries with a unique perspective, challenging viewers to examine the historical and philosophical underpinnings of a wide range of contemporary issues. Its productions have won honours at various international film and video awards competitions.

dhulme@visionmedia.org

Stephen Oppenheimer

Stephen Oppenheimer is at Green College, Oxford (UK). He read medicine at Oxford University, and later worked in New Guinea where he was the first to notice anti-malarial protection conferred by alpha-thalassaemia. That research subsequently led to his focus on the use of genetic markers to track migrations. His interests span archaeology, genetics, geology, and linguistics. His works include *Eden in the East: The Drowned Continent of Southeast Asia* (Phoenix Press, 1999) which became a Channel 4 (UK) TV programme; *The Real Eve: Modern Man's Journey Out of Africa* (Carroll & Graf, 2003) which became a Discovery Channel (UK) TV programme; and *Out of Africa: The Peopling of the World* (Constable and Robinson, 2004). His latest book is *The Origins of the British: A Genetic Detective Story* (Constable & Robinson, 2006).

Charles Pasternak

Charles Pasternak is the Director of the Oxford International Biomedical Centre (OIBC, UK). He read chemistry, followed by a DPhil in biochemistry, at Oxford University. In between he spent two years in National Service (commissioned into the Royal Artillery). He subsequently taught biochemistry at Oxford for sixteen years, before moving to London University (St George's Medical School) to become founder-chairman of a new department of biochemistry. His research interests are on biological membranes and infectious disease. Through OIBC he is active in promoting scientific research in developing countries, and in furthering an understanding of science by youngsters and the lay public. In regard to the latter he has written *The Molecules Within Us: Our Body in Health and Disease* (Plenum, 1998); and *Quest: The Essence of Humanity* (John Wiley, 2003; paperback 2004).

capasternak@oibc.org.uk

Thomas Suddendorf

Tom Suddendorf is in the School of Psychology at the University of Queensland (Australia). He received his PhD at the University of Auckland. His research interests are on the development and evolution of representational capacities with a focus on understanding of self, time and mind. He has contributed to several books, including (with Andrew Whiten) 'Reinterpreting the Mentality of Apes' (in J. Fitness and K. Sterelny, eds., *From Mating to Mentality: Evaluating Evolutionary Roots of Human Imagination*, Psychology Press, New York, 2003); and 'Great Ape Cognition and the Evolutionary Roots of Human Imagination' (in J. Roth, ed., *Imaginative Minds*, British Academy and Oxford University Press, in press).

tsuddend@psy.uq.edu.au

Ian Tattersall

Ian Tattersall is Curator in the Division of Anthropology at the American Museum of Natural History in New York City (USA). He received his undergraduate training in archaeology and anthropology at Cambridge University (UK) before gaining his doctorate in the Department of Geology and Geophysics at Yale University. He is a paleoanthropologist and primatologist. His current interests include the integration of the hominid fossil record with evolutionary theory, and the question of how a nonlinguistic, nonsymbolic precursor gave rise to the linguistic, symbolic *Homo sapiens* of today. His books include *The Fossil Trail: How We Know What We Think We Know About Human Evolution* (Oxford University Press, USA, 1997); *Being Human: Evolution and Human Uniqueness* (Oxford University Press, 2000); *The Human Odyssey: Four Million Years of Human Evolution* (with Donald C. Johanson; iUniverse 2001); *The Monkey in the Mirror: Essays on Science and What Makes Us Human* (Harcourt, 2001); and *The Human Fossil Record: Craniodental Morphology of Early Hominids* (with Jeffrey H. Schwartz; John Wiley, 2004).

iant@amnh.org

Andrew Whiten

Andrew Whiten, FRSE, FBA, is Professor of Evolutionary and Developmental Psychology and Wardlaw Professor of Psychology at the University of St Andrews (UK). His interests lie in how minds are shaped in the intertwined processes of evolution and development, with a particular focus on relationships between social cognition and social complexity in the lives of non-human primates and human children. His published works include *Natural Theories of Mind* (ed. Whiten; Basil Blackwell 1991; paperback 1992); *Foraging Strategies and Natural Diet of Monkeys, Apes and Humans* (with E. Widdowson, eds.; Oxford University Press, 1992); and *Machiavellian Intelligence II: Evaluations and Extensions* (with R. W. Byrne, eds.; Cambridge University Press, 1997); as well as several chapters in other books (see, for example, Thomas Suddendorf, above).

a.whiten@st-andrews.ac.uk

Lewis Wolpert

Lewis Wolpert, CBE, FRS, is Emeritus Professor of Biology as Applied to Medicine, Department of Anatomy, University College, London (UK). He is a developmental biologist with a particular interest in pattern formation, as well as in evolution. His published works include *The Unnatural Nature of Science* (Faber & Faber, 1992; paperback 2000); *Passionate Minds* (with Alison Richards, eds.; Oxford University Press, 1997); *Principles of Development* (with others; Oxford University Press, 1998; 2nd edition 2001; paperback 2006), *Malignant Sadness: The Anatomy of Depression* (Faber & Faber, 2001), and *Six Impossible Things Before Breakfast: The Evolutionary Origins of Belief* (Faber & Faber, 2006).

profwolpert@yahoo.com

Richard Wrangham

Richard Wrangham is Ruth Moore Professor of Anthropology at the Museum of Comparative Zoology, Harvard University (USA). He is a Fellow of the American Academy of Arts and Sciences. He read zoology at Oxford University and obtained his PhD in that subject from Cambridge University. For seventeen years he taught anthropology, biology, evolution, and human behaviour at the University of Michigan, Ann Arbor, and studied chimpanzee behaviour in Kibale Forest National Park, Uganda. In 1989 he moved to the Chair of Biological Anthropology at Harvard University. His wide interests are reflected in his publications, that include *Current Problems in Sociobiology* (with others, eds.; Cambridge University Press, 1982); *Ecology and Social Evolution: Birds and Mammals* (with D. I. Rubenstein, eds.; Princeton University Press, 1986); *Primate Societies* (with others, eds.; Chicago University Press, 1987); *Chimpanzee Cultures* (with others, eds.; Harvard University Press, 1994); and *Demonic Males: Apes and the Origins of Human Violence* (with Dale Peterson; Houghton Mifflin, Boston, 1996).

wrangham@fas.harvard.edu

1: Imitation Makes Us Human

Susan Blackmore

Introduction

To be human is to imitate.

This is a strong claim, and a contentious one. It implies that the turning point in hominid evolution was when our ancestors first began to copy each other's sounds and actions, and that this new ability was responsible for transforming an ordinary ape into one with a big brain, language, a curious penchant for music and art, and complex cumulative culture.

The argument, briefly, is this. All evolutionary processes depend on information being copied with variation and selection. Most living things on earth are the product of evolution based on the copying, varying and selection of genes. However, once humans began to imitate they provided a new kind of copying and so let loose an evolutionary process based on the copying, varying and selection of memes. This new evolutionary system co-evolved with the old to turn us into more than gene machines. We, alone on this planet, are also meme machines. We are selective imitation devices in an evolutionary arms race with a new replicator. This is why we are so different from other creatures; this is why we alone have big brains, language and complex culture.

There are many contentious issues here; the nature and status of memes, the validity of the concept of a replicator, the difference between this and other theories of gene-culture co-evolution, and whether memetics really is necessary, as I believe it is, to explain human nature. I shall outline the basic principles of memetics, show how memes could have driven human evolution, and consider some of these questions along the way.

The new replicator

Fundamental to all evolutionary processes is that some kind of information is copied with variation and selection (Campbell, 1960). As Darwin (1859) first pointed out, if you have creatures that vary, and if most of them die, and if the survivors pass on to their offspring whatever it was that helped them survive, then those offspring must, on average, be better adapted to the environment in which that selection took place than their parents were. It is the inevitability of this process that makes it such an elegant and beautiful explanation of the origins of biological design.

But it should not be confined to biology. Universal Darwinism (Dawkins, 1976; Plotkin, 1993) is the idea that the same principles apply to any system which has the three requisites – variation, selection and heredity. With these in place you *must* get evolution. Dennett calls this the 'evolutionary algorithm', a simple mindless procedure which produces 'Design out of Chaos without the aid of Mind' (Dennett, 1995, p. 50). Arguably it is the only process that produces design for function.

Dawkins coined the term 'replicator' to refer to the information which is copied with variations or errors, and whose nature influences its own probability of replication (Dawkins, 1976). Our most familiar replicator is the gene; a replicator that builds itself vehicles (Dawkins, 1976) or interactors (Hull, 1988) in the form of bodies that protect the genes and carry them around. Selection may take place at the level of the organism (and possibly at other levels too) but individual bodies die – it is the replicator that is copied reasonably intact through successive replications and is the ultimate beneficiary of the evolutionary process.

This is why replicators are called selfish. Genes are not selfish in the sense that they have human-like desires and intentions (obviously not – they are just information in chemicals). Rather, they are selfish in the sense that they will be copied and proliferate if they can, without concern for the organism that carries them, or indeed for anything else, unless it affects their own likelihood of being copied.

In explaining Universal Darwinism, Dawkins wanted to get people out of the habit of thinking only about genes and so he provided a new example of a replicator. He argued that whenever people copy skills, habits or behaviours from one person to another by imitation, a new replicator is at work.

> We need a name for the new replicator, a noun that conveys the idea
> of a unit of cultural transmission, or a unit of *imitation*. 'Mimeme'
> comes from a suitable Greek root, but I want a monosyllable that
> sounds a bit like 'gene'. I hope my classicist friends will forgive me if
> I abbreviate mimeme to *meme*. ... Examples of memes are tunes, ideas,
> catch-phrases, clothes fashions, ways of making pots or of building
> arches (Dawkins, 1976, p. 192).

This, then, was the origin of the term 'meme'. Its literal meaning is
'that which is imitated'. So other examples include gestures and
games, urban myths and financial institutions, scientific theories
and complex technologies. Most of these are not simple memes but
'co-adapted meme-complexes' or 'memeplexes'; groups of memes
that fare better together than they would individually, so they tend to
stick together, and get copied and passed on together, as in the rules,
equipment and clothing for a game, or the hardware, software, and
knowledge of how to use them for a mobile phone.

It is important to note that not everything you know or think about
is a meme. If you are unsure whether something is a meme or not, then
ask "was it copied from someone or something else?" If so, it is a
meme, otherwise it is not. So the skills you learn by yourself and for
yourself are not memes, nor are your memories of places you have seen
or people you know, nor are emotions that cannot be accurately conveyed to anyone else. But every word in your vocabulary, every story or
song that you know, and every idea you got from someone else is, and
when you combine these to make new stories or inventions to pass on
then you have created new memes.

Central to the idea of memes is that because they are replicators
evolution will happen for the benefit of the memes themselves rather
than for their carriers or for anything else. As Dennett (1995) emphasised, the ultimate beneficiary of any evolutionary process is whatever
it is that is copied. Everything that happens, and all the adaptations
that appear, are ultimately for the sake of the replicators. This idea is
what distinguishes memetics from related theories in sociobiology,
evolutionary psychology and gene-culture co-evolution theory. In
The Selfish Gene Dawkins complained of his colleagues that "In the
last analysis they wish always to go back to 'biological advantage.'"
(Dawkins, 1976, p. 193). This was certainly true, for example, when
Wilson, the founder of sociobiology, famously claimed that "the genes
hold culture on a leash" (Lumsden and Wilson, 1981) and took

inclusive fitness (advantage to genes) as the final arbiter. Perhaps more surprisingly it is still largely true now. Wilson still argues that myths and social contracts evolved because of their benefit to genes rather than to themselves (Wilson, 1998), as does Durham (1991). Even Richerson and Boyd (2005), whose 'costly information hypothesis' theory is probably closest to memetics, argue that cultural variants are not replicators and that "Culture is on a leash, all right" even if the dog on the end is big and clever. Deacon's (1997) theory comes close, especially in likening language to a personal symbiotic organism, but for him the turning point in human evolution was the acquisition of symbolic thought, not imitation. Donald's (2001) theory of 'mimesis' (note the spelling) sounds as though it may be similar to memetics but is not (Blackmore, 2005): in fact Donald rejects meme theory completely.

The bottom line here is that for all these theories culture is an adaptation, created by and for genes. But for memetics culture is not, and never was, an adaptation. Imitation was an adaptation, allowing individuals to learn from each other, but the memes it unintentionally let loose were not. Culture did not arise for our sake, but for its own. It is more like a vast parasite growing and living and feeding on us than a tool of our creation. It is a parasite that we cope with – indeed we and our culture have co-evolved a symbiotic relationship. But it is a parasite nonetheless.

To understand this we have to make the same mental flip that biologists did when they stopped thinking about evolution as being for the sake of the species or the individual and started taking the gene's eye view. We have to stop thinking of culture as an adaptation and start taking the meme's eye view.

Taking the meme's eye view

From the viewpoint of a meme, the important question is "How can I survive and get copied?" and usually this means "How can I get a human to pay attention to me, remember me, and pass me on?" Answers will be very varied but the general principle is that some memes succeed because they are good, useful, true, or beautiful, while others succeed even though they are false, useless or even harmful. From the meme's point of view their value to us or our genes is irrelevant, while to us it is critical. We try to select true ideas over false ones, and good over bad, but we do it imperfectly, and we leave all kinds of opportunities for other memes to get copied – using us as their copying machinery. In other words, there is an evolutionary arms race between us and the memes that we find ourselves copying.

There are many useless, false, or even harmful memes that survive very well. Simple examples are self-replicating viral sentences, chain letters and various kinds of email virus, such as those that make impossible threats and demand that you pass them on to warn your friends. Their basic structure is an instruction to "copy me" backed up by threats and promises; a structure that is seen in other, more serious, memeplexes.

Dawkins uses Catholicism as an example of a 'virus of the mind' (Dawkins, 1993); a vast memeplex that has succeeded for centuries in spite of being based on such falsehoods as miracles, virgin birth, and the Holy Mass, in which the wine is supposed to turn *literally* into the blood of Christ, even though the wine still smells and tastes as it did before and would not show up as Christ's blood in a DNA test. People infected with such a religion are exhorted to pass on their beliefs by converting others, bringing up lots of believing children, or punishing apostates. Compliance brings eternity in heaven (although of course it's invisible to us living creatures and so cannot be tested); rejection brings gruesomely described tortures, whether in the hell of *The Bible* or the special fires and torments of *The Qur'an*.

Many religions use the altruism trick (Blackmore, 1999) by which people are made to feel good by believing. This is particularly ironic since religious belief may be bad for societies. Evidence from comparing developed nations suggests that the more religious a country is, the higher are its rates of suicide, murder, teenage pregnancy, and abortion – precisely the things that most religions rail against (Paul, 2005). Believers must also spend much time praying, singing or reading holy works, and must give money not just to the poor but to build more churches, mosques, or synagogues that will inspire further meme hosts. Thus do memes make believers work for their propagation.

Some authors have emphasised viral memes (including cults, fads and alternative therapies that don't work) to the exclusion of all other memes. This is understandable given the importance of maladaptive cultural traits but it is important to remember that memes range from the completely viral through to the indispensable, and everything in between. In fact viral memes may be in a minority, with most of our culture consisting of memes that work at least as much for us as we do for them. These include our languages, the built environment, transport systems, communications technology and scientific theories. Without memes we could not speak, write, enjoy stories and songs, or do most of the things we associate with being human. Memes are the tools with which we think, and our minds and cultures are a mass of memes.

We can now take that big mental flip and see the world in a completely new way. Look out at the streets around you, the building you are in, or the cars passing by and now see them – all of them – as parts of a vast evolutionary system in which they are the winners in the competition to get copied and survive. Why is that house the way it is? Because those windows, that door, that style of roof, and all the many details that make it what it is, have won in the competition to get an architect to draw them, a builder to construct them, or an owner to buy them. Houses that people like fetch higher prices and so more like them get built. And so it goes on.

Step back a bit and think about a whole city. It is a spreading mass of copied memes – housing estates expanding; roads, railways and bus routes growing; the whole thing gobbling up resources, using humans as the willing meme machines that do the work.

Now step back a bit further and look at the whole planet. You might be looking down from an aeroplane at night, seeing those dense patches of lights, with curious streams of moving lights within them, or stretching out to other distant patches. They look like living creatures, and according to memetics that is precisely what they are. They were built on the basis of memes rather than genes, but the same principles apply.

This new view is different indeed from most people's normal way of looking at the world. Its power lies in its ability to unify all creative processes, both biological and cultural, within the same Darwinian framework. Yet after more than thirty years memetics is still not a thriving science.

There are many reasons for this. First, there are legitimate criticisms of memetics and many difficulties to be overcome (Aunger, 2000; Distin, 2005; Jablonka and Lamb, 2005). Second, there are repeated misunderstandings which cause people to abandon memetic explanations, such as thinking that memes must always exist as units, thinking that memetic inheritance is Lamarckian and therefore cannot occur, or thinking of memes as some kind of entity that may or may not exist rather than as the actual songs, stories or whatever is copied (Aunger, 2002; Midgley, 2000; Richerson and Boyd, 2005). Finally, some people seem to find memetics deeply unsettling in the way that it undermines free will, and the power of human creativity and consciousness (Midgley, 2000; Donald, 2001). I shall return to this point but for now simply note that fear is not a good reason for rejecting any theory. In my opinion memetics provides the best explanation of what makes us human.

How we got our big brains

One of the mysteries of human evolution is why our brains are so big. These outsize organs are expensive to build, dangerous to give birth to, and use a lot of energy to run, even during sleep. So there needs to be a very good reason.

Nearly all conventional theories start by assuming that the big brain was an adaptation (i.e. an advantage to human genes) but differ in what advantage it provided – for example it might have been implicated in complex social relationships, increased group size, gossip or more practical things like tool making (Deacon, 1997; Dunbar, 1996).

Memetics provides a completely different argument: that the increase in brain size was driven by and for the memes, as they transformed an ordinary brain into a meme machine. I have called this process memetic drive (Blackmore, 1999, 2001) and suggested that it would naturally begin as soon as our hominid ancestors were capable of imitating with sufficiently high fidelity to create the first memes. It does not matter what these were – possibly new ways of hunting, or lighting fires, or wearing clothes – but whatever they were they would change the environment in which human genes were being selected and give an advantage to individuals who could copy them.

Imagine a group in which someone discovered a new trick and some individuals were capable of copying it while others were not. If the trick was useful then the imitators would fare better, not only acquiring more useful survival tricks but higher status as others tried to copy them. They might also attract better mates and pass on (genetically) whatever it was that made them better imitators in the first place. Since imitation is a difficult skill (which is why most animals cannot do it), it is reasonable to assume that it requires a larger brain.

The result would be that brain size would increase. As imitation ability in the population increased more memes would flourish putting more pressure on individuals to be able to copy them. This process could continue until it became too costly.

Thus far the argument is not very different from many others. It becomes different when we think of memes as a second replicator evolving in its own right. So the presence of memes has another effect. I assumed that the first successful memes were useful ones (that is useful to the people who carried them or to their genes) but once imitation ability improved all sorts of memes would be copied, and people would have to choose what to copy and what not to copy. Seriously dangerous memes, like jumping off cliffs for fun or setting fire to yourself, would kill off their carriers and probably not get passed on (although, like martyrdom, they might), but plenty of neutral or even slightly harmful memes might easily thrive, giving an advantage to people who could select effectively between memes.

This suggests the beginnings of an arms race between the two replicators, with genetic pressure to keep the brain small and best at copying biologically useful memes, and memetic pressure to produce a brain capable of copying as many memes as possible as accurately as possible. It is this competition that makes a memetic explanation for the increasing brain size so different from other explanations. The resulting brain is not just larger but has been turned into a selective imitation device whose properties depend on the results of memetic competition.

The difference becomes even more obvious when we consider not just the size of the brain but the things it is best at copying – such as language.

The origins of language

All other theories of the origins of language – and the question has been hotly debated for centuries – assume that language is an adaptation. For memetics language is not an adaptation but a parasite turned symbiotic partner; an evolving system in its own right that fed off the humans who selected, remembered and copied sounds.

Let us suppose that our hominid ancestors began imitating the sounds each other made, perhaps the sort of sounds that other primates make – food calls, mating calls, danger signals, and so on. Other primates cannot imitate well, but these early humans would be able to start copying the nuances of each other's calls, perhaps imitating the more powerful individuals, or starting whole lineages of different copying trends. In a society where imitation was prized, the number of sounds being made would increase and soon people would have to choose which to copy. In other words, looking from the meme's eye view, there would be competition between the sounds. So which would be copied most?

A general principle is that higher fidelity replicators do better. There is nothing magic about this rule. It simply means (in this example) that sounds that are more accurately copied will tend to survive unchanged for longer, and so increase in the meme pool. Once again, individuals capable of high fidelity imitation will gain higher status, attract more desirable mates and so pass on any genes responsible for their superior copying ability. So fidelity of copying will generally increase.

This example shows memetic drive at its clearest, and emphasises the difference between this and other theories. Because the sounds are a replicator in their right, dependent on their living copying machines, they will evolve into a more complex system with higher fidelity sounds as time goes by. But according to the vagaries of circumstance they might evolve in different ways and – here is the critical point – according to which direction memetic evolution took, so genetic evolution would have to follow. If certain sounds became popular then brains would, over time, begin to get better at copying those kinds of sound. In other words the brain would gradually be transformed into one that was designed to copy the very kinds of sounds that had evolved in the meme pool.

In fact the redesign of the human larynx, throat and brain for language was quite dramatic and is one of the features that most distinguishes us from other apes. According to memetics this redesign was driven by pressure from the memes.

Of course language is more than just meaningless sounds; those sounds refer to things and people and actions. This would come about as people copied the sounds that others made while they were looking at a particular object or doing a particular action, or watching someone else perform an action.

If this all seems too speculative or far-fetched it is at least clearly testable. In *The Meme Machine* I argued that if memetic drive really were responsible for the evolution of language then the same process should happen with simple robots that can imitate each other's sounds. I called them 'copybots'. In fact very soon after that such robots were built. Steels' (2000) 'talking heads' robots looked at a board covered with simple shapes and colours and imitated the sounds they each made while looking at them. After many iterations of a copying game, not only did the robots begin to agree on certain sounds, but the space of possible vowel sounds became split into sounds they did and did not use, and words that referred to the things they were looking at emerged too. Interestingly no observer could tell just what they were saying, but clearly the beginning of language was evolving from a very simple copying system. There have since been studies of the emergence of grammar and syntax in robots (Steels et al., 2001) and much research on language as an evolutionary system (Christiansen and Kirby, 2003). It appears that the capacity for imitation really is something very special.

Art, music and the lure of religion

Language makes us unique, but there are many other curious aspects of human nature that require explanation. Unlike other animals we seem to love music and singing, dance and theatre, painting and sculpture. Yet none of these provides an obvious survival advantage. As Pinker explains, "As far as biological cause and effect are concerned, music is useless" (Pinker, 1997, p. 528); and Dennett (1999) says we "cannot avoid the obligation to explain how such an expensive, time-consuming activity came to flourish in this cruel world." So why and how did they come about?

Miller (2000) argues that art has been sexually selected: that the songs, paintings, and other artistic creations are the equivalent of a deer's impressive antlers or the famous peacock's tail, whose functions are to attract mates. He cites evidence that men are more artistic, and that women prefer to mate with creative men.

I have suggested that sexual selection plays a part in memetic drive, but the theories are otherwise quite different. According to Miller, artistic creations are aspects of the artist's phenotype and do not necessarily evolve in their own right. By contrast, according to memetics, artistic creations are memes that compete with each other and evolve. Dennett (1999) gives the beginnings of a memetic explanation by imagining how music might have begun – a just-so story about the first infectious sounds.

> One day one of our distant hominid ancestors sitting on a fallen log happened to start banging on with a stick – *boom boom boom*. For *no good reason at all*. This was just idle diddling ... mere nervous fidgeting, but the repetitive sounds striking his ears just happened to feel to him like a slight improvement on silence ... Now introduce some other ancestors who happen to see and hear this drummer. They might ... again *for no reason*, find their imitator-circuits tickled into action; they might feel an urge to drum along with musical Adam.

Dennett goes on to describe how drumming was copied and some drummings proved more infectious than others. It didn't matter why; the successful ones might have sounded nicer or been easier to copy but, whatever the reason, the drumming virus was born. He goes on to imagine that humming memes spread in the meme pool, the competition heated up, and hummings had to get more catchy, easier to hum, or more likely to gain attention, in order to get copied. By this time everyone lived in a music-filled culture.

The next step, which Dennett does not consider, is memetic drive. If drumming and humming became popular, and people who were good at them acquired status, then the pressures on hominid genes would change. It would then pay to have a brain that was good at copying drumming and humming, when previously it did not. Any genes that contributed to that ability would be favoured and so, gradually, hominid brains would be redesigned. The co-evolutionary process could continue indefinitely.

If this is how music evolved we can easily understand why modern humans have the sort of brains (and ears and hands) that help us enjoy making and listening to music. We are like that, not because music serves any biological function, but because musical memes long ago infected our ancestors and forced their brains to be redesigned. The same argument applies to any kind of art. So, for example, if techniques of cave painting or body decoration or singing evolved in competition with each other, then brains would be driven in the direction of getting better at copying the particular techniques that were successful. In other words, the direction taken by memetic evolution would drive the direction the genes had to take in building our bodies and brains.

Another related mystery is why we are so fond of religion and ritual. The answer could be that religious memes were highly successful in the past, putting pressure on people to enjoy religious behaviours and inclining them to believe religious ideas. If this is so it suggests a reason why, in spite of education and rational thought, and in spite of the harm done by religious war and oppression, it seems generally hard for people to live without religion.

This is really a general argument about the design of human nature. Whichever direction memetic evolution happened to take in the past, we humans would become better able to copy the memes that were successful – whether those were words, music, paintings, rituals or anything else. Our modern brains therefore carry the traces of all our past memetic evolution.

Human creativity

Creative design has always seemed to be somehow magical or special. The way it seems is that clever designs need something even cleverer to design them. Dennett (1995) calls this the "trickle down theory of creation", the idea that it takes a big fancy smart thing to make a lesser thing. As he points out, you never see a horseshoe making a blacksmith or a pot making a potter. So it seems obvious that design requires a designer, and that the designer must be something cleverer than the design.

We now know that there is no need for a designer in biological design: evolution works from the bottom up by the mindless power of natural selection. Yet the intuition remains powerful and drives belief in creationism and the theory of 'intelligent design'.

Turning to human thought and creativity, these too have been described as evolutionary processes (James, 1890; Popper, 1972), especially in the field of evolutionary epistemology (Campbell, 1960). Yet the intuition remains strong that somewhere inside ourselves there must be a designer, a conscious mind which originates novel ideas and creative output. Could we be wrong about this? I think so. Indeed I think it likely that *all* design works from the bottom up – human creativity included. Memetics shows how.

Let's take the meme's eye view again. Think about all the memes that have bombarded you today, from the words on your cereal packet and the news on the breakfast radio, to the ideas you dealt with at work, the e-mails, the phone calls, the letters and faxes, your favourite TV programme or bedtime reading. All day long memes are competing to get into your head. Those that succeed have some effect on your memory. They may be stored intact or twisted, but more importantly they get mixed up with all sorts of other memes. A human mind is a veritable factory for new memes. Every word in your vocabulary is a meme and you routinely mix them up to produce unique new sentences, but so are all the more complex ideas you come across. And if you are a creative person your new mixtures will be more interesting than other people's and will set off on their own with a chance of being copied again. This is, indeed, a creative process.

This is all that is happening as I write these words. All my ideas about evolution and memes have come from taking old ones and putting them together in new ways. It is certainly a creative process but not, I think, one that requires a conscious creator inside my head.

Or think of a painter or sculptor or potter who trains for years in techniques developed by others, practices for more years in putting paint to canvas or hands to clay, and then finds novel and exciting products emerging. In this context it is worth reflecting that artists are often surprised by their own creations. They can also be fiercely selective – destroying their own works if they don't like them. Many describe the state of mind in which their best work happens as a kind of 'flow' (Csikszentmihalyi, 1990) in which the self seems put into abeyance and the work creates itself. All this fits with the idea of human creativity as an evolutionary process working through human meme machines. It may seem rather sad to say that we don't really create anything through the power of conscious creativity, but it can be liberating, and I believe it is true.

Self and consciousness

Who then am I? One of the deepest mysteries of human nature is that we seem to be something like an inner conscious self who inhabits a body, rather than *being* the body. This has to be false.

It has to be false because there is no room in the brain for an inner self; there is no central place where the self could sit and receive impressions or from where it could send out the instructions to its arms and legs and mouth. The brain isn't even organised that way; it is a massively parallel system with no central controller and multiple systems all operating at once. Not only is there no place for a self, but there is no need for one. Although most people are dualists of one kind or another – believing in a non-material soul, spirit or inner self – philosophers have consistently argued that dualism cannot be made to work, and indeed there are almost no dualist philosophers today (Blackmore, 2003; Dennett, 1991; an exception is Chalmers, 1996).

The interesting question then becomes – if dualism is false why are we so easily deluded? If there is no inner self why does it seem as though there is?

Once again people have attempted biological explanations, for example arguing that it helps our survival to believe in a self who has to be protected. This does not work for the simple reason that the mystery is not why we protect our own bodies – every animal does that with or without belief in a soul – but why we think we are so much more than our physical shell, why it seems as though we are something that controls that body with our own free will, and may even survive after it is dead.

Memetics provides a possible answer by asking whether it would benefit the memes to construct a false idea of self and free will. I think it could. Imagine a child growing up and learning to speak. At first the word 'I' refers to this body rather than any other body, but soon the child, immersed in the world of natural language, learns to say lots more things – like 'I want', 'I think', 'I believe', or 'I know'. Sentences with 'I' in them proliferate, and take with them the false idea that there is a single inner self who is the 'I' referred to. More and more memes coalesce around this word until it seems just obvious that there must be an inner 'I' who has all these desires and wishes, plans and hopes, fears and intentions, when really there is just a meme machine mixing up old memes to make new ones and sending them on their way.

Living life as a meme machine

What makes us human? In the beginning it was imitation and the appearance of memes. Now it is the way we work as meme machines, living in the culture that the memes have used us to build.

Is it depressing to think of ourselves this way – as machines created by the competition between genes and memes, and in turn creating more genes and memes? I don't think so. We have got used to the idea that we need no God to explain the evolution of life, and that we humans are part of the natural world. Now we have to take a step further in the same direction and change yet again the way we think about ourselves, our consciousness and free will (Blackmore, 2006). But this is precisely what makes it so exciting being human – that as meme machines we can, and must, reflect on our own nature.

References

Aunger, R. A. (ed.) (2000) *Darwinizing Culture: The Status of Memetics as a Science*. Oxford, Oxford University Press.

Aunger, R. A. (2002) *The Electric Meme: A New Theory of How We Think*. New York, The Free Press.

Blackmore, S. J. (1999) *The Meme Machine*. Oxford, Oxford University Press.

Blackmore, S. (2001) Evolution and memes: The human brain as a selective imitation device. *Cybernetics and Systems*, **32**, 225–255.

Blackmore, S. (2003) *Consciousness: An Introduction*. London, Hodder & Stoughton; and (2004) New York, Oxford University Press.

Blackmore, S. (2005) A possible confusion between mimetic and memetic, in *Perspectives on Imitation: From Mirror Neurons to Memes*. Ed. S. Hurley and N. Chater. Cambridge, MA, MIT Press, Vol 2, 396–8.

Blackmore, S. (2006) It is possible to live happily and morally without believing in free will, in *What We Believe But Cannot Prove: Today's Leading Thinkers on Science in the Age of Certainty*. John Brockman (ed.). London & Sydney, Free Press, 41–2.

Campbell, D. T. (1960) Blind variation and selective retention in creative thought as in other knowledge processes. *Psychological Review*, **67**, 380–400.

Chalmers, D. (1996) *The Conscious Mind*. Oxford, Oxford University Press.

Christiansen, M. and Kirby, S. (eds.) (2003) *Language Evolution*. Oxford, Oxford University Press.

Csikszentmihalyi, M. (1990) *Flow: The Psychology of Optimal Experience*. New York, Harper & Row.

Darwin, C. (1859) *On the Origin of Species by Means of Natural Selection*. London, Murray.

Dawkins, R. (1976) *The Selfish Gene*. Oxford, Oxford University Press (new edition with additional material, 1989).

Dawkins, R. (1993) Viruses of the mind, in B. Dahlbohm (ed.) *Dennett and his Critics: Demystifying Mind*. Oxford, Blackwell.

Deacon, T. (1997) *The Symbolic Species: The Co-evolution of Language and the Human Brain*. London, Penguin.

Dennett, D. (1991) *Consciousness Explained*. Boston, Little, Brown.

Dennett, D. (1995) *Darwin's Dangerous Idea*. London, Penguin.

Dennett, D. (1999) The Evolution of Culture. Charles Simonyi Lecture, Oxford, February 17, 1999.

Distin, K. (2005) *The Selfish Meme: A Critical Reassessment*. Cambridge, Cambridge University Press.

Donald, M. (2001) *A Mind So Rare: The Evolution of Human Consciousness*. New York, Norton.

Dunbar, R. (1996) *Grooming, Gossip and the Evolution of Language*. London, Faber & Faber.

Durham, W. H. (1991) *Coevolution: Genes, Culture and Human Diversity*. Stanford, CA, Stanford University Press.

Hull, D. L. (1988) Interactors versus vehicles, in H. C. Plotkin (ed.) *The Role of Behaviour in Evolution*. Cambridge, MA, MIT Press.

Jablonka, E. and Lamb, M. J. (2005) *Evolution in Four Dimensions: Genetic, Epigenetic, Behavioral and Symbolic Variation in the History of Life*. Cambridge, MA and London, Bradford Books.

James, W. (1890) *The Principles of Psychology*. London, MacMillan.

Lumsden, C. J. and Wilson, E. O. (1981) *Genes, Mind and Culture*. Cambridge, MA, Harvard University Press.

Midgley, M. (2000) Why memes? in H. Rose and S. Rose (eds.) *Alas, Poor Darwin*. London, Cape, 67–84.

Miller, G. (2000) *The Mating Mind: How Sexual Choice Shaped the Evolution of Human Nature*. London, Heinemann.

Paul, G. S. (2005) Cross-national correlations of quantifiable societal health with popular religiosity and secularism in the prosperous democracies: a first look. *Journal of Religion and Society*, 7, 1–17.

Pinker, S. (1997) *How the Mind Works*. Harmondsworth, UK, Penguin.

Plotkin, H. (1993) *Darwin Machines and the Nature of Knowledge*. Cambridge, MA, Harvard University Press.

Popper, K. R. (1972) *Objective Knowledge: An Evolutionary Approach*. Oxford, Oxford University Press.

Richerson, P. J. and Boyd, R. (2005) *Not by Genes Alone: How Culture Transformed Human Evolution*. Chicago, University of Chicago Press.

Steels, L. (2000) Language as a complex adaptive system, in *Lecture Notes in Computer Science. Parallel Problem Solving from Nature* – PPSN-VI. Volume eds. Schoenauer, et al. Berlin, Springer-Verlag.

Steels, L., Kaplan, F., McIntyre, A. and Van Looveren, J. (2001) Crucial factors in the origins of word-meaning, in A. Wray, et al. (eds.) (2002) *The Transition to Language*. Oxford, Oxford University Press.

Wilson, E. O. (1998) *Consilience: The Unity of Knowledge*. New York, Knopf.

2: Memory, Time and Language

Michael C. Corballis and Thomas Suddendorf

Introduction

Natural selection is inevitably oriented toward the future. Many of the characteristics that are selected have to do with the ways in which animals behave – how they feed, fight, flee, and mate, or how they construct niches for successful living. If one animal, say a warthog, spends time digging a burrow whereas another does not bother, the first has a safe haven for the future survival of a lion attack and the second does not. Behaviours that increase reproductive fitness, ensuring that the individual's genes will be continued into future generations, will be selected at the expense of those that place future generations at greater risk, or that threaten reproduction itself. Behaviour itself is complex, and selected at many different levels. The way ants behave, for example, is rather different from the way an African lion disports itself on the savanna, or the way people behave on the New York Stock Exchange – although there are no doubt similarities as well as differences.

In this chapter, we start by proposing a hierarchy of behavioural adaptations, culminating in an adaptation that may help explain behavioural characteristics unique to our own species. This adaptation is mental time travel, and is based on the recording of specific events in the past, and the imagining of specific events in the future. Mental time travel is responsible for many human attributes, such as the ability to individually plan our futures in detail, and perhaps for phenomena such as religious belief and ideas about life after death. We argue that our ability to transcend time may lie at the heart of another capacity generally regarded as uniquely human. That capacity is language.

Behavioural adaptations: a hierarchy

At the most fundamental level, behaviour is dependent on bodily characteristics. For example, bodies built for strength or speed may have better chances of survival than those not so endowed, although this may be balanced against metabolic costs. There may be a trade-off between strength and speed, with predators specialized for attacking strength, their prey for speed or efficacy of escape. Cheaper substitutes for strength in attack may include deadly venoms or stings, and spikes may substitute for speed in defence. Size is another bodily characteristic, and selection may again lead to opposite adaptations; compare, for example, the ant and the hippopotamus. A large, heavy body may render an individual relatively impervious to attack or threat of injury, while a small, light body may offer more means of escape from predation, by climbing trees or hiding under rocks. Specific adaptations, like wings for flying or fins for swimming, may extend the range of habitats an animal might occupy, and so enhance reproduction and the survival of offspring. Such is the diversity of climate and terrain on the earth's surface that species have adapted in a kaleidoscope of different ways to their own niches.

At the next level of behavioural adaptation, animals may evolve specific patterns of behaviour. These can be quite complex, as in the building of webs or nests, or in migratory or hoarding behaviours. Many such behaviours are tuned to predictable regularities, such as the day-night cycle, the fluctuations of the seasons, or even the phases of the moon. Such instinctive patterns of behaviour are relatively fixed, and largely independent of learning or experience. A hibernator, for example, may hoard food for an impending winter even if it has never experienced a winter. Such instinctive behaviours may ensure reproductive fitness so long as the environmental pattern persists, but cannot deal with changes in long-term regularities, such as climate change, or with relatively unpredictable day-to-day events.

Learning provides another level of adaptation that is better tuned to specific features of the individual's environment. Learning may serve in part to fine-tune instinctive mechanisms, as in such phenomena as imprinting, or parameter setting. Other forms of learning are relatively independent of instinct (except insofar as learning itself may be regarded as an instinct), and operate at the level of the individual rather than the population. Classical conditioning, for example, may serve to elicit appropriate emotional or anticipatory responses to situations, animals, or objects that pose threats or promise rewards, and through operant conditioning animals develop behaviours that ensure reinforcements or escape from harm. These mechanisms are still relatively inflexible, and predictable according to quantitative laws of learning. Behaviour itself may not always be predictable, though, since behavioural modification, like evolutionary adaptation, depends on variations that allow the selection of those behaviours that prove adaptive (Skinner, 1966).

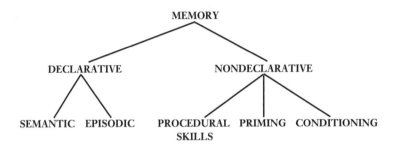

Figure 1 Taxonomy of memory systems (adapted and simplified from Squire, 2004).

Memory systems may permit still more flexible adaptation. Modern theories of memory recognize different levels of memory that themselves vary in flexibility. Figure 1 shows the now classic distinction between *declarative* and *nondeclarative* memory (sometimes known as implicit and explicit memory, respectively), and within declarative memory the distinction between *semantic* and *episodic* memory (Squire, 2004). Nondeclarative memory refers to the stimulus-driven, unconscious memory systems that drive such phenomena as procedural skills and habits, priming and perceptual learning, and simple classical conditioning. Declarative memory is so named because it can be declared. It is conscious, and corresponds to what we normally think of as "memory" in everyday language. Indeed, we suggest below that declarative memory provides the basis for language itself.

Declarative memory provides more flexible adaptation to the world than does simple learning or nondeclarative memory. First, it provides an explicit and often detailed model of the world in which we live. We know precisely where we live, the neighbourhoods, the geographical areas in which we work, play, and travel. As humans, we have a huge array of facts at our disposal that enable us to make precise plans for the future, and meet different obligations and contingencies. Second, declarative memories can be voluntarily triggered top-down from the frontal lobes, rather than bottom-up through perception (Miyashita, 2004). They can therefore be brought into consciousness "off-line" for flexible planning and decision-making. We can contrast and compare different pieces of knowledge, and choose knowledge relevant to a particular activity, such as planning a career, or a vacation.

Episodic memory

Over thirty years ago, Tulving (1972) drew the distinction within declarative memory between semantic memory, which is memory for facts, and episodic memory, which is memory for events. Roughly, semantic memory can be likened to a combined dictionary and encyclopaedia, while episodic memory can be likened to a personal diary. Of course part of our understanding of our personal past depends on semantic memory as well as on episodic memory, to make up what has been called *autobiographical memory*. The distinction between semantic and episodic memory has also been characterized as that between *knowing* and *remembering*, respectively (Tulving, 1985). For example, most of us know when we were born but do not remember the event, but may possibly remember events of the first day at school. Episodic memory is perhaps the ultimate in flexibility, since it records the particularities of one's life, and allows the fine-tuning of personal events in the future.

Relative to semantic memory, episodic memory is fragile and incomplete. In cases of amnesia, it is typically episodic memories rather than semantic memories that are lost. In one dramatic case, for example, a patient with extensive damage to the frontal and temporal lobes was unable to recall any specific episode from his life, yet retained semantic knowledge (Tulving et al., 1988). Even without brain injury, people probably remember only a tiny fraction of actual past episodes (Loftus and Loftus, 1980), and events are often remembered inaccurately, even to the point that people will claim with some certainty to have remembered events that did not in fact happen (Loftus and Ketcham, 1994; Roediger and McDermott, 1995).

Given the unreliability of episodic memory, often a bane to courts of law, it seems clear that it did not evolve primarily to serve as a record of the past. Schacter (1996) suggests rather that its function is to build up a personal narrative, which may provide the basis for the concept of self, as well as a basis on which to ground future behavioural choices. If semantic memory provides knowledge about relatively constant aspects of one's environment, episodic memory picks out singular events that can augment one's decisions about how to behave in similar circumstance in the future. Individual episodes provide a kind of vocabulary upon which to construct a self-narrative, and plan future episodes. To maintain a complete record, though, may be counterproductive, since this would occupy huge storage space, and involve needless repetition. As Anderson and Schooler (1971) note, forgetting itself can be adaptive, because it frees resources for future use and allows memory retrieval to continue quickly and efficiently.

Mental time travel

However incomplete, episodic memories are located in time, and so provide our mental lives with the time dimension. Episodic memory, then, can be regarded as part of a more general capacity for *mental time travel*, allowing us not only to mentally relive events in the past, but also to imagine the future in episodic detail (Suddendorf and Corballis, 1997). Developmentally this capacity to envisage future episodes appears to emerge in children at around the same time as episodic memory itself, between the ages of three and four (e.g. Atance and O'Neill, 2005; Busby and Suddendorf, 2005). Patients with amnesia are equally unable to answer simple questions about yesterday's events as to say what might happen tomorrow (Klein et al., 2002; Tulving, 1985). Amnesia for specific events, then, is at least in part a loss of the awareness of time.

The importance of mental time travel as a specific adaptation, enhancing the survival of the species, was anticipated by the legendary British psychologist, Kenneth Craik (1943):

> If the organisms carry a "small scale model" of external reality and of its own possible actions within its head, it is able to try out various

alternatives, conclude which are the best of them, react to future situations before they arise, utilize the knowledge of past events in dealing with the present and future, and in every way to react in a much fuller, safer and more competent manner to the emergencies which face it (p. 61).

Uniquely human?

It has been proposed that episodic memory (Tulving, 1983, 1985), and more generally mental time travel (e.g. Suddendorf and Corballis, 1997), are uniquely human. This has posed a challenge to animal researchers to show that these capacities exist in nonhuman species. Since the testing of episodic memory and mental time travel in humans typically involves language, it has proven difficult to design experiments to test episodic memory in non-linguistic species. Nevertheless there have been some concerted attempts to specify the necessary conditions for episodic memory, and then to test whether the conditions hold in a nonhuman animal.

To date, the most ingenious attempts have come from work with birds that cache items of food, and are later able to recover the food from the stored locations. In particular, scrub jays can select food locations not only according to the type of food that is stored there, but also according to how long it has been stored. For example, they will recover recently cached worms in preference to nuts, since fresh worms are more palatable, but if the worms have been cached for too long they will retrieve nuts, because the worms will have decayed and become unpalatable (Clayton et al., 2003). The mechanism underlying this behaviour has been dubbed www-memory (Suddendorf and Busby, 2003), because scrub jays seem to remember *what* has been cached, *where* it was cached, and *when* it was cached. In these respects, it seems to conform to the criteria of episodic memory. If observed caching food, scrub jays will later re-cache it, presumably to avoid the observer stealing the food. They will only do this, however, if they have themselves stolen food in the past – it takes a thief to know a thief (Emery and Clayton, 2001). Clayton et al. (2003) conclude that scrub jays can not only remember past events, but can also anticipate the future by taking steps to avoid future theft.

This work with scrub jays is perhaps the most convincing evidence to date for something resembling mental time travel in a nonhuman species. But is it enough? Certainly birds that cache food may show prodigious memory for location; Clark's nutcrackers seem to be among the most prolific, storing seeds in thousands of locations and recovering them with high (but not perfect) accuracy (e.g. Kamil and Balda, 1985). The question then is whether their ability to recover the cached food demonstrates knowing or remembering, in Tulving's (1985) distinction; in other words, do the birds actually remember caching the food, or do they simply know where it was cached? The ability of the scrub jays in Clayton et al.'s (2003) experiments to retrieve nuts or worms depending on how long they have been cached similarly does not prove memory for the act of caching, or even for the time of caching. A simple internal clock mechanism might be sufficient to specify how long a memory has been established, creating a kind of "use-by date" for retrieval. Moreover, caching in these birds is highly domain-specific, no doubt governed to a large extent by instinctive mechanisms, whereas declarative memory in humans is domain-general. We think it unlikely that caching birds have anything resembling autobiographical memory in humans.

Tool manufacture is sometimes taken as evidence for a sense of the future, especially when it is clear that a tool is manufactured on one occasion for later use. Again, birds seem to provide the most compelling evidence. For example, New Caledonian crows construct tools from pandanus leaves for the express purpose of extracting grubs from holes, and the design characteristics of these tools suggest a clear temporal distinction between construction and use (Hunt, 2000). In contrast, there is little evidence that nonhuman primates make tools with any sense of future planning. Chimpanzees and other great apes may improvise objects for use as tools, such as using stones to crack open nuts, and they can be taught to use tools in specific ways, and even show culturally determined variation on how they use these tools (Whiten et al., 2005), but there is little evidence that they construct tools for some given future purpose, although they may be capable of improvisation. Oakley (1961) wrote of Sultan, the most inventive of the chimpanzees observed by Kohler, that he "was capable of improvising tools in certain situations. Tool making occurred only in the presence of a visible reward, never without it. In the chimpanzee the mental range seems to be limited to present situations, with little conception of past or future" (p. 187). Perhaps this was too bleak a portrait, since a recent study by Mulcahy and Call (2006) suggests that orangutans and bonobos, at least, save tools for use up fourteen hours later, which might suggest mental time travel, although it is not entirely clear that the animals were not responding simply on the basis of associations (Suddendorf, 2006).

The evidence on mental time travel in nonhuman species remains scant, but might be taken to indicate some rudimentary ability to refer to specific past experiences or to imagine future ones. Convergent evolution may have produced various mechanisms designed to enhance future survival chances through cognitive capacities akin to mental time travel. Nevertheless the evidence pales beside the undoubted ability of humans to re-experience their past lives or to imagine the future in detail. The manufacture of tools by humans is clearly governed by design characteristics that are oriented toward future use, and there is a clear temporal separation between manufacture and use. We have even manufactured tools that record time itself, or that are programmed to operate at given points in time – such as ovens that can be programmed in the morning to have your meal ready for you in the evening when you come home. Indeed, our human lives seem dominated by time, not in the instinctive way that migrating or hoarding animals respond to seasonal changes, but rather in the day-to-day sense of specific things that need to be done or plans that need to be made.

When did mental time travel emerge?

It is the planned manufacture of tools, perhaps, that provides the earliest indication of mental time travel in hominid evolution. Stone tool industries in our hominid forebears have been dated from about 2.5 million years ago in Ethiopia (Semaw et al., 1997), and tentatively identified with *Homo rudolfensis*. Nevertheless these tools, which belong to the Oldowan industry, are primitive, and some have suggested that *H. rudolfensis* and *H. habilis*, the hominid traditionally associated with the Oldowan, should really be considered australopithecines (e.g. Wood, 2002). The true climb to humanity and human-like cognition probably began with the larger-brained *Homo erectus* around 1.8 million years ago, and the somewhat more sophisticated Acheulian tool industry dating from around 1.5 million years ago (Ambrose, 2001). Apparently, these tools were made and kept for repeated future use. The Acheulian industry even persisted into the culture of early *Homo sapiens* some 125,000 years ago (Walter et al.,

2000). Nevertheless, there was something of an increase in the sophistication of manufactured tools from about 300,000 years ago (Ambrose, 2001), and a more dramatic increase, as part of what has been termed the "human revolution," within the past 100,000 years (Mellars and Stringer, 1989). These developments may represent increasing sophistication in the understanding of time.

Our sense of time may have uniquely endowed us with the understanding of the inevitability of death, which may explain the universality of religion, involving such phenomena as ancestor worship, spirituality, and the concept of life after death. There is some evidence that the Neanderthals buried their dead, but ritualistic burial in which symbolic material is added to the grave may have been restricted to *Homo sapiens* (Pettit, 2002). Perhaps the earliest example is from a burial site at Qafzeh Cave in Israel, in which the head of a deer was placed on the body of a child who was buried. This burial is dated at about 100,000 years ago, and is associated with early anatomically modern humans (Andrews and Stringer, 1993).

The sense of time, and selection for episodic memory, may well have evolved, perhaps gradually, with the global shift to cooler climate after 2.5 million years ago, when much of southern and eastern Africa probably became more open and sparsely wooded (Foley, 1987). This left the hominids not only more exposed to attack from dangerous predators, such as sabre-tooth cats, lions, and hyenas, but also obliged to compete with them as carnivores. The solution was not to compete on the same terms, but rather to establish what Tooby and DeVore (1987) called the 'cognitive niche', relying on social cooperation and intelligent planning for survival. We succeeded. Masai in living in the savannah today still mature as warriors by cooperating as a hunting party to spear the king of the jungle. Accurate recording of specific events in a hostile environment may have been critical to effective and safe scavenging, and eventually to hunting as the manufacture of tools and weapons became more sophisticated. As Pinker (2003, p. 27) put it, it became increasingly important to encode information as to "who did what to whom, when, where, and why".

The progression toward what might be called episodic cognition might be tracked by the increase in brain size associated with the emergence of the genus *Homo*. When calibrated according to body size, the brains of the early hominids were of about the same size as those of modern great apes. According to estimates based on fossil skulls, for example, the average brain size of *Australopithecus afarensis*, a hominid species dating from some 3 to 4 million years ago, was around 433 cc compared with averages of 393 cc for the chimpanzee, 418 for the orangutan, and 465 for the gorilla (Martin, 1990). It rose to some 612 cc in *Homo habilis*, 854 cc in early *Homo erectus* (their African cousins are also known as *Homo ergaster*), and 1016 cc in later *Homo erectus*. After a period of stasis, there appears to have been a secondary increase from about 500,000 years ago, reaching about 1552 cc in the Neanderthals (*Homo neanderthalensis*), and a slightly smaller 1355 cc in *Homo sapiens* (Wood and Collard, 1999). This secondary increase might represent the arrival of a full sense of time, along with rituals associated with death and religion.

Language and memory: shared structures

The human capacity that is most widely regarded as uniquely human is language (e.g. Chomsky, 1975; Descartes, 1647/1985; Hauser et al., 2002; Pinker, 2004). Though some argue that all that is unique about human cognition can be traced to language (e.g. Macphail, 1996), we have argued that the evolution of mental content must have preceded the evolution of means to communicate such content. Language shares a number of critical properties with mental time travel, and may derive from the need to communicate about events that occur in other places and at other times. Indeed, the link between language and memory is implicit in the very term 'declarative memory', with the implication that our memories are accessible only through language – or what can be declared. Although declarative memory and mental time travel cannot be considered synonymous with language (i.e. one can talk without travelling in time and one can picture past and future without language), they do have a number of important characteristics in common. These include the following.

Combinatorial structure

The combinatorial structure of what we may call episodic thought arises, at least in part, because the same elements, including people, actions, contexts, and so forth, are repeated in different episodes in different combinations. The uniqueness of an episode, then, like the uniqueness of a sentence, depends more on the specific combination of the familiar than on the insertion of the unfamiliar. Given the repetition of elements, it is not surprising that the brain would establish these as part of semantic memory, which would be increasingly elaborated as we register more information about how individuals behave, how scenarios play out, how situations constrain events, and so on. Elements also belong naturally to different classes, the most fundamental being objects and actions. Each episode, whether remembered as a past event or imagined as a future one, can therefore be considered a particular combination of events belonging to different categories.

Language exhibits these same properties; every episode is a potential sentence, or combinations of sentences. According to the eighteenth-century English philologist John Horne Tooke (1857), the earliest 'language' consisted only of nouns and verbs ("necessary words"), corresponding at the most fundamental level to objects and actions. Structural complexity would then be built from the combinations of objects and actions, experienced as events, and represented in language as nouns and verbs. The added complexity would then allow individuals to register and express, in Pinker's phrase, "who did what to whom, when, where, and why". Within language, at least, this complexity has been attributed to a process of 'grammaticalization' (Hopper and Traugott, 2003), driven by environmental pressure. Christiansen and Dale (2004) have suggested that the structure of the brain did not adapt to accommodate language, as generally supposed, but rather that language adapted to biological constraints, and connectionist systems are increasingly successful in simulating the acquisition of language (e.g. Chang et al., 2006; Christiansen and Dale, 2004), without the necessity to postulate any pre-existing, innately determined universal grammar, such as proposed by Chomsky (1975). If this is so, then language may depend partly on the structure of knowledge and episodic memory, although there are also adaptations specific to language itself.

A real-life example of the 'discovery' of a combinatorial principle is provided by Nicaraguan Sign Language (NSL), which first emerged some twenty-five years ago when a school was established for deaf children. In an experimental study, users of NSL were asked to describe the action of rolling down a slope. Those from the first cohort mimicked both the rolling and the down motions in a single gesture. The majority of those in the second and third cohorts indicated the motion in two gestures, one to indicate a rolling motion and the other to indicate downward motion (Senghas et al., 2004). This is a living example of grammaticalization. The discovery of combinatorial structure may be as much a part of memory as a part of language itself. That is, through episodic experiences, one may come to parse events in more refined ways, and so begin to record different episodes as different combinations of the same elements.

Generativity

We argued earlier that episodic memory did not evolve to provide an accurate record of one's individual past, but rather to supply a vocabulary from which to construct a personal narrative and means for generating potential future episodes, and even to embellish or invent past ones. The generative nature of mental life is also well illustrated in fictional story-telling, whether orally, through books, or television soaps. Our imaginations are relentlessly generative, as we fantasize about what was, what might have been, and what hopefully will be. Indeed, the generative component allows us to understand time that precedes birth and that continues after death, giving rise to history, theories about the origins of the universe, and the concept of life after death.

Hockett (1960), who called it 'productivity', regarded generativity as one of the defining properties of human language. To Chomsky (e.g. 1975) generativity is the critical component of human language that distinguishes it from animal communication, and further implies that language cannot be reduced to associative learning, or to a finite-state system. More recently, Chomsky and colleagues have proposed that the critical ingredient underlying generativity is recursion (Hauser et al., 2002), which is a computational procedure that invokes itself, or that invokes an equivalent kind of procedure. It is recursion, then, that allows phrases to be embedded in phrases, as in sentences like *The dog that the cat scratched was subdued*. Recursion is as much a property of human episodic memory as of language, since events can be embedded in events.

The role of time

As outlined earlier, episodic memory introduced the dimension of time into mental life, thereby vastly increasing demands on storage. A life lived in the present can be accommodated largely through instinct and learned adaptations. The time dimension is a characteristic property of language, in the form of tense, enabling us to talk about past, present, or future. Most languages have developed subtle variations on the simple notion of time as a continuum from the past to the future. In English there are as many as thirty different tenses. For example, the future perfect (e.g. *he will have walked*) illustrates our ability, not only to project ourselves mentally into the future, but also to imagine an event that will be in the past at some future date. This again illustrates the generative, recursive nature of both language and thought.

Again, there is evidence that tense is not some innately given component of language, but depends on environmental or cultural contingencies. The language spoken by the Pirahã, a tribe of some 200 people in Brazil, has no perfect tense and only a very primitive way of talking about relative time (Everett, 2005). Correspondingly, the Pirahã are said to live in the present, with no creation myths, no art or drawing, no individual or collective memory for more than two generations past. Their language also has no numbers or system of counting and no colour terms. The grammar itself is simple, with no embedding of phrases, and the system of pronouns is the simplest yet recorded. They have remained monolingual despite more than 200 years of trading with Portuguese-speaking Brazilians and speakers of other native languages. One might be tempted to believe that they suffer from some genetic defect, but this idea is rejected by Everett, who describes them as "some of the brightest, pleasantest, and most fun-loving people that I know" (p. 621).

Evolution of language

Given the commonalities between language and mental time travel, it seems reasonable to assume that they are linked. Logically, one might suppose mental time travel to have preceded language. It was during the Pleistocene, perhaps, that the mind became structured to record individual events in time, affording a more finely tuned capacity to adapt to future events. Nevertheless, survival undoubtedly depended also on cooperation between individuals, and the sharing of episodic information. This may have led to the evolution of a form of communication designed to refer to events that were separated in both time and space from the present. To some degree at least, then, the structure of events dictated the structure of sentences, involving nouns and verbs to designate objects and actions. Since events are located in space and time, language also incorporated spatial markers as well as tense.

Although mental time travel may have been a prerequisite for language, the two must also have coevolved. Gärdenfors (2004) writes similarly that, in his view, "there has been a coevolution of cooperation about future goals and symbolic communication" (p. 243). Indeed language itself adds to the capacity for mental time travel, since it provides a means by which people can create the equivalent of episodic memories in others, and therefore contributes to episodic thinking. By telling you what happened to me, I can effectively create an imagined episode in your mind, and this added information might help you adapt more effectively to future conditions. Through story telling, there has no doubt been a long tradition in all cultures of creating potential scenarios that contribute to our ability to envisage future scenarios, both for ourselves and for others. Thus mental time travel and language can interact to vastly increase the storehouse of episodic information, leading also to the elaboration and refinement of semantic information. Mental time travel and language are costly compared to the more ancient mechanisms of instinct and learning, and probably depended on increases in the size of that metabolically expensive organ, the brain. Nevertheless they permit fine tuning to the specific environments that we humans inhabit, and may have been necessary in a world that, since the beginning of the Pleistocene, has become increasingly dangerous – although present-day threats derive more from our own species than from the killer cats of the savannah.

The formation of a combinatorial system to represent past episodes or to generate potential new ones may be the basis of what Pinker (1994) calls 'mentalese', the internal language of thought. Actual language, however, requires further adaptations, since the medium of thought is not the same as the various media of communication. Speech, for example, requires *linearization*, so that an episode that has both spatial and temporal components is converted into a temporal string of speech sounds. Signed languages can include both spatial and temporal components, perhaps allowing a more flexible mapping. For example, tense in speech depends on discrete words or morphemes, but signed language can be conveyed in a more continuous fashion by locating signed events at varying distances behind (*past*) or in front of (*future*) the body. The bigger the distance, the more

remote from the present. Many of the trappings of grammar are practical and conventionalized solutions to the problem of conveying
episodic information. With increasingly sophisticated visual media,
such as film and television, episodic information can be conveyed
even more directly, although we still need symbolic markers to indicate temporal and locational information.

Conclusions

Mental time travel and human language have been proposed as
uniquely human capacities. The main theme of this chapter is that
they are related, and indeed interdependent. The basic structure of
language, we argue, is rooted in declarative memory, which permits
the generation of specific episodes, whether past or future, actual or
imagined. Language then allows this information to be shared. This
does not mean, of course, that our language and thought consist
entirely of episodic information, or the semantic knowledge gained
from it, since language and thought both have undoubtedly expanded
to include abstract thought, logic, and the like. Nevertheless it has
been proposed that even processes as abstract as deductive logic may
depend on 'mental models' that often involve visual images (Johnson-
Laird and Byrne, 1991), which in turn may derive from the ability to
imagine events.

In neuroanatomical terms, the key to the evolution of both mental
time travel and language may lie in the mesial temporal lobe, and more
particularly the hippocampus. O'Keefe and Nadel (1978) provided
detailed evidence showing that the infrahuman hippocampus com-
prises a 'cognitive map', in which particular locations are stored for
future use. O'Keefe (1996) suggests that this model must be extended
to account for evidence on the role of the hippocampus in human, in
two ways. First, time itself must be incorporated into the model to
allow for the storage of spatiotemporal information, thus providing
for episodic memory. Second, the model must be extended to account
for lateralization of function, with much of the left hemisphere taken
over by language functions. In humans, damage to the right mesial
temporal lobe results in amnesia for episodic visuospatial material,
while left-sided damage results in amnesia for linguistic material (e.g.
Frisk and Milner, 1990). Thus the right hippocampus receives inputs
from analysis of the physical world, while the left hippocampus

receives inputs from language centres. Implicit in this notion is that language itself has a fundamentally spatial structure, an idea advocated by a group of linguists known as 'localists' (e.g. Anderson, 1971; Cook, 1989). O'Keefe notes, for instance, that most prepositions in English, such as *at, about, around, between, among, along, across, opposite, against, from, to*, and *through*, are fundamentally spatial, and can apply to any of the three spatial dimensions, although a few prepositions, such as *since* or *until*, apply only to the time dimension. Nevertheless spatial prepositions can also be applied to time, as in *from Monday through Friday*, and even to logical expressions that are symbolic rather than spatial, as in *A follows from B*, or *The argument against A is B*.

Evidence for a close link between grammar and space also comes from developmental studies. Mandler (1996) has argued that language is structured spatially because preverbal infants have already constructed spatial representations. The developmental links between language and spatial concepts is explored more fully in the edited volume by Bloom et al. (1996). One might suppose that the time dimension is added later, allowing the development of episodic memory and the emergence of tense in language. Perhaps the most compelling argument for the use of a spatial structure underlying language comes from signed languages, which are themselves fundamentally spatial (Emmorey, 2002). One of us (MCC) has argued elsewhere that speech evolved from manual gesture, suggesting an evolutionary scenario for the close link between language and space (Corballis, 2002; Gentilucci and Corballis, this volume).

In this chapter, we have merely sketched the idea that two characteristics that appear to be uniquely human might be fundamentally related. These characteristics are mental time travel, and language. Given that language seems so admirably designed to convey information about events that are located in space and time, we suggest that the relations between the two should be further explored.

References

Ambrose, S. H. 2001. 'Paleolithic technology and human evolution', *Science*, 291, 1748–1752.

Anderson, J. M. 1971. *The Grammar of Case: Towards a Localist Theory*. Cambridge: Cambridge University Press.

Anderson, J. R. and Schooler, L. J. 1991. 'Reflections of the environment in memory', *Psychological Science*, 2, 396–408.

Andrews, P. and Stringer, C. 1993. 'The primates' progress', in *The Book of Life*, ed. S. J. Gould. London: Norton, pp. 219–251.

Atance, C. M. and O'Neill, D. K. 2005. 'The emergence of episodic future thinking in humans', *Learning and Motivation*, 36, 126–144.

Bloom, P., Peterson, M. A., Nadel, L. and Garrett, M. F. (eds.). 1996. *Language and Space*. Cambridge, MA: MIT Press.

Busby, J. and Suddendorf, T. 2005. 'Recalling yesterday and predicting tomorrow', *Cognitive Development*, 20, 362–372.

Chang, F., Dell, G. S. and Bock, K. 2006. 'Becoming syntactic', *Psychological Review*, 113, 234–272.

Chomsky, N. 1975. *Reflections on Language*. New York: Pantheon.

Christiansen, M. H. and Dale, R. 2004. 'The role of learning and development in language evolution: A connectionist perspective', in *Evolution of Communication Systems*, ed. D. K. Oller and U. Griebel. Cambridge, MA: MIT Press, pp. 91–109.

Clayton, N. S., Bussey, T. J., and Dickinson, A. 2003. 'Can animals recall the past and plan for the future?', *Nature Reviews Neuroscience*, 4, 685–691.

Cook, W. A. 1989. *Case Grammar Theory*. Washington, DC: Georgetown University Press.

Corballis, M. C. 2002. *From Hand to Mouth: the Origins of Language*. Princeton, NJ: Princeton University Press.

Craik, K. 1943. *The Nature of Explanation*. Cambridge: Cambridge University Press.

Descartes, R. 1985. 'Discourse on method, in J. Cottingham, R. Stootfoff, and D. Murdock (ed. and tr.), *The Philosophical Writings of Descartes*. Cambridge: Cambridge University Press (orig. pub. 1647).

Emery, N. J. and Clayton, N. S. 2001. 'Effects of experience and social context on prospective caching strategies by scrub jays', *Nature*, 414, 443–446.

Emmorey, K. 2002. *Language, Cognition, and Brain: Insights from Sign Language Research*. Hillsdale, NJ: Erlbaum.

Everett, D. L. 2005. 'Cultural constraints on grammar and cognition in Pirahã', *Current Anthropology*, 46, 621–646.

Foley, R. 1987. *Another Unique Species: Patterns in Human Evolutionary Ecology*. Harlow: Longman Scientific and Technical.

Frisk, V. and Milner, B. 1990. 'The role of the left hippocampal region in the acquisition and retention of story content', *Neuropsychologia*, 28, 349–359.

Gärdenfors, P. 2004. 'Cooperation and the evolution of symbolic communication', in *Evolution of Communication Systems*, ed. D. K. Oller and U. Griebel. Cambridge, MA: MIT Press, pp. 237–256.

Gentilucci, M. and Corballis, M. C. 2007. 'The hominid that talked' (*this volume*).

Hauser, M. D., Chomsky, N., and Fitch, W. T. 2002. 'The faculty of language: What is it, who has it, and how did it evolve?', *Science*, 298, 1569–1579.

Hockett, C. F. 1960. 'The origin of speech', *Scientific American*, 203, 88–96.

Hopper, P. J. and Traugott, E. C. 2003. *Grammaticalization* (2nd edition). Cambridge: Cambridge University Press.

Horne Tooke, J. 1857. 'Epea pteroenta or the diversions of Purley'. London: Tegg.

Hunt, G. R. 2000. 'Human-like, population-level specialization in the manufacture of pandanus tools by New Caledonian crows *Corvus moneduloides*', *Proceedings of the Royal Society of London B*, 267, 403–413.

Johnson-Laird, P. N. and Byrne, R. M. J. 1991. *Deduction*. Hillsdale, NJ: Erlbaum.

Kamil, A. C. and Balda, R. P. 1985. 'Cache recovery and spatial memory in Clark's nutcrackers (*Nucifraga columbiana*)', *Journal of Experimental Psychology: Animal Behavior Processes*, 85, 95–111.

Klein, S. B., Loftus, J., and Kihlstrom, J. F. 2002. 'Memory and temporal experience: The effects of episodic memory loss on an amnesiac patient's ability to remember the past and imagine the future', *Social Cognition*, 20, 353–379.

Loftus, E. and Ketcham, K. 1994. *The Myth of Repressed Memory*. New York: St. Martin's Press.

Loftus, E. F. and Loftus, G. R. 1980. 'On the permanence of stored information in the human-brain', *American Psychologist*, 35, 409–420.

Macphail, E. M. 1996. 'Cognitive function in mammals: The evolutionary perspective', *Cognitive Brain Research*, 3, 279–290.

Mandler, J. 1996. 'Preverbal representation and language', in *Language and Space*, ed. P. Bloom, M. A. Peterson, L. Nadel, and M. F. Garrett. Cambridge, MA: MIT Press, pp. 365–384.

Martin, R. D. 1990. *Primate Origins and Evolution: A Phylogenetic Reconstruction*. Princeton, NJ: Princeton University Press.

Mellars, P. A. and Stringer, C. B. (eds.) 1989. *The Human Revolution: Behavioural and Biological Perspectives on the Origins of Modern Humans*. Edinburgh: Edinburgh University Press.

Miyashita, Y. 2004. 'Cognitive memory: Cellular and network machineries and their top-down control', *Science*, 306, 435–440.

Mulcahy, N. J. and Call, J. 2006. 'Apes save tools for future use', *Science*, 312, 1038–1040.

Oakley, K. P. 1961. 'On man's use of fire, with comments on tool-making and hunting', in *Social Life of Early Man*, ed. S. L. Washburn. Chicago: Aldine, pp. 176–193.

O'Keefe, J. 1996. 'The spatial prepositions in English, vector grammar, and the cognitive map theory', in *Language and Space*, ed. P. Bloom, M. A. Peterson, L. Nadel, and M. F. Garrett. Cambridge, MA: MIT Press, pp. 277–316.

O'Keefe, J. and Nadel, L. 1978. *The Hippocampus as a Cognitive Map*. Oxford: Clarendon Press.

Pettit, P. 2002. 'When burial begins', *British Archaeology*, issue 66 (August).

Pinker, S. 2004. *The Language Instinct*. New York: Morrow.

Pinker, S. 2003. 'Language as an adaptation to the cognitive niche', in *Language Evolution*, ed. M. H. Christiansen and S. Kirby. Oxford: Oxford University Press, pp. 16–37.

Roediger, H. L. and McDermott, K. B. 1995. 'Creating false memories – remembering words not presented in lists', *Journal of Experimental Psychology: Learning Memory and Cognition*, 21, 803–814.

Schacter, D. L. 1996. *Searching for Memory: The Brain, the Mind, and the Past*. New York: Basic Books.

Semaw, S. P., Renne, P., Harris, J. W. K., Feibel, C. S., Bernor, R. L., Fessweha, N. et al. 1997. '2.5-million-year-old stone tools from Gona, Ethiopia', *Nature*, 385, 333–336.

Senghas, A., Kita, S., and Özyürek, A. 2004. 'Children creating core properties of language: Evidence from an emerging sign language in Nicaragua', *Science*, 305, 1779–1782.

Skinner, B. F. 1966. 'Phylogeny and ontogeny of behaviour', *Science*, 153, 1205–1213.

Squire, L. R. 2004. 'Memory systems of the brain: A brief history and current perspective', *Neurobiology of Learning and Memory*, 82, 171–177.

Suddendorf, T. 2006. 'Foresight and evolution of the human mind', *Science*, 312, 1006–1007.

Suddendorf, T. and Busby, J. 2003. 'Mental time travel in animals?', *Trends in Cognitive Sciences*, 7, 391–396.

Suddendorf, T. and Corballis, M. C. 1997. 'Mental time travel and the evolution of the human mind', *Genetic, Social, and General Psychology Monographs*, 123, 133–167.

Tooby, J., and DeVore, I. 1987. 'The reconstruction of hominid evolution through strategic modeling', in *The Evolution of Human Behavior: Primate Models*, ed. W. G. Kinzey. Albany, NY: SUNY Press.

Tulving, E. 1972. 'Episodic and semantic memory', in *Organization of Memory*, ed. E. Tulving and W. Donaldson. New York: Academic Press, pp. 381–403.

——. 1983. *Elements of Episodic Memory*. London: Oxford University Press.

——. 1985. 'Memory and consciousness', *Canadian Psychology*, 26, 1–12.

Tulving, E., Schacter, D. L., McLachlan, D. R., and Moscovitch, M. 1988. 'Priming of semantic autobiographical knowledge: A case study of retrograde amnesia', *Brain and Cognition*, 8, 3–20.

Walter, R. C., Buffler, R. T., Bruggemann, J. H., Guillaume, M. M. M., Berhe, S. M., Negassi, B. et al. 2000. 'Early human occupation of the Red Sea coast of Eritrea during the last interglacial', *Nature*, 405, 65–69.

Whiten, A., Horner, V., and de Waal, F. B. M. 2005. 'Conformity to cultural norms of tool use in chimpanzees', *Nature*, 437, 737–740.

Wood, B. 2002. 'Hominid revelations from Chad', *Nature*, 418, 134–135.

Wood, B. and Collard, M. 1999. 'The human genus', *Science*, 284, 65–71.

3: Why Are Humans Not Just Great Apes?

Robin Dunbar

Humans are a very odd species, at least by comparison with all the others that we know about. To be sure, we share a long history with, and many similarities to, our primate cousins. As a result, most of the differences between us and great apes (our sister species) in terms of our anatomy, physiology and genetics are trivial. We differ, as has so often been pointed out, by only about 2 per cent in terms of our DNA from chimpanzees, whose own direct ancestors we shared around 5–6 million years ago. But there are some anatomical oddities. We are bipedal, for example, and have unusually large brains.

For a long time, these persuaded biologists to classify humans in a separate group among the apes. Conventional wisdom had it that we shared only a very deep ancestry with the other great apes, perhaps as long as 20 million years ago, long before even the orangutan's lineage branched off from its common ancestor with the other three great apes (the chimpanzee, bonobo and gorilla – or, strictly speaking as it has now turned out, the two gorilla species). The human lineage, which included all the australopithecines from Africa, had a long and – we supposed – distinguished history that was separate from the other apes. After all, if nothing else, we walked upright and all the other apes walked on all fours.

But appearances can be deceptive. As the genetic revolution unfolded through the 1980s, it became increasingly obvious that, no matter how different we might *appear* from the other apes, our genetic make-up was rather similar. In fact, more than just rather similar: it was all but identical. By the end of that decade, our whole understanding of ape evolutionary history had been turned on its head. So far from being a separate evolutionary lineage with deep roots, we humans were in fact embedded within the great ape family. Indeed, we were not just embedded within the great ape family, we were kith and kin to the chimpanzees – genetically more closely related to the two chimpanzee species (the common chimpanzee and the bonobo) than any of the three of us was related to the gorilla. Indeed, it has since turned out that we are more closely related to each other than the two species of gorilla (the physically barely distinguishable eastern and western gorillas) are related to each other! The universally accepted position is now that the big split in the great ape family is not between humans and the other great apes, but between the Asian orangutan and the four (or should it be five?) species of African great apes (one of which is us humans). Humans are now, strictly speaking, firmly ensconced within the chimpanzee family.

Yet, despite this, we are very different from all our ape cousins. Despite all the fuss being made about cultural traditions in chimpanzees and orangutans (and occasionally among whales, too), only one species has built the Great Wall of China, put men on the moon, thought up Pythagoras's theorem, conceived the existence of life after death, written the plays of Shakespeare and composed the music of Johann Sebastian Bach. In short, is in humans' capacity for culture, to live in a world constructed by ideas, that we really differ from the other apes. So just how are we different from the other apes (and, by extension, all other forms of life), and why should this have come to be?

How humans are different

So let me begin with the easier question: in exactly what ways are humans different from other species? I want to argue that the real differences lie in our capacity to live in an imagined world. In respect of almost everything else, including the basic features of our cognition – like memory and causal reasoning – we are all but indistinguishable from great apes. What we can do, and they cannot, is to step back from the real world and ask: could it have been otherwise than we experience it? In that simple question lies the basis for everything that we would think of as uniquely human. Literature depends on our capacity to imagine a set of events, a world that is different from the one we personally inhabit on a day to day basis. Science depends on our capacity to imagine that the world could have been different, and then to ask why it has to be the way it is. Curiosity about distant places has led us to explore the furthest reaches of the planet, and even to venture hesitantly out into space.

By contrast, all other creatures alive today seem to have their noses thrust so firmly up against the grindstone of everyday experience that they cannot step back far enough to ask these kinds of questions. The world is as it is, and that seems to be all there is to it. They cannot explore the world of the imagination in the way that is so fundamental and so necessary to everything we would naturally identify as being the core to the human condition – what it means to be human.

But there is one aspect of our cultural life that merits particular comment in this context. And this is our capacity to contemplate alternative universes. As a result of this, we have developed theories about transcendent spirit worlds, about life before birth and after death, about beings who live in a parallel universe who can influence the world in which we live. In short, it is the world of religion. There is something genuinely odd about our apparent capacity to live our lives partly in an inner world that is half-connected with the real world. I would argue that this capacity has a particularly close association with our capacity to produce literature. Both share the curious feature of requiring us to imagine fictional worlds with such intensity that we can believe in their veracity.

Given this, the question we have to ask is why apes, for example, cannot create these imagined worlds. At least, so far as I know, no one has yet produced convincing evidence that they can do so and pretty well most scientists working in this area are rather pessimistic that anyone is ever likely to do so in the future. Apes certainly do not produce any of the externally visible signs of being able to do so. They do not build structures, or organise festivals to worship gods or plan (never mind go on) expeditions to far distant places. And, crucially, they do not speak. Language is critical in this context, because if we do not communicate our ideas and thoughts about this inner world, it might as well not exist. This is not to say that language creates or gives rise to these inner worlds. Far from it: my point is only that language is necessary to *communicate* our discoveries about these inner worlds to each other. If we cannot share these experiences with others, we cannot build those communal intellectual edifices that we think of as the essence of human culture – dramas, histories, the rituals of religion, metaphysics and theologies. So, what is it about apes' minds that prevents them from doing so?

Theory of mind and intentionality

There is a growing consensus among both developmental and comparative psychologists that the phenomenon known as 'theory of mind' (the capacity to imagine another individual's 'mind states') is a critical difference between humans and other animals. It is widely accepted now that most animals (certainly higher animals) have knowledge of their own mind states. In terms of philosophy of mind, this is what is usually referred to as first order intentionality. 'Intentionality' is a general term covering those mind states that involve beliefs. They are evidenced by the use of words like *believe* [that something is the case], *know*, *suppose*, *intend*, *want*, *desire*, *wish*, etc. They imply that we have a certain level of awareness about the contents of our minds, that we are aware that we believe, in some intuitive sense, that something is the case.

This state of self-knowledge is the world inhabited by very young children. This is not necessarily the same thing as *self*-consciousness, but it is certainly a form of consciousness – and probably one that is shared with a wide range of birds and mammals, at the very least. However, at around the age of four years, children develop the capacity to reflect on other's minds as well as their own. This capacity is now referred to as 'theory of mind' (literally intended to mean that they have a theory about minds, a theory about other people's capacities to have beliefs). It may even be the key to self-consciousness in some formal sense: they can believe that they themselves believe that something is the case.

The key distinction in this respect lies in two particular aspects of young children's behaviour. Once they have acquired the capacity for theory of mind, they are able to engage in fictive play (to imagine that a dolly can drink tea from a teacup, even though the cup is empty) and they can lie with conviction. This is not to say that children cannot lie before the age of four years: of course they can. Rather it is the *quality* of the lying that changes. Before the age of four, they are what we might think of as good ethologists: they are good at reading observable behaviour, at noticing the correlations between events in the world, at learning how to manipulate the world to get what they want. But the way they do this is by working at a relatively superficial level. They know that if you say something with utter conviction, adults will give you the benefit of the doubt nine times out of ten. But they don't understand *why* adults do that, only the fact that they do. In the tradition of Gilbert Ryle's philosophy of mind (Ryle, 1967), they understand *that* but they don't understand *how* (or *why*). From the age of about four, they begin to appreciate that other people have minds like their own, and that sometimes these minds see the world differently, and so can have different beliefs about the world. As a result, they can begin to exploit those minds by feeding them false information in order to deliberately mislead them. And this raises the ante considerably, because the skill and effectiveness with which they can lie is greatly magnified. There is still much to learn from practice, but the point is that the acquisition of theory of mind takes their mental world onto a new and higher plane.

With theory of mind in the mental tool kit of young children, they become good psychologists – they understand the mind behind the behaviour, and they begin to understand how false information can mislead that mind. They are in what philosophers of mind would call second order intentionality – they *believe* that someone else *believes* [that something is the case]. Before this, they have always assumed that everyone else shares the same knowledge about the world as they do. But now, with theory of mind, they are able to realise that others can hold false beliefs (or, rather, beliefs that they suppose to be false).

There is no evidence to suggest that any species of animals other than humans – not even dolphins – has theory of mind. The only case where this might be so (and the evidence is weak and open to dispute) is chimpanzees (and, by extension, probably the other great apes). In my view, the evidence is suggestive enough to imply that chimpanzees are about at the same level as children aged four to five – i.e. the point at which children are acquiring theory of mind, but are still not wholly proficient at it in the way that, for example, six-year-olds are.

This is enough, I think, to suggest that great apes may indeed be a cut above the average monkey, dolphin, lion, and rat. But in the grand scale of things, they are still a long way short of what adult humans can do. If we consider intentionality as a naturally reflexive scale that extends to infinity – I *believe* that you *suppose* that we *want* to ensure that everyone else *understands* that we would *like* them all to *believe* that we *know* [.... what we are talking about] – then we can compare how well humans of different ages do on understanding these kinds of tasks. When we have done this, we find that on the scale babies have first order intentionality and five-year-olds have second order, normal adult humans scale in at fifth order. We can cope competently with thoughts as convoluted as "I *believe* that you *suppose* that we *want* to ensure that everyone else *understands* that we would *like* them ...", but after that we get lost. It seems that this is not just a memory problem (i.e. remembering long strings of words in sentences) but one of keeping track of the various mind states.

Even so, by comparison with what human toddlers and chimpanzees can do, even fifth order intentionality is in a different and very grand league. It's the difference between running a computer programme on your Nintendo *Gameboy* and running it on a powerful modern PC. It makes it possible to do certain things that simply cannot be done on the smaller computer. Let me illustrate this with a strictly literary example.

Shakespeare and *Othello*

Consider Shakespeare sitting down to write his play *Othello*. To make this play work, he has to have at least three core characters: Othello himself, Iago and the ill-fated Desdemona. This involved Shakespeare persuading his audience (when they eventually got to see the play) that Iago *intended* that Othello *believe* that Desdemona *was in love* with someone else. That involves three separate mind states on the stage. But to make the story really convincing, he really has to add in Casio, the apparent object of Desdemona's desires. If Desdemona merely fantasised about Casio, Othello would, surely, have been much less bothered by it all. It might have led to a bit of leg-pulling in the garden, but why should Othello have been so exercised about the intelligence that Iago offered him if he believed that Casio was not involved. The answer is that Othello is led to believe that Casio reciprocates Desdemona's interest. It is this that racks up the intensity of Othello's angst and causes him to do what he eventually did. So, to make the story really sell, Shakespeare has to handle four mind states on the stage: Iago *intends* that Othello *believes* that Desdemona *loves* Casio and Casio *loves* her.

So just to put the bones of the story together on the stage, Shakespeare has to handle four sets of minds, and that means working at fourth order intentionality. But this is not the end of the story, because Shakespeare has to persuade the audience to believe all this stuff. If they are not taken in by it, the play will be dead in the water, and the impressario of the Globe Theatre won't be coming back to him for another play as the current run draws to its end. So Shakespeare has to factor the minds of the audience (or, at least, the virtual mind of a nominal member of the audience) into his calculations. And last, but not least, he has to be doing the imagining of all this himself. So when he sat down with his quill pen poised above a sheet of foolscap one wet Monday morning in Elizabethan London, he had to be able to work – minimally – at sixth order intentionality: he had to *intend* that the audience *believed* that Iago *wanted* Othello to *suppose* that Desdemona *loved* Casio and that Casio, in turn, *loved* her (and hence that they planned to run away together).

That's no mean feat, because he is already working at one level of intentionality above what the average adult human can cope with. Notice that he is also pushing his audience to its limits – fifth order intentionality. It is probably precisely because Shakespeare could work successfully at this level, and so challenge his audience to their limit, that he came to be such a successful playwright.

However, the real issue for our present concerns is that only a human could have done this. With their cognitive limits set firmly at second order intentionality (at best!), even the proverbial chimpanzee sitting down at its typewriter could never have produced the script for *Othello*. If it had actually done so after many millions of years of typing, it would have been a purely statistical accident, and not a very interesting one at that. For the ape typist would not have *intended* the action of the play, and it certainly would never have pondered the audience's capacity to follow the unfolding story as it did so. It might have appreciated that Iago intended to say something to Othello ("I *believe* that Iago *intends* ..."), but it would not have been able to understand how, in addition, Othello interpreted Iago's words – that would have required third order intentionality that it could never aspire to.

So the lesson for us is that the flights of fancy that we engage in when dabbling in literature, even when just telling stories around the campfire, are far beyond the cognitive capacities of any other species of animal currently alive. Great apes might be able to imagine some-one else's state of mind, and so they might even be able to construct a very simple story, but it could never be much more than a narrative involving one character. Only adult humans could ever intentionally produce literature of the kind that we associate with human culture. It is possible, of course, to produce stories with third and even fourth order intentionality (perhaps the cognitive equivalent of eight- and eleven-year-old children), but they would inevitably lack the sophisti-cation of the stories told by the average adult, never mind those of a Shakespeare or a Molière.

The argument for religion

I want to suggest that we can make exactly the same argument for reli-gion. Just as we can construct stories with different levels of inten-tionality, so we can construct religions at different levels of intentionality. But without the capacity for intentionality, we could not even begin to imagine a world that involves spirits that have no corporeal substance. We minimally require competent second order intentionality to do that: I *believe* that the world is other than I *believe* it to be from my direct experience – in other words, that there is some kind of parallel spirit world that can influence the world I live in. But, at best, that simply gives us a rather solipsistic form of religion. I can have a personal belief, but no more.

If we add a third level of intentionality, we can do a bit better per-haps. I can try to persuade you about my beliefs: I *intend* that you *believe* that these spirit beings are *willing* to intervene in our world (if we ask them nicely enough). But we are really still not that much better off. I can tell you about my beliefs, but there is nothing to per-suade you to acquiesce. I could try fourth order: I *intend* that you *believe* that the spirits *are willing* to intervene in a way that we *want* them to ... Now I think we have a form of *social* religion: you and I can agree about what is involved in this spirit world. But still we are not quite there yet, for there is nothing in all this to persuade you that *you* have to acquiesce: you can shrug your shoulders, look puzzled and walk away – if I want to believe all this, that's fine, but ... Add a fifth order of intentionality, however, and it seems to me we are suddenly in a different league: I *intend* that you *believe* that we *want* the spirits *to be willing* to intervene in the world in the way we *want* them to. Now we have what I would call *communal* religion, because if you accept the truth of this statement, it commits you to the same beliefs as me. Fourth order does not: you can accept a fourth order statement as being true (you can agree that I believe all this), but without any need to feel committed to that belief yourself.

So, I would argue that to have religion in the sense that we understand it – religion as we actually experience and practise it – you have to have fifth order intentionality. Anything less, and what you get can certainly be described as religion, but it is a form of religion that is more personal, and would certainly not be strong enough to create the kinds of communal commitment to dogma that we associate with religion in its modern sense. We would not, I suggest, find mass acts of worship, mass acts of belief about religious phenomena. There would be no miraculous apparitions at Lourdes, no witch hunts at Salem, no wailing at the Temple wall in Jerusalem.

When, and why, did humans become human?

'Why' questions are usually easier to answer than 'When' questions, so let me begin with the 'Why'. Humans are intensely social animals, just like all our monkey and ape cousins. We live in tightly bonded social groups, and it is this sociality that has been the secret of our success, just as it has been the secret of primates' evolutionary success as a family. Primate societies are implicit social contracts: their members, in effect, agree to cooperate in solving the everyday problems of life and death collectively. Doing so allows them to solve these problems more effectively. But such cooperation comes at a price. Social contracts are always at risk of freeriders – those who take the benefits of the contract, but decline to pay all the costs. A social contract obliges you to be willing to forgo some of your immediate selfish desires in the interests of being able to find enough common ground to allow cooperation to work. Failure to do so will inevitably create dissension and distrust, and ultimately lead to the dissolution of the contract. It very quickly becomes everyone for themselves once again. Freeriders destabilise social contracts because they trade on and exploit our willingness to trust each other to do our bit.

Because freeriders are so destructive, all social contracts require mechanisms to control or police freeriders. So long as they can be held in check most of the time, cooperation can work, even if, very occasionally, individuals get exploited. It is probably impossible to get rid of freeriders altogether, but at least we can minimise their impact. Although detection, policing and punishing are effective ways of dissuading individuals from doing too much freeriding, the carrot is always better than the stick. And one of the most effective carrots we have in our social armoury is creating a sense of communality, of belonging, of membership in the group. Rousing the emotional commitment to the common weal is much more effective than threatening even the most dire sanctions. This is because, if we commit ourselves to the group, our consciences do a very good job of policing our behaviour. If we merely threaten punishment, then there is always the temptation to try and get away with it if we can – not least because the risk of punishment always depends on the uncertainty of detection. Even in the house of *Big Brother* it is never possible to watch everyone all the time.

So, the solution to the freerider problem is easy: just persuade everyone to commit themselves to the group and its ideals and common interests. And it is here that I think story-telling and religion come into play: they are two particularly effective ways in which we try to create this sense of belonging, of groupishness.

Story-telling works at two levels. One of these is very direct, because stories – and especially stories in traditional societies – are often about group origins. Origin stories play a prominent role because they remind us all who we are, and how we came to be here. Usually, that involves reminding us that we are all descended from the same common ancestor, whether that ancestor be real or entirely mythical. By reminding us that we are all family, we call up strong ancient emotions, especially the evolutionarily very ancient emotions associated with behaving altruistically towards kin. But such stories also create a sense of belonging indirectly. Shared knowledge plays an important role in creating a sense of group membership, and probably especially so in identifying common kinship. You and I share a common fund of knowledge about the world because we grew up together and learned all this at the same set of mothers' knees, and we grew up together because, at least statistically, we are all related. Being able to tell a story depends on being able to call on a vast array of implicit shared knowledge among the listeners, so that the story-teller does not have to explain every last detail. Indeed, it seems as though it is the listeners' ability to fill in the gaps that makes the experience all the more exciting and emotional. And by stirring up the emotions, we create a sense of bonding between those involved.

The rituals of religion work in much the same way: they stir up powerful emotions, sometimes even by imposing pain, sometimes by creating terror, sometimes just through the use of song and dance. The more intense the pain, the more frightening the occasion, the more intense the emotion; and if this is done as a group, everyone emerges from it feeling that they belong to a band of brothers (or sisters, as the case may be). This is the nature of crowd effects. One sees it in rites of passage in traditional societies, one sees it in its more extreme forms even in the modern doctrinal world religions (think of the flagellants in medieval Christianity and their many imitators in the centuries since; think of the annual rituals of Shia Islam associated with the martyrdom of the Iman Husain at Kabala and elsewhere).

But religion needs more than just rituals: it needs reasons for people to gather together and perform the rituals, and it is here that the intellectual component comes in. We need a theology to persuade us to keep turning up and engaging in these bonding rituals, or we become lazy. And the theology, in turn, requires the intentionality capacities that we discussed in the preceding section. We need to be able to work at fifth order intentionality to have the intellectual commitment to make us turn up for our weekly dose of religious ritual.

So if religion came into existence as part of the complex of mechanisms designed to create a sense of group membership, when did it first evolve? Well, since we can in principle have religion at any level of intentionality, the short answer is that it might have existed from the moment our ancestors had third order intentionality. But, while that may be true, we have to recognise that the nature of the religious experience that our ancestors could have had would have depended crucially on the levels of intentionality that they could habitually aspire to. Third order religion would probably not have involved rituals and communal beliefs of the kind that would be effective in group bonding. For that, we really seem to need fifth order intentionality.

So when might fifth order intentionality have appeared? And since this is also the level of intentionality we find in modern humans, in effect we are asking: when did the modern human mind first appear? This seems like a difficult question to answer, but as it happens anatomy springs to our aid, at least to provide a tentative answer. We do not have a great deal of hard data to go on, but what there is suggests that there is a fairly simple relationship between achievable levels of intentionality and the size of the frontal lobe, at least across the monkeys, apes and humans. Though somewhat tentative, we can set an equation through these data and use this equation to predict intentionality levels for our ancestral fossil populations from the sizes of their brains.

If we do this, we find that fifth order intentionality did not appear before the appearance of our own species (usually known to archaeologists as 'anatomically modern humans' to differentiate them from people like the Neanderthals), and the genetic evidence suggests that they first originated about 200,000 years ago. The archaic humans who preceded us (among whom the Neanderthals are now numbered) would certainly have had fourth order intentionality, and that would surely have meant that they could have had religion in some more muted form. But full-blown religion, with its rituals and panoply of commonly held beliefs and commitments, would have sprung into life only with the emergence of modern humans, somewhere in Africa, a mere 10,000 generations ago. In the grand scale of human evolution stretching back to our last common ancestor with the apes some five and a half million years ago, that's not all that long ago.

Conclusions

I have tried to make three claims here. One is that humans really differ from other monkeys and apes in just one key respect, the world of the imagination. That capacity to live in a virtual world makes possible both literature and religion, perhaps the two most central aspects of culture that define our humanity. The other is that religion and story-telling evolved in order to enable our large and otherwise rather fragmented social groups to be bonded into effective communities so that they could do their intended job of fostering our survival and evolutionary success. Last, but perhaps by no means least, I have suggested that there is some indirect evidence to suggest that those capacities might have arisen rather late during the course of human evolution – indeed, that they explicitly demarcate and define the appearance of our particular species, modern humans.

Reference

Ryle, G. 1967. *The Concept of Mind*. London: Hutchinson.

4: The Hominid that Talked

Maurizio Gentilucci and Michael C. Corballis

Introduction

It is commonly argued that the primary characteristic that distinguishes our species from other hominids is language (e.g. Bickerton, 1995; Crow, 2002; Pinker, 1994). In this chapter, we argue that it was not language *per se* that distinguished *Homo sapiens* from our immediate, but now extinct, ancestors. Rather, it was the conversion from a primarily visual form of language to one that is conveyed primarily through the medium of sound. What distinguished our species was the power of speech.

The argument derives initially from the question of how language evolved in the first place. Language is composed of symbols that bear little or no physical relation to the objects, actions, or properties they represent. How, then, did these abstract symbols become associated with aspects of the real world? One theory proposed by Paget (1930), called "schematopoeia," holds that spoken words arose initially from parallels between sound and meaning. Nevertheless most of the things we talk about cannot be represented iconically through sound, and with very few exceptions the actual sounds of most words convey nothing of what they mean. This raises the paradox that was well expressed by Rousseau (1964/1775), who remarked that "Words would seem to have been necessary to establish the use of words" (pp. 148–149).

A possible solution to this problem is suggested by the theory that language evolved from manual gestures rather than from vocalizations. This theory goes back at least to the eighteenth-century philosopher Condillac (1971/1756), but has been put forward, with variations, many times since (e.g. Arbib, 2005; Armstrong, 1999; Armstrong et al., 1995; Corballis, 1992, 2002; Donald, 1991, Gentilucci and Corballis, 2006; Givòn, 1995; Hewes, 1973; Rizzolatti and Arbib, 1998; Ruben, 2005). Unlike spoken words, manual actions can provide more obvious iconic links with objects and actions in the physical world. In the course of evolution pantomimes of actions might have incorporated gestures that are analogue representations of objects or actions (Donald, 1991), but through time these gestures may have lost the analogue features and become abstract. The shift from iconic gestures to arbitrary symbols, which appears to be common to both human and animal communication systems, is termed *conventionalization*, and is probably driven by increased economy of reference (Burling, 1999).

Nevertheless, the gestural theory of language origins has not received widespread acceptance. One of the reasons for this has been well expressed by the linguist Robbins Burling:

> ... the gestural theory has one nearly fatal flaw. Its sticking point has always been the switch that would have been needed to move from a visual language to an audible one (Burling, 2005, p. 123).

We argue below that, on the contrary, the transition can be readily understood in both neurophysiological and evolutionary terms. The switch, we propose, was a gradual one, and even today speech is typically accompanied by manual gestures that help convey a speaker's full meaning. Nevertheless the capacity to convey the major part of the message entirely through the vocal medium, as on radio or telephone, may have evolved only in our own species, and may explain the so-called "human revolution" that has allowed our species to dominate the planet. It may also explain the demise of the Neanderthals, who in other respects seem to have been the cognitive equals of *Homo sapiens*. The questions of where, how, when, and why language might have been transformed from something resembling gesture language to vocal speech are considered in the following sections.

Where ...

Neurophysiological evidence suggests that nonhuman primates have little if any cortical control over vocalization, which is critical to speech. This implies that the common ancestor of humans and chimpanzees was much better preadapted to develop a voluntary communication system based on visible gestures rather than sounds. Ploog (2002) documents two neural systems for vocal behavior, a cingulate pathway and a neocortical pathway. In nonhuman primates vocalization is largely, if not exclusively, dependent on the cingulate system. The neocortical system was progressively developed for voluntary control of manual movements, including relatively independent finger movements, from monkeys to apes to humans, and is indispensable for voluntary control (e.g. Hepp-Raymond, 1988). Only in humans is the neocortical system developed for precise voluntary control of the muscles of the vocal cords and tongue.

Monkeys do make extensive use of facial expressions for communication, but these are more obviously gestural than language-like (Van Hooff, 1962, 1967). Attempts to teach vocal language to great apes have achieved much greater success in communicating in language-like fashion through manual signs than in acquiring anything resembling vocal language (e.g. Gardner and Gardner, 1969; Savage-Rumbaugh et al., 1998), which is further evidence that voluntary control is more highly developed manually than vocally in our closest primate relatives. The human equivalents of primate vocalizations are probably emotionally-based sounds like laughing, crying, grunting, or shrieking, rather than words. With the emergence of bipedalism in the hominid line some 6 million years ago, the hands were freed from locomotion, providing a potential boost to the evolution of manual communication.

The gestural theory is supported by the discovery of neurons, the "mirror neurons", in area F5 in the ventral premotor cortex of the monkey that fire when the animal makes movements to grasp an object with the hand and also when the animal observes another individual making the same movements (Ferrari et al., 2003; Gallese et al., 1996; Rizzolatti et al., 1996. Another set of neurons fire when the animal performs the grasping action with either the hand or the mouth (Rizzolatti et al., 1988). More recent discoveries, based on both neurophysiological recordings in primates and functional brain imaging in humans, have identified a more general mirror system, involving temporal, parietal, and frontal regions that are specialized for the perception and understanding of biological motion (Rizzolatti et al., 2001). In monkeys this system has been demonstrated primarily for reaching and grasping movements, although it also maps certain movements, such as tearing paper or cracking nuts, onto the sounds of those movements (Kohler et al., 2002), suggesting that the mirror system was also preadapted in the primate brain for cross-modal mapping. So far, though, there is no clear evidence from nonhuman primates for a mapping of the production of vocalizations onto the perception of vocalizations. However, this mapping is implicit in humans in the so-called motor theory of speech perception (Liberman et al., 1967), which holds that we understand spoken speech in terms of how it is produced rather than in terms of its acoustic properties. This raises the possibility that vocalization was incorporated into the mirror system after the split between the ape and hominid lineages.

More detailed study of area F5 suggests further specializations of relevance to the understanding of manual action. F5 is located in the rostral part of the ventral premotor cortex, and consists of two main sectors, one located on the dorsal convexity (F5c), the other on the posterior bank of the inferior arcuate sulcus (F5ab). Both sectors receive a strong input from the second somatosensory area (SII) and area PF. In addition, F5ab is the selective target of parietal area AIP (for a review, see Rizzolatti and Luppino, 2001). Single-neuron recording studies have shown not only that F5 neurons code specific actions, such as "grasping", "holding", or "tearing", but also that many of them code specific types of hand shaping, such as the precision grip. It is worth noting that hand shape is an important component of human signed languages (e.g. Emmorey, 2002). F5 neurons frequently discharge when the grasping action is performed with the mouth as well as with the hand (Gallese et al., 1996; Rizzolatti et al., 1988). These neurons may be functionally involved in preparing the mouth to grasp the object when the hand grasps it (Gentilucci et al., 2001), thereby encoding the goal of the action (taking possession of the object, Rizzolatti et al., 1988). From an evolutionary point of view, they may have been instrumental in the transfer of the gestural communication system from the hand to the mouth (see below).

F5 neurons can fire during specific phases of the grasp, and some of them, known as canonical neurons, are activated simply by the presentation of a graspable object (Murata et al., 1997; Rizzolatti et al., 1988). Canonical neurons, which are mostly located in the sector F5ab, are distinct from the mirror neurons described above, which are found generally in sector F5c. Nevertheless, mirror neurons also frequently respond to grasping actions, whether executed or observed, and may be sensitive to the particular type of grip used in the action (Gallese et al., 1996), but they do not respond to the mere presentation of a graspable object. Recently, Nelissen et al. (2005) using functional magnetic resonance imaging (fMRI) found other sections of the monkey premotor cortex and prefrontal cortex that were active during the observation of grasp actions. Specifically, the anterior regions responded to more abstract representations of grasp actions and even to presentation of objects probably coding their *graspability*. As of now, no fMRI study has been conducted to demonstrate that these anterior regions are active during both the observation and execution of grasping movements.

Because the mirror system is activated when observing and executing the same hand action, it can be considered to be involved in understanding the action meaning (Gallese et al., 1996). It might therefore have provided the link between actor and observer that also exists between sender and receiver of messages. Rizzolatti and Arbib (1998) proposed that the mirror system was used as an initial communication system in language evolution. Indeed, a comparable mirror system has also been inferred in present-day humans, based on evidence from electroencephalography (Muthukumaraswamy et al., 2004), magnetoencephalography (Hari et al., 1998), transcranial magnetic stimulation (TMS) (Fadiga et al., 1995), and fMRI (Iacoboni et al., 1999). Area F5 is also considered the homologue of Broca's area in the human brain (Rizzolatti and Arbib, 1998), and the mirror system in general corresponds quite closely with the cortical circuits, usually on the left side of the human brain, that are involved in language, whether spoken or signed. The perception and production of language might therefore be considered part of the mirror system, and indeed part of the more general system by which visuo–motor (and audio–motor) integration is used in the understanding of biological motion.

How ...

As noted earlier, a critical question for the theory that language evolved from manual gestures is how the medium of language shifted from a manuo–visual system to a vocal–acoustic one. It is likely that this switch was not an abrupt one, but was rather a gradual change, in which language evolved initially as a largely manual system, but facial and vocal elements were gradually introduced, and evolved to the point that vocalization became the predominant mode (Corballis, 2002). McNeill (1992) has pointed out, though, that even today speech-synchronized manual gestures should be considered part of language, so the dominance of speech is not complete.

An important step in the argument that vocal language evolved from gesture is the insight that speech itself is fundamentally gestural. This idea is captured by the motor theory of speech perception (Liberman et al., 1967), and by what has more recently become known as *articulatory phonology* (Browman and Goldstein, 1995). In this view speech is regarded, not as a system for producing sounds, but rather as a system for producing articulatory gestures, through the independent action of the six articulatory organs – namely, the lips, the velum, the larynx, and the blade, body, and root of the tongue. This approach derives from the discovery that the basic units of speech, known as phonemes, do not exist as discrete units in the acoustic signal (Joos, 1948), and are not discretely discernible in mechanical recordings of sound, as in a sound spectrograph (Liberman et al., 1967). One reason for this is that the acoustic signals corresponding to individual phonemes vary widely, depending on the contexts in which they are embedded. In particular, the formant transitions for a particular phoneme can be quite different, depending on the neighboring phonemes. Yet we can perceive speech at remarkably high rates, up to at least 10–15 phonemes per second, which seems at odds with the idea that some complex, context-dependent transformation is necessary. Even relatively simple sound units, such as tones or noises, cannot be perceived at comparable rates, further suggesting that a different principle underlies the perception of speech. The conceptualization of speech as *gesture* overcomes these difficulties, at least to some extent, since the articulatory gestures that give rise to speech partially overlap in time (co-articulation), which makes possible the high rates of production and perception (Studdert-Kennedy, 2005).

MacNeilage (1998) has drawn attention to the similarity between human speech and primate sound-producing facial gestures such as lipsmacks, tonguesmacks, and teeth chatters. Ferrari et al. (2003) recorded discharge both from mirror neurons in monkeys during the lipsmack, which is the most common facial gesture in monkeys, and from other mirror neurons in the same area during mouth movements related to eating. This suggests that nonvocal facial gestures may indeed be transitional between visual gesture and speech. One interesting class of mouth gestures constitute what is known as *echo phonology*, in which movements of the mouth parallel movements of the hand. For example, the mouth may open and close in synchrony with the opening and closing of the hand (Woll, 2002). Indeed Woll and Sieratzki (1998) have suggested that echo phonology might provide the link between gesture and speech.

There are intimate connections between hand and mouth in monkeys as well as in humans. As we have seen, the mirror system in the monkey is related to both arm (Gallese et al., 1996; Rizzolatti et al., 1996) and mouth actions (Ferrari et al., 2003). This suggests that gestures of the mouth might have been added to the manual system to form a combined manuofacial gestural system. Up to now a mirror system has been documented only for arm and mouth actions, and the anatomical closeness of hand and mouth cells in the premotor cortex may relate to the involvement of both effectors in common goals. Since food is acquired by using mainly hand and mouth, it is important for animal maintenance to extract the meanings and goals of actions from visual analysis. Area F5 of the monkey premotor cortex includes also a class of neurons that discharge when the animal grasps an object with either the hand or the mouth (Rizzolatti et al., 1988). Gentilucci et al. (2001) infer a similar neuronal system in humans. They showed that when subjects were instructed to open their mouths while grasping objects, the size of the mouth opening increased with the size of the grasped object, and conversely, when they open their hands while grasping objects with their mouths, the size of the hand opening also increased with the size of the object. In the evolution of communication, this mechanism of double command to hand and mouth could have been instrumental in the transfer of a communication system, based on the mirror system, from movements of the hand to movements of the mouth.

Grasping movements of the hand also affect the kinematics of speech itself. Grasping larger objects (Gentilucci et al., 2001) and bringing them to the mouth (Gentilucci et al., 2004a) induces selective increases in parameters of lip kinematics and voice spectra of syllables pronounced simultaneously with action execution. Even observing another individual grasping or bringing to the mouth larger objects affects the lip kinematics and the voice spectra of syllables simultaneously pronounced by the viewer (Gentilucci, 2003; Gentilucci et al., 2004a, 2004b). Again, then, action observation induces the same effects as action execution. The effects on voicing and lip kinematics depend on the arm movement itself, and not on the nature of the grasped objects. Indeed, the same effects were found when either fruits or geometrical solids were presented, and even when no object was presented (i.e. the action was pantomimed, see Fig. 3). By using the mirror system, an individual observing an arm action can automatically and covertly execute the same action in order to interpret its meaning. For manual actions functionally related to orofacial actions the motor command is sent also to the mouth, and reaches the threshold for execution when the mouth is already activated to pronounce the syllable.

Gentilucci and colleagues (Gentilucci, 2003; Gentilucci et al., 2001; Gentilucci et al., 2004b) found that execution/observation of the grasp with the hand activates a command to grasp with the mouth, which modifies the posture of the anterior mouth articulation, according to the hand shape used to grasp objects of different size. This, in turn, affects formant 1 (F1) of the voice spectra, which is related to mouth aperture. Conversely, execution/observation of the bringing-to-the-mouth action probably induces an internal mouth movement (as for example chewing or swallowing), which affects tongue displacement according to the size of the object being brought to the mouth (Gentilucci et al., 2004a, 2004b). This, in turn, modifies speech formant 2 (F2), which is related to tongue position. On the basis of these results it was proposed that, early in language evolution, communication signals related to the meaning of actions (e.g. taking possession of an object by grasping, or bringing an edible object to the mouth) might have been associated with the activity of particular masticatory organs of the mouth that were later co-opted for speech.

The possibility that actions directed to a target might have been used to communicate is supported by the finding that the observation of pantomimes influences speech in the same way that observation of the corresponding real actions does (Gentilucci et al., 2004a). The strict relationship between representations of actions and spoken language is supported also by neuroimaging studies, which show activation of Broca's area when representing meaningful arm gestures (Buccino et al., 2001; Decety et al., 1997; Gallagher and Frith, 2004;

Grèzes et al., 1998). Motor imagery of hand movements has also been shown to activate both Broca's and left premotor ventral areas (Gerardin et al., 2000; Grafton et al., 1996; Hanakawa et al., 2003; Kuhtz-Buschbeck et al., 2003; Parsons et al., 1995).

We suggest that this system, which relates transitive manual actions to actions of the mouth, provides an obvious link between manual gestures and spoken words. From a behavioral point of view, words and manual gestures are communicative signals, which, according to McNeill (1992) are parts of the same communication system. Further support comes from Bernardis and Gentilucci (2006), who showed that voice spectra parameters of words pronounced simultaneously with execution of the corresponding-in-meaning gesture increased in the comparison with those resulting from word pronunciation alone. This was not observed when the gesture was meaningless. Conversely, pronouncing words slowed down the simultaneous execution of the gesture, which did not occur when pseudo-words were pronounced. These effects of voice enhancement and arm inhibition were interpreted as due to a process of transferring some aspects (such as the intention to interact closely) from the gesture to the word (Bernardis and Gentilucci, 2006). On the other hand, the verbal response to a message expressed by the combination of word and gesture is different from that to either communication signal alone. In fact, the voice spectra of words pronounced in response to simultaneously listening to and observing the speaker making the corresponding-in-meaning gesture are enhanced, just as they are by the simultaneous production of both word and gesture (Bernardis and Gentilucci, 2006). Broca's area is probably involved in the simultaneous control of symbolic gestures and word pronunciation. Indeed, the effects of gesture observation on word pronunciation, described above, were extinguished during temporary inactivation of this area using repetitive TMS (Gentilucci et al., 2006).

In summary, the connections between hand and mouth reviewed above may have been established initially in the context of ingestive movements of the mouth, and the acts of grasping and bringing food to the mouth, but adapted later for communication. MacNeilage (1998) has suggested that speech itself originated from repetitive ingestive movements of the mouth. This may well be correct, but we suggest that it is only half the story, since it neglects the important role, in primates at least, of hand and arm movements in eating.

When ...

Although the connections between hand and mouth were probably well established in our primate forebears, fully articulate vocalization may not have been possible until fairly late in hominid evolution, and perhaps not until the emergence of our own species, *Homo sapiens*. As we have seen, there is little if any cortical control over vocalization in nonhuman primates (Ploog, 2002), and it has proven virtually impossible to teach chimpanzees anything approaching human speech (Hayes, 1952). Moreover, fossil evidence suggests that the alterations to the vocal tract (e.g. D. Lieberman, 1998; P. Lieberman et al., 1972) and to the mechanisms of breath control (MacLarnon and Hewitt, 1999, 2004) necessary for articulate speech were not completed until late in hominid evolution, and perhaps only with the emergence of our own species, *Homo sapiens*, which is dated at some 170,000 years ago (Ingman et al., 2000).

A further clue comes from study of an extended family in England, known as the KE family. Half of the members of this family are affected by a disorder of speech and language, which is evident from the affected child's first attempts to speak and persists into adulthood (Vargha-Khadem et al., 1995). The disorder is now known to be due to a point mutation on the *FOXP2* gene (forkhead box P2) on chromosome 7 (Fisher et al., 1998; Lai et al., 2001). For normal speech to be acquired, two functional copies of this gene seem to be necessary. The nature of the deficit, and therefore the role of the *FOXP2* gene, have been debated. Some have argued that the *FOXP2* gene is involved in the development of morphosyntax (Gopnik, 1990), and it has even been identified more broadly as the "grammar gene" (Pinker, 1994) – although Pinker (2003) has since recognized that other genes probably also played a role in the evolution of grammar. Subsequent investigation suggests, however, that the core deficit in affected members of the KE family is one of articulation, with grammatical impairment a secondary outcome (Watkins et al., 2002a). It may therefore play a role in the incorporation of vocal articulation into the mirror system, but have little to do with grammar itself (Corballis, 2004a).

This is supported by a study in which fMRI was used to record brain activity in both affected and unaffected members of the KE family while they covertly generated verbs in response to nouns

(Liégeois et al., 2003). Whereas unaffected members showed the expected activity concentrated in Broca's area in the left hemisphere, affected members showed relative *under* activation in both Broca's area and its right-hemisphere homologue, as well as in other cortical language areas. They also showed *over* activation bilaterally in regions not associated with language. However, there was bilateral activation in the posterior superior temporal gyrus; the left side of this area overlaps Wernicke's area, important in the comprehension of language. This suggests that affected members may have generated words in terms of their sounds, rather than in terms of articulatory patterns. Their deficits were not attributable to any difficulty with verb generation itself, since affected and unaffected members did not differ in their ability to generate verbs overtly, and the patterns of brain activity were similar to those recorded during covert verb generation. Another study based on structural MRI showed morphological abnormalities in the same areas (Watkins et al., 2002b).

The *FOXP2* gene is highly conserved in mammals, and in humans differs in only three places from that in the mouse, but two of the three changes occurred on the human lineage after the split from the common ancestor with the chimpanzee and bonobo. A recent estimate of the date of the more recent of these mutations suggests that it occurred "since the onset of human population growth, some 10,000 to 100,000 years ago" (Enard et al., 2002, p. 871). If this is so, fully articulate vocal language may not have emerged until *after* the appearance of our species, *Homo sapiens*, some 170,000 years ago in Africa. This is not to say that the *FOXP2* gene was the only gene involved in the switch to an autonomously vocal system; rather, it was probably just the final step in a series of progressive changes.

Why …

Selective changes to the vocal tract, breathing, and cortical control of vocal language suggest that there must have been selective pressure to replace a system that was largely based on manual and facial gestures to one that could rely almost exclusively on vocalization, albeit with manual accompaniments. This pressure must have been strong, since the lowering of the larynx to enable articulate speech increases the risk of choking to death. What, then, were the adaptive advantages associated with the switch from visible gestures to auditory ones? We think that there were several:

> First, a switch to autonomous vocalization would have freed the hands from necessary involvement in communication, allowing increased use of the hands for such activities as grooming, carrying things, and the manufacture and tool use. Indeed vocal language allows people to speak and use tools at the same time, leading perhaps to pedagogy (Corballis, 2002, pp. 193–194).

Second, speech allows communication over longer distances, as well as communication at night or when the speaker is not visible to the listener. The San, a modern hunter-gatherer society, are known to talk late at night, sometimes all through the night, to resolve conflict and share knowledge (Konner, 1982). Boutla et al. (2004) have shown that the span of short-term memory is shorter for American Sign Language than for speech, suggesting that voicing may have permitted longer and more complex sentences to be transmitted – although the authors claim that the shorter memory span has no impact on the linguistic skill of signers. Auditory stimuli also have greater attentional impact than visual stimuli, and at first grunts may have accompanied signing to attract attention rather than to convey information.

Third, speech is much less energy-consuming than manual gesture. Anecdotal evidence from courses in sign language suggests that the instructors require regular massages in order to meet the sheer physical demands of sign-language expression. In contrast, the physiological costs of speech are so low as to be nearly unmeasurable (Russell et al., 1998). In terms of expenditure of energy, speech adds little to the cost of breathing, which we must do anyway to sustain life. Paradoxically, though, humans frequently gesticulate while speaking, although perhaps with less expenditure of energy than is required in signed languages. Goldin-Meadow (2005) proposed that, when accompanying speech, gesture assumes a global and synthetic form, conveying information that differs from that conveyed by speech. Indeed, the combined use of speech and manual gesture allows the transmission of information on how people learn, remember, and solve problems. The apparent paradox might then be explained in that more information can be conveyed by speech and gesture combined than by gesture alone, with little if any extra cost.

A possible scenario for the switch, then, is that there was selective pressure for the face to become more extensively involved in gestural communication as the hands were increasingly engaged in other activities. Our hominid forebears had been habitually bipedal from some 6 or 7 million years ago, and from some 2 million years ago were developing tools, which would have increasingly involved the hands. The face had long played a role in visual communication in primates, and plays an important role in present-day signed languages (e.g. Neidle et al., 2000). Consequently, there may have been pressure for intentional communication to move to the face, including the mouth and tongue. Gesturing may then have retreated partly into the mouth, so there may have been pressure to add voicing in order to render movements of the tongue more accessible – through sound rather than sight. In this scenario, speech is simply gesture half swallowed, with voicing added. Adding voicing to the signal could have had the extra benefit of allowing a distinction between voiced and unvoiced phonemes, increasing the range of speech elements.

Even so, lip-reading can be a moderately effective way to recover the speech gestures. The importance of visible movements of the face is also illustrated by the so-called McGurk effect, in which dubbing a syllable (e.g. "ba") onto a mouth that is saying something different (e.g. "ga") shifts the perception to some intermediate syllable (e.g. "da"), and sometimes completely to the visual ("ga") (McGurk and MacDonald, 1976). Sometimes the viewer/listener does report the acoustic stimulus ("ba"), but even here the different syllable mimicked by the visually presented face influences perception. This is shown by the variation in the voice spectra of the syllable repeated in response to the presented audiovisual stimulus (Gentilucci and Cattaneo, 2005). That is, speech remains partly visual, even though we can convey linguistic messages, albeit with some loss of information, through the acoustic medium, as on telephone or radio.

And the consequences were ...

The advantages of incorporating sound, at least to the point that the message can be conveyed without visible access to the speaker, may explain the so-called "human revolution" (Mellars and Stringer, 1989), manifest in the dramatic appearance of more sophisticated tools, bodily ornamentation, art, and perhaps music, dating from some 40,000 years ago in Europe, and probably earlier in Africa (McBrearty and Brooks, 2000; Oppenheimer, 2003). Freed from communicative duty, the hands were free to express themselves! These dates correspond reasonably closely to the estimated date of the mutation of the *FOXP2* gene, which may have been the final step in the evolution of autonomous speech. This raises the possibility that the final incorporation of vocalization into the mirror system was critical to the emergence of modern human behavior in the Upper Paleolithic (Corballis, 2004b). It may also have been responsible for the eventual demise of the Neanderthals in Europe and *Homo erectus* in Asia. These species may well have had a form of language that was part gestural and part vocal, but the emergence of autonomous speech in our own forebears may have created a sufficient advantage, technological as well as communicative, to enable our own species to prevail.

The human revolution is commonly attributed to the emergence of symbolic language itself rather than to the emergence of speech (e.g. Klein et al., 2004; Mellars, 2004). This implies that language must have evolved very late, and quite suddenly, in hominid evolution. Some have associated it with the arrival of our own species, *Homo sapiens*, about 170,000 years ago. Bickerton (1995), for example, writes that "... true language, via the emergence of syntax, was a catastrophic event, occurring within the first few generations of *Homo sapiens sapiens*." Crow (2002) has similarly proposed that the emergence of language was part of the speciation event that gave rise to *Homo sapiens*. The association of the evolutionary explosion with the human revolution suggests that language may have emerged even later, as proposed by Klein et al. (2004), although there is still debate over the extent and time frame of the human revolution (e.g. McBrearty and Brooks, 2000).

Given the complexity of syntax, still not fully understood by linguists, it seems unlikely that these "big bang" theories of language evolution can be correct. It seems much more likely that language evolved incrementally, perhaps beginning with the emergence of the genus *Homo* from around 2 million years ago. Pinker and Bloom (1990) argue, contrary to earlier views expressed by Chomsky (1975), that language evolved incrementally through natural selection, and Jackendoff (2002) has proposed a series of stages through which this might have occurred. In something of a change of stance for Chomsky, he and his colleagues have also highlighted a continuity between primate and human communication, again suggesting the gradual evolution of human language (Hauser et al., 2002) – although they do not consider the possibility that language evolved from manual and facial gestures, nor do they speculate as to precisely when the uniquely human component (what they call "faculty of language in the narrow sense") emerged in hominid evolution. If syntactic language evolved gradually over the past 2 million years, then it seems reasonable to suppose that it was already well developed by the time *Homo sapiens* appeared a mere 170,000 or so years ago. As we have seen, it now seems likely that the *FOXP2* gene has to do with oral–motor control rather than with syntax.

One may question whether the switch to an autonomous vocal language could have brought about an effect as apparently profound as the human revolution. As noted above, speech would have freed the hands, enhancing pedagogy, which itself may be a uniquely human characteristic (e.g. Csibra and Gergely, in press). More generally, changes in the medium of communication have had deep influences on our material culture. Without the advent of writing, and the later development of mathematical notation, for example, we would surely not have had our modern contrivances such as the automobile, or the supersonic jet. We suggest, then, that the switch from a manuo-facial to a vocal means of communication would have especially enhanced material culture, including the manufacture and use of tools – not to mention weapons of war. Indeed, it is primarily in material culture that the human revolution is manifest, whereas the earlier evolution of language itself may have been expressed in, and perhaps driven by, complex social interaction, or what has been called cultural cognition (Tomasello et al., 2005). The social component may be less visible in the archaeological record. The human revolution may therefore give a false impression of the evolution of the human mind itself.

In summary, language may well uniquely distinguish our species from any other extant species, but need not have distinguished us from the Neanderthals or other late species of the genus *Homo*. We suggest that what really distinguished us from all other hominids was the honing of language into a cost-efficient mode that freed the hands and arms for other activities, and allowed humans to communicate in a wider range of environmental contexts than is possible in a purely visual medium. That mode was speech.

References

Arbib, M. A. 2005. From monkey-like action recognition to human language: An evolutionary framework for neurolinguistics. *Behavioral and Brain Sciences*. 28:105–168.

Armstrong, D. F. 1999. *Original Signs: Gesture, Sign, and the Source of Language*. Washington, DC: Gallaudet University Press.

Armstrong, D. F., Stokoe, W. C., and Wilcox, S. E. 1995. *Gesture and the Nature of Language*. Cambridge, MA: Cambridge University Press.

Bernardis, P. and Gentilucci, M. 2006. Speech and gesture share the same communication system. *Neuropsychologia*, 44:178–190.

Bickerton, D. 1995. *Language and Human Behavior*. Seattle, WA: University of Washington Press,

Boutla, M., Supalla, T., Newport, E. L. and Bavelier, D. 2004. Short-term memory span: insights from sign language. *Nature Neuroscience*, 7:997–1002.

Browman, C. P. and Goldstein, L. F. 1995. Dynamics and articulatory phonology. In T. van Gelder & R. F. Port (eds.), *Mind as Motion*. Cambridge, MA: MIT Press, pp. 175–193.

Buccino, G., Binkofski, F., Fink, G. R., Fadiga, L., Fogassi, L., Gallese, V., Seitz, R. J., Zilles, K., Rizzolatti, G., and Freund, H. J. 2001. Action observation activates premotor and parietal areas in a somatotopic manner: an fMRI study. *European Journal of Neuroscience*, 13:400–404.

Burling, R. 1999. Motivation, conventionalization, and arbitrariness in the origin of language. In B. J. King (ed.). *The Origins of Language: What Nonhuman Primates Can Tell Us*. Santa Fe, NM: School of American Research Press, pp. 307–350.

Burling, R. 2005. *The Talking Ape*. New York: Oxford University Press.

Chomsky, N. 1975. *Reflections on Language*. New York: Pantheon.

Condillac, E. Bonnot de 1971. *An Essay on the Origin of Human Knowledge: Being a Supplement to Mr. Locke's Essay on the Human Understanding*. A facsimile reproduction of the 1756 translation by T. Nugent of Condillac's 1747 essay. Gainesville, FL: Scholars' Facsimiles and Reprints.

Corballis, M. C. 1992. On the evolution of language and generativity. *Cognition*, 44:197–226.

Corballis, M. C. 2002. *From Hand to Mouth: The Origins of Language*. Princeton, NJ: Princeton University Press.

Corballis, M. C. 2004a. *FOXP2* and the mirror system. *Trends of Cognitive Science*, 18: 95–96.

Corballis, M. C. 2004b. The origins of modernity: Was autonomous speech the critical factor? *Psychological Review*, 111:543–552.

Crow, T. J. 2002. Sexual selection, timing, and an X-Y homologous gene: Did *Homo sapiens* speciate on the Y chromosome? In T. J. Crow (ed.) *The Speciation of Modern* Homo Sapiens. Oxford: Oxford University Press, pp. 197–216.

Csibra, G. and Gergely, G. In press. Social learning and social cognition: The case for pedagogy. In M. H. Johnson and Y. Munakata (eds.) *Processes of Change in Brain and Cognitive Development, Attention and Performance XXI*. Oxford: Oxford University Press.

Decety, J., Grezes, J., Costes, N., Perani, D., Jeannerod, M., Procyk, E., Grassi, F., and Fazio, F. 1997. Brain activity during observation of actions. Influence of action content and subject's strategy. *Brain*, 120:1763–1777.

Donald, M. 1991. *Origins of the Modern Mind*. Cambridge, MA: Harvard University Press.

Emmorey, K. 2002. *Language, Cognition, and Brain: Insights from Sign Language Research*. Hillsdale, NJ: Erlbaum.

Enard, W., Przeworski, M., Fisher, S. E., Lai, C. S. L., Wiebe, V., Kitano, T., Monaco, A. P., and Paabo, S. 2002. Molecular evolution of FOXP2, a gene involved in speech and language. *Nature*, 418:869–871.

Fadiga, L., Fogassi, L., Pavesi, G., and Rizzolatti G. 1995. Motor facilitation during action observation – a magnetic stimulation study. *Journal of Neurophysiology*. 73:2608–2611.

Ferrari, P. F., Gallese, V., Rizzolatti, G., and Fogassi, L. 2003. Mirror neurons responding to the observation of ingestive and communicative mouth actions in the monkey ventral premotor cortex. *European Journal of Neuroscience*, 17:1703–1714.

Fisher, S. E., Vargha-Khadem, F., Watkins, K. E., Monaco, A. P., and Pembrey, M. E. 1998. Localisation of a gene implicated in a severe speech and language disorder. *Nature*, 18:168–170.

Gallese, V., Fadiga, L., Fogassi, L., and Rizzolatti, G. 1996. Action recognition in the premotor cortex. *Brain*, 119:593–609.

Gallagher, H. L. and Frith, C. D. 2004. Dissociable neural pathways for the perception and recognition of expressive and instrumental gestures. *Neuropsychologia*, 42:1725–1736.

Gardner, R. A. and Gardner, B. T. 1969. Teaching sign language to a chimpanzee. *Science*, 165:664–672.

Gentilucci, M. 2003. Grasp observation influences speech production. *European Journal of Neuroscience*, 17:179–184.

Gentilucci, M., Benuzzi, F., Gangitano, M. and Grimaldi, S. 2001. Grasp with hand and mouth: a kinematic study on healthy subjects. *Journal of Neurophysiology*, 86:1685–1699.

Gentilucci, M., Bernardis, P., Crisi, G., and Dalla Volta, R. 2006. Repetitive transcranial stimulation of Broca's area affects verbal responses to gesture observation. *Journal of Cognitive Neuroscience*, 18:1059–1074.

Gentilucci, M. and Cattaneo, L. 2005. Automatic audiovisual integration in speech perception. *Experimental Brain Research*, 167:66–75.

Gentilucci, M. and Corballis, M. C. 2006. From manual gesture to speech: A gradual transition. *Neuroscience and Behavioral Reviews*, 30: 949–960.

Gentilucci, M., Santunione, P., Roy, A. C., and Stefanini, S. 2004a. Execution and observation of bringing a fruit to the mouth affect syllable pronunciation. *European Journal of Neuroscience*, 19:190–202.

Gentilucci, M., Stefanini, S., Roy, A. C., and Santunione, P. 2004b. Action observation and speech production: study on children and adults. *Neuropsychologia*, 42:1554–1567.

Gerardin, E., Sirigu, A., Lehericy, S., Poline, J. B., Gaymard, B., Marsault, C., Agid, Y., and Le Bihan, D. 2000. Partially overlapping neural networks for real and imagined hand movements. *Cerebral Cortex*, 10:1093–1104.

Givòn, T. 1995. *Functionalism and Grammar*. Philadelphia, PA: Benjamins.

Goldin-Meadow, S. 2005. The two faces of gesture: Language and thought. *Gesture*, 5:241–257.

Gopnik, M. 1990. Feature-blind grammar and dysphasia. *Nature*, 344:715.

Grafton, S. T., Arbib, M. A., Fadiga, L., and Rizzolatti, G. 1996. Localization of grasp representations in humans by positron emission tomography. 2. Observation compared with imagination. *Experimental Brain Research*, 112 :103–111.

Grèzes, J., Costes, N., and Decety, J. 1998. Top-down effect of strategy on the perception of human biological motion: a PET investigation. *Cognitive Neuropsychology*, 15:553–582.

Hanakawa, T., Immisch, I., Toma, K., Dimyan, M. A., Van Gelderen, P., and Hallett, M. 2003. Functional properties of brain areas associated with motor execution and imagery. *Journal of Neurophysiology*, 89:989–1002.

Hari, R., Forss, N., Avikainen, S., Kirveskari, E., Salenius, S., and Rizzolatti, G. 1998. Activation of human primary motor cortex during action observation: A neuromagnetic study. *Proceeding of National Academy Science, USA*, 95:15061–15065.

Hauser, M. D., Fitch, W. T., and Chomsky, N. 2002. The faculty of language: What is it, who has it, and how did it evolve? *Science*, 298:1569–1579.

Hayes, C. 1952. *The Ape in Our House*. London: Gollancz.

Hepp-Raymond, M. C. 1988. Functional organization of motor cortex and its participation in voluntary movements. In H. D. Steklis and J. Erwin (eds.) *Comparative Primate Biology, Vol. 4: Neurosciences*. New York: Alan R. Liss, pp. 501–624.

Hewes, G. W. 1973. Primate communication and the gestural origins of language. *Current Anthropology*, 14:15–24.

Iacoboni, M., Woods, R. P., Brass, M., Bekkering, H., Mazziotta, J. C., and Rizzolatti, G. 1999. Cortical mechanisms of human imitation. *Science*, 286:2526–2528.

Ingman, M., Kaessmann, H., Pääbo, S., and Gyllensten, U. 2000. Mitochondrial genome variation and the origin of modern humans. *Nature*, 408:708–713.

Jackendoff, R. 2002. *Foundations of Language: Brain, Meaning, Grammar, Evolution*. Oxford: Oxford University Press.

Joos, M. 1948. *Acoustic Phonetics. Language Monograph No. 23*. Baltimore, MD: Linguistic Society of America.

Klein, R. G., Avery, G., Cruz-Uribe, K., Halkett, D., Parkington, J. E., Steele, T., Volman T. P., and Yates, R. 2004. The Ysterfontein 1 Middle Stone Age site, South Africa, and early human exploitation of coastal resources. *Proceeding National Academy Science, USA*, 101:5708–5715.

Kohler, E., Keysers, C., Umiltà, M. A., Fogassi, L., Gallese, V., and Rizzolatti, G. 2002. Hearing sounds, understanding actions: Action representation in mirror neurons. *Science*, 297:846–848.

Konner, M. 1982. *The Tangled Wing: Biological Constraints on the Human Spirit*. New York: Harper.

Kuhtz-Buschbeck, J. P., Mahnkopf, C., Holzknecht, C., Siebner, H., Ulmer, S., and Jansen, O. 2003. Effector-independent representations of simple and complex imagined finger movements: a combined fMRI and TMS study. *European Journal of Neuroscience*, 18:3375–3387.

Lai, C. S., Fisher, S. E., Hurst, J. A., Vargha-Khadem, F., and Monaco A. P. 2001. A novel forkhead-domain gene is mutated in a severe speech and language disorder. *Nature*, 413:519–523.

Lieberman, D. 1998. Sphenoid shortening and the evolution of modern cranial shape. *Nature*, 393:158–162.

Liberman, A. M., Cooper, F. S., Shankweiler, D. S., and Studdert-Kennedy, M. 1967. Perception of the speech code. *Psychological Review*, 74:431–461.

Lieberman, P., Crelin, E. S., and Klatt, D. H. 1972. Phonetic ability and related anatomy of the new-born, adult human, Neanderthal man, and the chimpanzee. *American Anthropology*, 74:287–307.

Liégeois, F., Baldeweg, T., Connelly, A., Gadian, D. G., Mishkin, M., and Vargha-Khadem, F. 2003. Language fMRI abnormalities associated with FOXP2 gene mutation. *Nature Neuroscience*, 6:1230–1237.

MacLarnon, A. and Hewitt, G. 1999. The evolution of human speech: The role of enhanced breathing control. *American Journal of Physic Anthropology*, 109:341–363.

MacLarnon, A. and Hewitt, G. 2004. Increased breathing control: Another factor in the evolution of human language. *Evolution Anthropology*, 13:181–197.

MacNeilage, P. F. 1998. The frame/content theory of evolution of speech. *Behavioral Brain Science*, 21:499–546.

McBrearty, S. and Brooks, A. S. 2000. The revolution that wasn't: A new interpretation of the origin of modern human behavior. *Journal of Human Evolution*, 39:453–563.

McGurk, H. and MacDonald, J. 1976. Hearing lips and seeing voices. *Nature*, 264:746–748.

McNeill, D. 1992. *Hand and Mind: What Gestures Reveal about Thought*. Chicago: University of Chicago Press.

Mellars, P. A. 2004. Neanderthals and the modern human colonization of Europe. *Nature*, 432:461–465.

Mellars, P. A. and Stringer, C. B. (eds.) 1989. *The Human Revolution: Behavioural and Biological Perspectives on the Origins of Modern Humans*. Edinburgh: Edinburgh University Press.

Murata, A., Fadiga, L., Fogassi, L., Gallese, V., Raos, V., and Rizzolatti, G. 1997. Object representation in the ventral premotor cortex (area F5) of the monkey. *Journal of Neurophysiology*, 78:2226–2230.

Muthukumaraswamy, S. D., Johnson, B. W., and McNair, N. A. 2004. Mu rhythm modulation during observation of an object-directed grasp. *Cognitive Brain Research*, 19:195–201.

Neidle, C., Kegl, J., MacLaughlin, D., Bahan, B., and Lee, R. G. 2000. *The Syntax of American Sign Language*. Cambridge, MA: MIT Press.

Nelissen, K., Luppino, G., Vanduffel, W., Rizzolatti G., and Orban, G. A. 2005. Observing others: Multiple action representation in the frontal lobe. *Science*, 310:332–336.

Oppenheimer, S. 2003. *Out of Eden: The Peopling of the World*. London: Constable.

Paget, R., 1930. *Human Speech: Some Observations, Experiments and Conclusions as to the Nature, Origin, Purpose and Possible Improvement of Human Speech*. New York: P. Kegan, T. Trench, Trubner & Co.

Parsons, L. M., Fox, P. T., Downs, J. H., Glass, T., Hirsch, T. B., Martin, C. C., Jerabek, P. A., and Lancaster, J. L. 1995. Use of implicit motor imagery for visual shape discrimination as revealed by PET. *Nature*, 375:54–58.

Pinker, S. 1994. *The Language Instinct*. New York: Morrow.

Pinker, S. 2003. Language as an adaptation to the cognitive niche. In M. H. Christiansen and S. Kirby (eds.) *Language Evolution*. Oxford: Oxford University Press, pp. 16–37.

Pinker, S. and Bloom, P. 1990. Natural language and natural selection. *Behavioral and Brain Sciences*, 13:707–784.

Ploog, D. 2002. Is the neural basis of vocalisation different in non-human primates and *Homo sapiens?* In T. J. Crow (ed.) *The Speciation of Modern Homo Sapiens.* Oxford: Oxford University Press, pp. 121–135.

Rizzolatti, G. and Arbib, M. A. 1998. Language within our grasp. *Trends in Neuroscience*, 21:188–194.

Rizzolatti, G., Camarda, R., Fogassi, L., Gentilucci, M., Luppino, G., and Matelli, M. 1988. Functional organization of inferior area 6 in the macaque monkey. II. Area F5 and the control of distal movements. *Experimental Brain Research*, 71:491–507.

Rizzolatti, G., Fadiga, L., Gallese, V., and Fogassi, L., 1996. Premotor cortex and the recognition of motor actions. *Cognitive Brain Research*, 3:131–141.

Rizzolatti, G., Fogassi, L., and Gallese, V. 2001. Neurophysiological mechanisms underlying the understanding and imitation of action. *Nature Review Neuroscience*, 2:661–670.

Rizzolatti, G. and Luppino, G. 2001. The cortical motor system. *Neuron*, 31:889–901.

Rousseau, J. J. 1775/1964. Discours sur l'origine et les fondements de l'inégalité parmi les hommes. In B. Gagnebin and M. Raymond (eds) *Oeuvres Complètes, Vol. 3.* Paris: Gallimard.

Ruben, R. J. 2005. Sign language: Its history and contribution to the understanding of the biological nature of language. *Acta Oto-Laryngologica*, 125:464–467.

Russell, B. A., Cerny, F. J., and Stathopoulos, E. T. 1998. Effects of varied vocal intensity on ventilation and energy expenditure in women and men. *Journal of Speech, Language, Hearing Research*, 41:239–248.

Savage-Rumbaugh, S., Shanker, S. G., and Taylor, T. J. 1998. *Apes, Language, and the Human Mind.* New York: Oxford University Press.

Studdert-Kennedy, M. 2005. How did language go discrete? In M. Tallerman (ed.) *Language Origins : Perspectives on Evolution.* Oxford: Oxford University Press, pp. 48–67.

Tomasello, M., Carpenter, M., Call, J., Behen, T., and Moll, H. 2005. Understanding and sharing intentions: The origin of cultural cognition. *Behavioral and Brain Sciences*, 28:635–673.

Van Hooff, J. A. R. A. M. 1962. Facial expressions in higher primates. *Symposium of Zoological Society London*, 8:97–125.

Van Hooff, J. A. R. A. M. 1967. The facial displays of the catarrhine monkeys and apes. In D. Morris (ed.) *Primate Ethology.* London: Weidenfield and Nicolson, pp. 7–68.

Vargha-Khadem, F., Watkins, K. E., Alcock, K. J., Fletcher, P., and Passingham, R. 1995. Praxic and nonverbal cognitive deficits in a large family with a genetically transmitted speech and language disorder. *Proceeding National Academy Science, USA*, 92:930–933.

Watkins, K. E., Dronkers, N. F., and Vargha-Khadem, F. 2002a. Behavioural analysis of an inherited speech and language disorder: Comparison with acquired aphasia. *Brain*, 125:452–464.

Watkins, K. E., Vargha-Khadem, F., Ashburner, J., Passingham, R. E., Connelly, A., Friston, K. J., Frackowiak, R. S., Mishkin, F., and Gadian, D. G. 2002b. MRI analysis of an inherited speech and language disorder: structural brain abnormalities. *Brain*, 125:465–478.

Woll, B. 2002. The sign that dares to speak its name: Echo phonology in British Sign Language (BSL). In P. Boyes-Braem and R. Sutton-Spence (eds.) *The Hands are the Head of the Mouth: The Mouth as Articulator in Sign Languages*. Hamburg: Signum-Verlag, pp. 87–98.

Woll, B. and Sieratzki, J. S. 1998. Echo phonology: Signs of a link between gesture and speech. *Behavioral and Brain Sciences*, 21:531–532.

5: Half Ape, Half Angel?

The Rt Revd Richard Harries

We are physical but not just physical

Modern science has hugely increased our knowledge of how human beings came about and how we are made up. A range of scientific disciplines point to the conclusion that we have developed over a period of more than 13½ billion years by a gradual process of evolution from very simple and unconscious beginnings involving, in its later stages, incremental change brought about by random mutation and natural selection. We also know that we are made up of some 30,000 genes with their three billion base letters. We know that humans and chimpanzees shared a common ancestor some six million years ago and that we have 99.4 per cent of our genes in common with them. So we are bound up in the bundle of life with all living creatures, for example sharing nearly 40 per cent of our genes with lettuces. All this has important implications for the kind of respect we should show the natural world and the value of each particular species. So it's not insulting or disrespectful, as Victorians tended to think, to say that we are half ape if what we mean is what I have described.

We are also, as my title suggests, half angel. There are two ways in which this is sometimes denied, both of which I believe are false. First, reductionism. This is the view that we are nothing but our genes – or our atoms, or our subatomic particles, whatever is thought to be the most basic unit of our make-up. All forms of reductionism, what has been termed "nothing buttery", fail to acknowledge that a whole is greater than its parts and cannot be reduced to it. It is as though we said that a computer was nothing but the sand out of which its chips are made. A computer is a hugely complex whole and it operates as a unity. It's as absurd to say that human beings are nothing but their genes as it is to say that a computer is nothing but sand.

The second false idea, often linked with reductionism, is determinism. This suggests that our genes, or whatever is the fashionable subject of the moment, determines all we do and say and think. Now don't get me wrong. A very great part of what we are is clearly shaped by factors outside our control. Almost every day I read of some new research suggesting this, most recently, that there is a gene which determines whether you have waxy or dry ears, whether you have a natural capacity for dancing and so on. We are clearly shaped in our behaviour far more than we are aware of. But the idea that everything is determined is self refuting: because if it *were* true the statement that everything is determined would itself be determined, and you couldn't therefore appeal to people to decide whether it was true or false.

In addition to being self-contradictory absolute determinism would leave no role for consciousness and from an evolutionary point of view that would be unprecedented. Clearly consciousness has evolved for some purpose, that is, it has helped us to survive (or as Richard Dawkins would put it, it has helped our genes to survive and replicate). The purpose of consciousness is to transmute our instinctual drives in such a way that the result of conscious reflection and decision-making, as expressed in our behaviour, doesn't simply reflect the strength of the instinctual input. Or, to put it more simply, if you feel aggressive towards someone and want to punch them in the face, conscious reflection can enable you to channel your anger in a more constructive way. However often we fail and act purely instinctively, rational reflection is fundamental to what it is to be a human being. However much we are shaped by our genes, or other factors such as our upbringing and our culture, absolute determinism is false, being both self-contradictory and leaving no evolutionary explanation for the emergence of human consciousness.

If we reject reductionism and determinism the way is open to affirm two truths. First, mind or consciousness is not simply reducible to the brain. We know of course there is a very close relationship between the brain and the mind – the whole of neuroscience is based on that premise. We can alter states of mind by drugs or by operations on different parts of the brain. But though the relationship between our brains and our minds is clearly close, and how we understand their relationship is a very complex, philosophical conundrum on which there is no consensus, I believe it right to reject reduction-ism and determinism in relation to the brain, as in relation to our genes or any other aspect of our physical make-up. Consciousness isn't simply the spume given off by electrical discharges in the brain. It is an initiator, a centre of reflection and choice leading to action.

This points to the second truth, that of top-down causality. Every gene, cell and multi-cellular structure in our body is beavering away being itself and combining with other elements to enable them to beaver away being themselves. All this is our physical make-up. But our conscious mind, thinking, evaluating and deciding is also a factor – I would say the crucial factor – influencing our whole physical being from the top or the centre if you like.

A fundamental feature of human rational reflection is that we are aware of values and principles. We don't just decide to act, we decide to act in the light of what we think is to our advantage or disadvantage, and what we think is right or wrong. This capacity for rational reflec-tion in the light of our principles and values is first of all what I mean by the phrase "Half angel", or to put it in more traditional Christian language, what I mean by being made in the image of God. Although I give it that description, the account I have given so far of what it is to be a human would I think be shared by the majority of agnostics and atheists. It does not at all follow that because you have no religious belief you are thereby a reductionist or a determinist. Richard Dawkins, to take just one example, a passionate believer in the theory of evolution, is no less passionate in affirming that human beings don't simply have to act on the basis of the survival of the fittest, and indeed they shouldn't. In so far as genes are selfish, we can con-sciously go against the grain of the gene universe in this respect and, if we choose, act unselfishly.

Called to be something more

That said, by the phrase "Half angel", I also mean something more, which not all will share. I believe, alongside Charles Pasternak, that human beings have a capacity not only to quest in general [see Chap-ter 8 of this volume], but to engage in an intellectual and spiritual quest, to relate to God, that is to pray, and that we are called to deepen that relationship, as we are also called to deepen and enlarge our care for our fellow human beings. Jesus summed up the whole of religion in two great principles, to love God with all that we are and to love our neighbours as ourselves. In this he stands very much in the tradition of the Hebrew scriptures. As the prophet Micah put it:

> He has showed you, O man, what is good;
> And what does the Lord require of you but to do justice, and to love kindness,
> And to walk humbly with your God? (Micah 6: 8)

Nothing could be clearer and more basic than that. The New Testament is also based on the conviction that the process of growth in self-transcendence and appreciation of others, though it must begin here, has a consummation beyond space and time. So to be half angel means not just that we are capable of rational reflection and morally based decision and action, but that we have a spiritual orientation and destiny to grow in love.

I do not think that this spiritual orientation and destiny can be proved. From the standpoint of pure logic, all the traditional proofs of the existence of God can be disputed. Furthermore, I think that from a theological point of view, not only do such proofs not work but in principle they could not work. However, and this is no less important, nor can it be proved that there is no God. All philosophical considerations, as I will come on to, leave the issue open. But before that, if there are no proofs that work, how can a rational person come to make such a crucially important decision that there is indeed a wise and loving power behind the universe? Pascal's answer, known as Pascal's wager, that if it is true we have everything to gain, and if it is untrue we have nothing to lose, teasingly clever though it is, has never appealed to me.

I begin with the experience of the religious believer. Here I must emphasise two points, because the mention of religious experience can give rise to misunderstandings. By religious experience I don't mean anything exotic, miraculous or highly emotional. I refer to the daily experience of the average Christian believer of offering her life day by day to God, making decisions in a prayerful spirit and seeking grace to live more Christianly. Secondly, I'm not at all suggesting that because a person claims that God is upholding, guiding and strengthening them, this proves that there is a God. The believer could be under an illusion. What I'm trying to do is indicate what it is for a believer to believe. Most would say that at some point in their lives, gradually or suddenly, religious truth has taken hold of them, they find themselves a believer. For the thoughtful person, rational reflection will have been part of this process, but as John Henry Newman put it, the whole person moves, paper logic is but the record of it. So, gradually or suddenly depending on temperament and circumstances, with a great deal or reflection or little, a person finds themselves living within a milieu of faith, rather than outside.

From this two things follow, and here I quote the Oxford theologian Austin Farrer (1970, p. 61): "Because we have God under the root of our being we cannot help but acknowledge him at the root of all the world's being." The Christian believes that her being is moment by moment held in existence by the fount of all being, that she is utterly dependent on the ground and fount of all that exists. If this is the believer's personal experience, she cannot help but acknowledge the same power as the ground and source of the length and breadth of the universe, including its origin *ex nihilo* some 13½ billion years ago.

Secondly, as Farrer put it:

> To make you or me, God must make half a universe. A man's body and a man's mind form a focus in which a world is concentrated, and drawn into a point. It may be in that point that I know existence; but it is an existence which involves the world (1967, p. 30).

To quote Farrer again:

> If we are concerned about a Creative Cause, it is because, in creating all things he is creating us; and it concerns us to enter into the making of our souls, and of one another's. To enter into the action of God thus is what we mean by religion; and it is something we do, it is a matter of experience (1966, p. 66).

In short, a believer seeks to align their life with the divine illumination and leading. But because we exist as the product of evolution, that divine illumination and leading has been present at every point of the whole process. We read back from our own interaction with the divine will that there is a divine will working in and through all secondary causes, all those causes that can be mapped out by scientific exploration. The divine leading cannot of course be located by scientific scrutiny. But the religious believer who claims to be aware of this will in their own life cannot but help posit this will as the basis of all life, cannot help in the sense that consistency of thought demands it.

R. S. Thomas gets the paradoxical nature of that divine leading in a late poem when he writes

> To yield to an unfelt pressure that, irresistible
> In itself, had the character of everything
> But coercion? (p. 353)

How the believer believes

It's described as a pressure, but unfelt. It's described as irresistible but it has the character of everything but coercion. That's what a believer believes and how she comes to believe it. Let me now say why I think proofs of the existence or non-existence of God don't work as strict logic. The most familiar is the argument from causality. Everything that happens in life has a cause or series of causes; so, it is suggested, must the universe itself be traced back to an uncaused first cause, which is what we mean by God. The argument of Kant against this (in his *Critique of Pure Reason*) is that we simply don't know whether the kind of reasoning that applies to events within the world apply to the universe itself. To widen the argument out slightly: it would indeed make rational good sense to think that there is a rational purpose behind the universe. Everything would fall into place. But we can't prove this – or disprove it – because it assumes that our understanding of rationality applies to the universe as a whole, which is to assume precisely what we wish to prove, and can't. All we can say is that it would be very nice if there was a rational purpose behind everything. It would correspond to our appreciation of the rational. But we simply don't know whether this is the case or not.

The other argument is the argument for design particularly associated with Archdeacon William Paley in the eighteenth century. You see a watch on the beach and you conclude that there must be a watchmaker. The universe is amazingly complex and intricate so, as this line of argument goes, there must be a divine designer. The problem with this is that to say that something is designed you have to have a standard of comparison. You have to have some idea as to what is designed and what is undesigned. If on the beach we see not a watch but a piece of driftwood, we conclude it has been bought to shore and shaped that way by the elements of wind, sea and sand – not a woodcarver. If on closer inspection the driftwood turns out to be part of an old table leg, then we draw the appropriate conclusion about the existence of a carpenter. The trouble with the argument from design is that by definition we only have one universe. We don't have one box marked designed universes and another box marked undesigned universes between which we can choose to place this universe. Again, we simply don't know. The important implication of this is that we similarly can't say for certain that the universe is undesigned. We know that everything that is living came about through a process of evolution. But we don't know if that whole process is designed or not. Nearly everything that has happened over the last 13 and a half billion years was inherent, in some sense contained, in that original explosion. It might have been designed that way – or it might not. From a philosophical point of view the matter remains open.

There is another important implication of all this. In recent decades we've heard a fair amount about the so-called anthropic principle. This points out that the universe is very finely tuned and even the tiniest variation would have meant that human life as we know it would not have emerged. So everything seems, as it were, to lead up to the emergence of human beings. I've never found this argument at all convincing. The fact is that if we are here at all, as we are, then of course everything seems as though it has been designed to produce us. But seeming to be so is very different from being designed to do so. The anthropic principle fails for the same reason as the argument from design. We don't have two sets of universes, one finely tuned to lead up to human beings and one not so finely tuned. By definition there is only one universe that we can have experience of and we have nothing with which to compare it. (If, as Martin Rees suggests, there is a wider multiverse, it is not one that we experience.)

So I come back to what a believer believes and why she believes it. On the basis of her own experience of being utterly dependent on a ground of all being and orientated towards the goal of human longing, seeking to line her personal purpose with the divine wisdom received within, she posits a ground and purpose for the universe as a whole. What we can say is that this makes sense of things, for making sense from our point of view means wise and rational purpose. There is no logical proof that things ought to make sense. But it makes sense not only of our own sense of personal purpose, it makes sense of our capacity for moral awareness, for what we believe is rooted in a divine wisdom that is conceived as sheer, unutterable goodness. It makes sense of our aesthetic sense, for we believe that it is rooted in one whom St Augustine addressed as "O thou beauty most ancient and withal so fresh" (Chadwick, 1992). It makes sense of our quest for truth in maths and the sciences. One of the features of the universe that has emerged very strongly in recent years is the way that what you might call the higher maths can actually map out the universe and do so in a way which is remarkably concise and elegant. Professor Roger Penrose, the former Professor of Maths at Oxford gave a set of lectures in which he referred to the "extraordinary accuracy of the appropriate theories – Newton's, Maxwell's and Einstein's – as well as their mathematical elegance". Two points were made in that sentence: the accuracy of the theories and their elegance. From the standpoint of religious faith this is because the logos, the divine reason, is reflected in the very structure of the universe, and can be apprehended by rational minds. Again, this does not prove that there is a wisdom at the very heart of things but it does set our awareness of truth and beauty, as well as our sense of goodness, in a wider explanatory framework.

I have yet to mention the great stumbling block to religious belief, the amount of anguish and evil in the world. The size of this stumbling block cannot be exaggerated. There is, alas, no time to explore that issue here except to indicate the Christian approach, with its conviction that God himself in Christ shares human anguish to the full, even to the extent of being forsaken, whilst giving us a hope that through the resurrection of Christ the divine purpose of love will finally win through. Although I cannot deal with this issue here, I need to mention it simply to stress that I think that this is where the real difficulty lies and why. The argument goes that although it would be very nice to think that there is a wise, rational and loving purpose at the heart of things, in the light of the extent of human suffering and evil, it can't be seen as something more than what would be nice; it can only be wishful thinking. That, I think, is where the real difficulty lies. For, as I've already suggested, I think it natural that there should be an initial trust that a universe that yields itself to rational exploration, has a wise and rational power and purpose behind it.

One further aspect must be briefly mentioned, the subject of increasing interest at the moment, namely the evolutionary basis of religion. Why did religion evolve, and what evolutionary purposes does it serve? The earliest surviving evidence of religious belief, in terms of grave gods and goddesses, dates from the Paleolithic period, about 25,000 years ago. So religion evolved between 100,000 and 200,000 years ago, or at least that's what we can surmise. From an evolutionary perspective it emerged, and has persisted, because it helped our survival. I'm not qualified to answer the question of evolutionary purpose. But I have read with great interest Robin Dunbar's (2006) essay in *New Scientist* recently and his hypothesis seemed to make great sense. But I can say that whatever the answer, there are still further questions to be considered. Our need to eat and drink clearly has evolutionary significance. Without it we would not be here. But a whole range of culinary cultures have emerged – Indian, Chinese, French and so on – for eating and drinking has taken on an enormous cultural significance. Within those cuisines people make distinctions about what is and is not nutritious, what is and is not tasty, even what is aesthetically pleasing. So with religion. Whatever its evolutionary significance, its cultural significance is even greater. Within and between cultures we seek to discriminate between good religion and bad, between that which helps living humanely and that which hinders it. We also try to make evaluations about truth.

So, I come back to my title. We are indeed half ape: the product of evolution, sharing our genes with all other living creatures. We are also, I argue, half angel. We are rational beings capable of transcending egoism, acting altruistically and serving the well-being of others. More than that, I have suggested we have a capacity for entering into the divine purpose for our lives, a purpose which we read back both into the evolution of life and the origin of the universe in the first place. The wisdom beyond our own wisdom that we know in our own experience, we posit it as being behind, beyond and within all things. Such a belief has even greater explanatory power than the theory of evolution, to which of course it is not opposed, for it helps us to understand our sense of values, our appreciation of beauty and our desire to get at the truth of things. There is no rational proof that I know of which can impel someone by sheer force of logic to enter the milieu of faith, or indeed to leave it. Religious belief is a mysterious matter, involving the whole person and the sum of their life experience. A believer wants to affirm that, despite the anguish and evil of the world, existence remains a blessing, and its ills, though not willed by God, can often be made to yield a further blessing. For in the end, evaluating life's purpose is more than a utilitarian calculus of pain and pleasure. So I end with a verse by the Orkney poet Edwin Muir, in which he contrasts the unsullied paradise of Eden with the dark world we know now. In relation to that contrast Muir writes

> But famished field and blackened tree
> Bear flowers in Eden never known.
> Blossoms of grief and charity
> Bloom in these darkened fields alone.
> What had Eden ever to say
> Of hope and faith and pity and love
> Until was buried all its day
> And memory found its treasure trove?
> Strange blessings never in paradise
> Fall from these beclouded skies (p. 227).

Despite everything, it is better to exist than not to exist. To live as a thinking, choosing, intellectually and spiritually questing, loving and praying being remains a blessing. It is to that fact that the designation "Half Angel" points.

Postscript

There's a painting by El Greco called *An Allegory with a Boy Lighting a Candle in the Company of an Ape and a Fool*, painted in the late 1580s or early 1590s and now in the National Gallery of Scotland in Edinburgh. It shows a boy, with his face fully lit by reflection from the candle he is holding and lighting it from some kind of torch. On his right is an ape, perhaps a chimpanzee, with some faint reflection of the light on his face. To the boy's left is a fool, someone who would once have been described as mentally subnormal, looking down, also with a faint reflection of the light round his mouth, though not at all round his eyes or the rest of his face. It brings out well the continuity between the chimpanzee and humanity. But if light is taken as a symbol of consciousness, of reflective self-awareness, then there seems not just a quantitative difference but a qualitative one between the full light on the boy's face on the one hand and the faint light on the chimpanzee, and the fool on the other.

References

Chadwick, H. (trans.) (1992) "Late have I loved you, beauty so old and so new", St Augustine, *Confessions*. Oxford University Press, p. 201.

Dunbar, R. (2006) We believe ... *New Scientist* 189, No. 2536 [28.01.06], pp. 30–33.

Farrer, A. (1970) *A Celebration of Faith*. ed. Leslie Houlden. Hodder and Stoughton, p. 61.

——. (1967) *Saving Belief*. Hodder and Stoughton, p. 30.

——. (1966) *A Science of God?* Geoffrey Bles, p. 66.

Muir, E. (1976) "One Foot in Eden", *Collected Poems*. Faber, p. 227.

Newman, J. H. (1959) *Apologia Pro Vita Sua*. Fontana/Collins, p. 225.

Pasternak, C. A. (2003) *Quest: The Essence of Humanity*. John Wiley, pp. 249–276.

Paley, W. *Natural Theology*. (First published in 1802.)

Thomas, R. S. (1993) "Perhaps", *Collected Poems, 1945–1990*. J. M. Dent, p. 353.

6: Material Facts from a Nonmaterialist Perspective

David Hulme, Ph.D.

Ask "What makes us human?" and a range of responses is guaranteed from materialist and nonmaterialist scientist and religious thinker alike. From self-awareness to free moral agency, from conscience to the capacity to imagine, such traits are put forward as distinguishing us from nonhuman species. There's also the capacity for spoken language, which some say is the most distinctive difference, even innate. On a more troubling level, some might list the deliberate decision not to reproduce ourselves, and more darkly still, the willing invention of weapons that assure mutual mass destruction, threatening extinction of the species.

That all of these characteristics have a connection with human consciousness is clear. But the definition and operation of human consciousness is not. Despite the fact that a US presidential proclamation declared the 1990s "the decade of the brain," with the assurance that "a new era of discovery is dawning in brain research,"[1] little has been achieved in understanding the brain-mind relationship. Addressing a 2005 neuroscience conference, Stephen Morse, Professor of Psychology and Law in Psychiatry at the University of Pennsylvania, candidly noted,

> Here's a dirty little secret: We have no idea how the brain enables the mind. We know a lot about the localization of function, we know a lot about neurophysiological processes, but how the brain produces mental states – how it produces conscious, rational intentionality – we don't have a clue. When we do, it will revolutionize the biological sciences.[2]

While we wait for that moment, it might be opportune to focus on what makes us human from a much overlooked nonmaterialist perspective. Why is this worthy of consideration in an age when the soul and even the secular self are no longer in vogue as explanatory concepts?[3] The answer lies in Morse's admission that the materialist replacement for nonmaterial explanations faces an impasse of its own: human consciousness (and thus its associated self-awareness) remains a mystery. This would come as no surprise to brain researcher Robert L. Kuhn, who wrote almost forty years ago:

> The human brain cannot account for the yawning chasm between [the] utterly unique characteristics of humans and the repetitive instincts of animals.
>
> Therefore, a non-physical addition must unite with the human brain, converting it into the human mind.
>
> ... The human brain *cannot* explain the human mind – there must be a non-physical ingredient, beyond our microscopes, test tubes, electrodes and computers. To the truly open-minded individual, it is fruitless to physically rationalize the uniqueness of mind. There must be a non-physical essence – a 'spirit' – in man.
>
> ... Evolutionary theorists point to the similarity among human and ape brains to corroborate their views. It is ironic that, in reality, they have stumbled on to the most significant scientific observation in history, irrefutably attesting to the non-physical component which converts the output of the human brain into mind. Without this non-physical factor, man could be nothing more than a super-ape, more intelligent than the chimp to the *same* degree that the chimp is more intelligent than a less complex mammal.[4]

Philosopher of mind John Searle has remarked that in the absence of agreement on the subject of consciousness, he welcomes discussion from all perspectives, including the nonmaterialist, to further the search for an explanation.[5] Thus, it might be helpful to re-examine some of the wisdom of the past for answers of a different order. By this I do not intend a repetition of what has become the conventional Western religious conceptualization of the human being – body and soul – but rather an examination of the largely forgotten wisdom of the ancient Hebrews. In so doing, we might light upon an alternative explanation that could inform present efforts.

The body and soul of Greek philosophy

Before detailing that early Hebrew perspective, it is helpful to consider the origin of the concept of the soul and the self. In a recent
examination of the intellectual history of personal identity, professors
Raymond Martin and John Barresi remind us:

> What Pythagoras and Empedocles seem to have shared, and what
> they encouraged in thinkers who would come later, was belief in a
> soul, or self, that existed prior to the body, that could be induced to
> leave the body even while the body remained alive, and that would
> outlast the body.

> These ideas were extremely consequential. Directly or indirectly,
> they seem to have powerfully influenced Plato and, through Plato,
> various church fathers, including Augustine and, through Augus-
> tine, Christian theology and, through Christianity, the entire mind-
> set of Western civilization, secular as well as religious. It is ironic,
> perhaps, that ideas that eventually acquired such an impressive ratio-
> nal pedigree may have originated in the dark heart of shamanism,
> with its commitment to magic and the occult.[6]

It is a far-reaching proposition that merits serious contemplation –
that our entire Western mindset, *religious and secular*, on the matter of
how we have understood ourselves, may have originated not from a
rational process but from notions within magic and the occult. More
specifically, it is arresting that those regarded as some of the founda-
tional thinkers of Western civilization, *religious and secular*, could have
succumbed to ideas with such dubious origins.

What, then, of the separately originated Hebrew account of consciousness, self-awareness, and human uniqueness? The following
discussion provides the opportunity to clarify the differences between
the Greek and Hebrew mindsets on these issues and to examine the
often misunderstood biblical record.

"For dust you are ..."

In another resource about origins or beginnings, the book of Genesis,
the reader is invited to consider a very different perspective.[7] In the
second chapter's account of creation, we learn from the Jewish Publication Society's Tanakh translation that "the LORD God formed man
from the dust of the earth. He blew into his nostrils the breath of life,

and man became a living being" (Genesis 2:7).[8] This differs from the King James Version of the Holy Bible, beloved of English-speaking Christians, whose translators rendered the Hebrew *nephesh* not as "a living being" but as "a living soul" (from the Latin *solus*, "sole" or "alone"). A better choice in Latin would have been *anima* from the Greek *anemos* ("air" or "breath").[9] But in this verse, the King James Version's translators betrayed their bias toward the ancient Greek philosophers and their intellectual descendants, the early church fathers, for whom the soul was the essential part of the human being. For example, according to Irenaeus,

> ... the prophetic word declares of the first-formed man, "He became a living soul," [Genesis 2:7] teaching us that by the participation of life the soul became alive; so that the soul, and the life which it possesses, must be understood as being separate existences.[10]

While most modern English translations have adopted the term "a living being," there are some that seem disinclined to let go of the ancient Greek notion of the immortal soul. *The Message: The Bible in Contemporary Language* reads, "God formed Man out of dirt from the ground and blew into his nostrils the breath of life. The Man came alive – a living soul!"[11] Unfortunately, according to the Hebrew, the "soul" of any person (even a translator!) can never be anything but material. But the availability of more accurate translations does not necessarily bring changes in established doctrine or popular belief. The soul as immortal has not disappeared from theological discourse, liturgical practice, or everyday imagination.[12]

One scholar whose view differs is Jon D. Levenson, annotator of Genesis for *The Jewish Study Bible*. He comments on Genesis 2:7 that "the human being is not an amalgam of perishable body and immortal soul, but a psychophysical unity who depends on God for life itself."[13] What does he intend by a "psychophysical unity" that is not "an amalgam of perishable body and immortal soul?" Further, is this terminology consistent with the rest of the Hebrew Scriptures, and is it perpetuated in the Apostolic Writings of the early followers of Jesus? By setting this unity against the ancient Greek/traditional Christian conceptualization of the human being as temporary body plus eternal soul, Levenson draws attention to an entity that, although physical, is also mental. And by his definition both aspects are temporary. To repeat, this is a far cry from Pythagoras, Empedocles, Plato,

Augustine, various church fathers, traditional Christianity, and the entire mindset of Western civilization, religious and secular.

Tracing this Hebrew conceptualization further, the book of Job, written as early as the patriarchal period (circa 2100–1900 BCE),[14] addresses the psychological part of this unity, when one of the suffering man's counselors explains that "it is the spirit in man, the breath of the Almighty, that makes him understand" (Job 32:8).[15] Here is an obvious connection with Genesis 2:7, but now the psychological or mental part of the psychophysical unity is termed "the spirit in man." Its function, originating with God, is to provide the human being with the capacity to understand.

"… and to dust you shall return"

Thus far we have a nonmaterial, conscious, mentally empowering, physically bounded aspect of the human being that ceases at death. This is confirmed in the book of Psalms, where we learn of man, "His spirit departs, he returns to the earth; in that very day his thoughts perish" (146:4),[16] and in the Hebrew wisdom book of Ecclesiastes, "The living know they will die [self-awareness]. But the dead know nothing [no continuing post-death consciousness]; they have no more recompense, for even the memory of them has died. Their loves, their hates, their jealousies have long since perished" (9:5–6a).[17]

Solomon, the likely tenth-century-BCE author of Ecclesiastes, explains that humans and animals meet the same fate: "as the one dies so dies the other" (3:19).[18] What, then, becomes of this unique spirit in man at death? He writes, "The dust returns to the ground as it was, and the lifebreath returns to God who bestowed it" (12:7).[19]

Thus, according to this Hebrew perspective, there is no immortal soul and no immortal "spirit in man" either. The body decays and the spirit returns to God.

The Jewish Encyclopedia confirms, "The belief that the soul continues its existence after the dissolution of the body is a matter of philosophical or theological speculation rather than of simple faith, and is accordingly nowhere expressly taught in Holy Scripture."[20]

Despite the seeming finality of death for the psychophysical unity, termination of life was nevertheless understood by the ancient Hebrews as temporary and as a kind of sleep. Later there would come a time of awakening when the body would be reconstituted and the spirit revived. This resurrection to life is of two kinds – physical and nonphysical. The prophet Ezekiel speaks of a resurrection of physical people to physical life: "Thus said the Lord GOD to these bones: I will cause breath to enter you and you shall live again. I will lay sinews upon you, and cover you with flesh, and form skin over you. And I will put breath into you, and you shall live again. And you shall know that I am the LORD!" (Ezekiel 37:5–6).[21] The prophet Daniel writes about people who are raised to live or die forever, "And many of those who sleep in the dust of the earth shall awake, some to everlasting life, some to shame and everlasting contempt" (Daniel 12:2).[22] Daniel himself is told that he will "rest [die] and will arise [be resurrected] ... at the end of the days" [far in the future] (Daniel 12:13).[23] But none of these references speak about an immortal soul, only about the raising of previously physical people who have ceased to exist for some time.

Continuing in the spirit of Hebrew tradition

The concept of the spirit in man and of resurrection to life recurs in the Apostolic Writings, in the first letter to the church at Corinth. Paul, a Hellenistic Jew and self-described "Hebrew of the Hebrews," writes to people living in a world dominated by Greek philosophy, "What man knows the things of a man except the spirit of the man which is in him?" (1 Corinthians 2:11a).[24] It is by means of the nonmaterial, uniquely human spirit that human beings gain understanding of the human realm. Eschewing any debt to Greek thinkers, and as a Hebraic scholar, Paul simply reiterates the ancient Hebrew concept of a material-spiritual psychophysical unity.

While we might claim from this alone that, according to Paul, the spirit in man separates humans from the other species, is there any more evidence of human uniqueness in his writings?

Paul was certainly aware of the Genesis account in which each lifeform is separated from others by its unique identity – its "kind." Vegetation is said to be different in kind from fish and birds, which are different from each other and from wild and domestic animals and reptiles. And each in turn differs from humankind. He confirms this understanding when he writes, "Not all flesh is the same, but there is one kind for humans, another for animals, another for birds, and another for fish" (1 Corinthians 15:39).[25] Thus, for Paul, human

uniqueness was evident on at least two levels, mental and physical –
Levenson's psychophysical unity.

What did Paul understand to happen at death? Not surprisingly,
the Hebrew scholar hews to the now familiar line. He says that though
some of the followers of Jesus "have fallen asleep," they "will arise
first" (1 Thessalonians 4:13, 16).[26] In chapter 15 of his first letter to
the church at Corinth, he explains that the psychophysical entity
ceases ("in Adam all die"), but that there is still a future resurrection
to life, through the agency of Jesus Christ ("in Christ all shall be made
alive").[27] He appeals to Genesis 2:7 when he writes, "The first man
Adam became a living being," and he expresses the means of resurrection by saying: "The last Adam [Christ] became a life-giving
spirit."[28] The Greek for "living being" is *psuche*, the equivalent of the
Hebrew *nephesh*, while "life-giving spirit" is *pneuma*, the counterpart
of the Hebrew *ruach*. Again, there is nothing here to suggest that Paul
accepted the Platonic notion of an immortal soul.

From this Hebraic perspective, what makes humans unique is
the nonphysical component, "the spirit in man." It is this that must
give rise to our notable differences from all other species. While it
may be conceded that levels of consciousness may exist in other
living systems, from animals to birds to reptiles to insects, etc., it is
very difficult to find evidence of humor or ecstasy, of inspiration,
of free moral agency or self-sacrificing love in any other species.
The only way that the ancient Hebrew tradition could explain the
difference between humans and the closest mammals in brain
size and complexity is by reference to a nonmaterial spirit that
empowers this quantitatively similar brain to produce a huge qualitative difference.

Having referred to the unique spirit in man, Paul writes to the
people at Corinth that "no one knows the things of God except the
Spirit of God" (1 Corinthians 2:11).[29] In the next verse, he goes on to
say that the followers at Corinth have received this same Spirit, "that
we might know the things that have been freely given to us by God."
Here, then, is the possibility of an additional nonphysical and unique
aspect of the human brain. In a later letter, this time to believers in
Rome, he says that the spirit in man can interface with this Spirit of
God. He writes, "For his Spirit joins with our spirit to affirm that we
are God's children" (Romans 8:16).[30]

The science of change

As a final comment on contributions to the ongoing debate about what makes us human, it is worth considering an aspect of human behavior rarely mentioned in such discussions. Part of our uniqueness concerns the capacity to show remorse and to change radically for the better. We are not irreversibly programmed by our genes or by our early environment. We can make changes in our existence by conscious, willed thought leading to action. This, too, has a connection with an ancient Hebrew concept, as we will see.

Researchers have thought for years that the brain came prewired – that its development from birth through adolescence was the result of a gradual unfolding of its already existing potential, and that by adulthood it was set. But recent findings show that the brain's circuitry is wired as the individual develops and can be *rewired* by the conscious thought of the individual. Because of the brain's neuroplasticity, we can change our own patterns of thought and behavior by our self-directed will. The evidence of this is observable in physical changes in the neural pathways of the brain. These new circuits can replace previous pathways and become fixed.

The first inklings of this phenomenon came with work on stroke victims and with people suffering from obsessive-compulsive disorder (OCD). It became clear that certain patients, parts of whose brain circuitry had been compromised by cerebral hemorrhage leaving them unable to perform specific tasks, could be retrained. Their brain circuits would rewire a way around the particular problem. This took intensive training, but it produced positive and permanent changes. Those suffering from OCD (for example, uncontrollable handwashing resulting from a fear of germs) found relief once they understood that part of their brain circuitry was causing the problem. They were trained in the technique of using self-directed free will to rewire their faulty circuitry.

It goes without saying that such breakthroughs are needed in other mental and behavioral impasses. The new findings have profound implications for improvement in the most difficult and sensitive human problems, from depression to addictions of all kinds and even protracted national and international deadlocks. The severely depressed can be helped by undertaking a program in which they learn to recognize what is happening inside their brains and take appropriate self-directed or self-willed actions. In other findings, there is the possibility of using the self-directed will to shut down the sexual response in those obsessed with pornography.

There is a nonmaterial or spiritual parallel to these new findings. That there are nonphysical principles behind physical change in the brain is clear when we take into consideration the ancient Hebrew verb *shub*, which means "to (re)turn." One of its additional meanings is to repent of wrong actions by turning away from evil. The word combines two aspects of repentance: to turn from evil and to turn to the good. This means retracing our steps to find the right way again.

In the case of the ancient Israelites, God wanted them to change their ways by first changing their minds. One theological wordbook explains further about *shub* that "by turning, a God-given power, a sinner can redirect his destiny."[31] We may define sin very broadly as anything that damages our relationship with God or with human beings (including oneself). When the brain's circuits are wired incorrectly, either through damage or conscious choice, harm is done. Change, or rewiring, is the only way forward, the way to health both physically and spiritually. In other words, those activities of our minds and bodies that harm us, those around us, and our relationship with God are evil. They need to be changed first at the level of the mind, by the use of the will to do good. Another way of saying it is that sin can be overcome through change at the conscious level of the mind when the will is engaged.

In the Apostolic Writings, the Greek equivalent of *shub* is *metanoeo*. It includes the concept of changing one's mind, or of coming to a new way of thinking. What we have not understood until recently is the role of the physical brain in this process. Once the will to change is engaged and specific actions are taken, new neural pathways are created and new attitudes and new behaviors result. The more we take the new action, the more lasting the behavior becomes. We've had clues about rewiring the brain and our behavior before: it's a common notion that it takes three weeks to break a habit and instill a new one. We know, too, that when we act in harmful or wrong ways regularly, our consciences become hardened and evil gains our acceptance. The way out of human problems as diverse as obsessive-compulsive disorder, bad habits, racial prejudice, hate crimes, depression, brutality, and the exploitation of others remains a fundamental change of mind. The Hebrew Scriptures and the Apostolic Writings have said that, in principle, all along.

That same tradition speaks of repentance as introspecting and changing our way of doing so that change is lasting. According to brain researcher Jeffrey Schwartz, whose therapeutic technique for treating OCD[32] is very much akin to the biblical concept of repentance, "you cannot form trustful relations with others without acknowledging error, without sincerity. And repentance is just, when you get right down to it, a form of sincerity. It's saying, 'I realize I made errors. I'm not perfect. There are things I could try to do better.' "[33]

What makes humans unique? Consider that from the ancient Hebrew perspective, it is the spirit in man, the spirit of God, and the capacity to change for the better that flows from self-directed, conscious, willed action.

Endnotes

1. Library of Congress/National Institute of Mental Health "Decade of the Brain" Project, "Presidential Proclamation 6158" (July 17, 1990), http://www.loc.gov/loc/brain/proclaim.html.

2. Stephen Morse (address, "The New Neuromorality," W. H. Brady Program in Culture and Freedom Conference, American Enterprise Institute, Washington, D. C., June 1, 2005). Video available online at http://www.aei.org/events/eventID.1072/event_detail.asp.

3. See Raymond Martin and John Barresi, *The Rise and Fall of Soul and Self: An Intellectual History of Personal Identity* (New York: Columbia University Press, 2006).

4. Robert Kuhn, "The Human Mind," *Probe '69* (Johannesburg: University of Witwatersrand, 1969).

5. "What Is Consciousness?" *Closer to Truth* (2000). Video available online at http://www.closertotruth.com/videoarchive/.

6. Martin and Barresi, *Rise and Fall*, 11.

7. Parallel to the current discussion about what makes humans unique, it's intriguing to note that the ancient Hebrew psalmist David pondered, "What is man that You are mindful of him?" (Psalm 8:4, New King James Version). This question was repeated about a thousand years later by the author of the book of Hebrews, believed by many to be the apostle Paul.

8. *Tanakh: A New Translation of The Holy Scriptures, According to the Traditional Hebrew Text* (Jerusalem: The Jewish Publication Society, 1985).

9. See *The Companion Bible*, appendix 13 (London: The Bullinger Publications Trust, in association with Marshall, Morgan and Scott, 1974).

10. *Against Heresies*, 2.34.4, in Alexander Roberts and James Donaldson, eds., *The Ante-Nicene Fathers: Translations of the Writings of the Fathers Down to* A.D. 325, vol. 1 (Edinburgh: T&T Clark, 1884; Grand Rapids, MI: Eerdmans Publishing Company, 1996).

11. Eugene H. Petersen, *The Message: The Bible in Contemporary Language, Numbered Edition* (Colorado Springs: NavPress, 2005).

12. It is interesting that the word *nephesh* is also used many times of animals, in the sense of "a living creature" – and the Bible certainly doesn't accord immortality to animals.

13. Adele Berlin and Marc Zvi Brettler, eds., *The Jewish Study Bible*, Jewish Publication Society Tanakh Translation (Oxford: Oxford University Press, 2004).

14. John F. Walvoord and Roy B. Zuck, *The Bible Knowledge Commentary*, "Job" (Wheaton, IL: Victor, 1985).

15. English Standard Version (ESV).

16. New American Standard Bible, 1995 Update.

17. Tanakh.

18. Ibid.

19. Ibid.

20. *The Jewish Encyclopedia*, s.v. "Immortality of the Soul" (by Kaufman Kohler), http://www.jewishencyclopedia.com/view.jsp?artid= 118& letter=I (accessed December 5, 2006).

21. Tanakh.

22. New King James Version (NKJV).

23. Ibid.

24. Ibid.

25. ESV.

26. NKJV.

27. 1 Corinthians 15:22, NKJV.

28. Ibid., verse 45.

29. NKJV.

30. New Living Translation.

31. R. Laird Harris, Gleason L. Archer Jr., and Bruce K. Waltke, *Theological Wordbook of the Old Testament* (electronic edition), entry no. 2340 (Chicago: Moody Press, 1980, 1999).

32. Jeffrey M. Schwartz, M. D., and Sharon Begley, *The Mind and the Brain: Neuroplasticity and the Power of Mental Force* (New York: HarperCollins, Regan Books, 2002).

33. Jeffrey M. Schwartz, M. D., interview by author, "Fusing Mind and Matter," *Vision – Journal for a New World* 6, no. 3 (2004), http://www.vision.org/visionmedia/article.aspx?id=295.

7: What Makes Us Human? – Our Ancestors and the Weather

Stephen Oppenheimer

The facile answer is that we are the only living species that could or would want to ask such a question. Yet we are not the only animal that needs to identify its own species or sub-group by visual, vocal and behavioural signals. The extraordinary range of answers to this commonly posed question, and our occasional sinister ambivalence about the humanity of other 'races', reveal as much about our primate origins as about our philosophical, biological and religious backgrounds.

Having a biological background, I naturally find resonance with the rational views expressed by both Charles Pasternak and Simon Fisher, and others (this volume), which imply that we are, as it were, 'more monkey than man' both genetically and, to an unacknowledged extent, behaviourally. The small degree to which we differ genetically from apes may be largely the result of a constellation of relatively small adaptive genomic modifications in the DNA regulating the relative growth of our organs (ontogeny), particularly the DNA affecting the growth of our brain. It is these minor mutations that should be examined by those who would look for meaningful differences between chimps and ourselves.

As Fisher points out, the majority of the workhorse genes which act as templates for the creation of unique proteins, our building blocks, are conserved and held in common between our species, with little variation. The blind mutational accidents of 'ontogenetic' control and regulation hold the blueprints for our recent spectacular change in shape and behaviour. They, in turn, have been blindly selected for in the survivors of our ever-changing battle with climate and food resources. The needs of our increasingly exploratory and adaptive behaviour have fed back into the size of the organ responsible for that behaviour, our brain, and its virtual client our complex language ability. The latter is our giraffe's neck, our special organ, which may have had its origins long before we became human.

I would like to answer the question of our humanity by looking backwards at what *made* an already intelligent ape evolve into a walking, talking creature who rapidly moved from fashioning stone tools to exploring every corner of the Earth and then the moon. The forces that drove our adaptive survival against heavy odds in the African savannah are the keys to our nature and to our extraordinary story. An objective view of the fossil and genetic evidence supports the rationalist argument, held long before Darwin, that we were not simply 'put' here fully formed, walking, talking, and unique among animals. It further appears that we were selected, as a result of certain pre-existing skills and habitat, and moulded by a fierce, blind, unthinking environment. Like all evolving species, we had ancestors and cousins who shared some of our abilities but went extinct. Our physical and behavioural adaptations, the most striking being our brain size and language, were focused on surviving the struggle with our greatest enemy, the worsening climate.

The appearance of new and more successful human species have coincided with severe glaciations and expansions of the African savannah during the past 2.5 million years. But climate was a major force behind hominid evolution for much longer than that. Primates have, in general, more dextrous hands, relatively larger brains, more varied diets, and more complex social lives than most other contemporary mammals. Ten million years ago, Africa was a lush paradise with vast forests and home to a number of species of ape. Africa's grassland has expanded progressively since then, as the world's climate has cooled and dried in cyclical fits and starts of increasing frequency and severity, associated with a dramatic reduction in the number of ape species.

Walking apes

Habitual bi-pedalism, evidenced by changes in our legs, marks a split between our ancestors and those of chimps, but antedates humans by several million years. At present, the first clear evidence for bi-pedal-ism is seen only in skeletons of *Australopithecus anamensis*, a walking ape dating from 4 million years ago and found on the shores of Lake Turkana, although such claims have been made for *Ardipithecus ramidus* at 4–5 million years (White et al., 1994) and *Orrorin tugenensis* at 6 million years ago (Senuta et al., 2001) (see Figure 1).

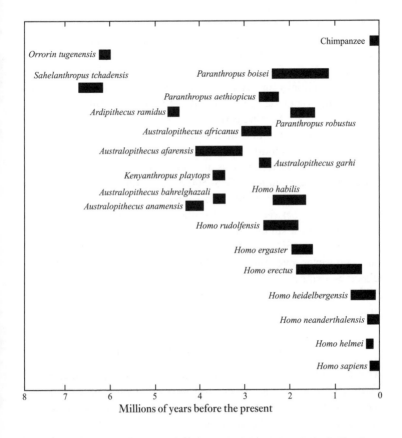

Figure 1 Over the past 8 million years of hominid evolution (including here only our nearest relatives, chimps), several species usually co-existed at any one time, so drawing a tree of direct descent on the basis of chance fossil finds may be misleading – hence the lack of branches on this tree. (Figure from Oppenheimer, 2003)

Many think that there was a cause–and–effect relation between the spread of the grasslands and the change from quadruped forest–living to easy walking around the savannah. Others have suggested alternative theories of the change, such as habitual wading through water, or walking tall, literally to keep a cool head (Wheeler, 1993), or keeping an eye out for predators on the plain. However, our ancestors' brains, although larger than those of most other land mammals, were no bigger than that of our cousin the chimpanzee, so there was less danger of them overheating. Nor is standing upright – which many mammals do, including monkeys, chimpanzees, bears, and meerkats – the same thing as habitually walking on two legs for long periods. The idea of leaving hands free for manipulation, such as wielding heavy sticks for hunting (or initially for defence against predators, since our ancestors were mainly vegetarian), is more attractive as an evolutionary force. Unfortunately we have no direct proof, since wood is perishable and stone tools are not found from that time.

Those early walking apes, including 'Lucy' (*Australopithecus afarensis*) were shorter than us and still closer to chimps above the neck with brain volumes of 375–500 cm^3, although they had smaller canine teeth. A different two-legged version (*Australopithecus africanus*) lived between 2 and 3 million years ago and, although the same size, had a slightly larger average brain size than chimps at between 420 and 500 cm^3. Their teeth were also smaller and more like ours. However, over the few million years in which the australopithecines ('southern apes') and their immediate ancestors walked Africa's grasslands, we see only a moderate, not a dramatic, increase in brain size (see Figure 2).

Growing brains in the big dry

Two and a half million years ago the world started getting colder. Within a million years, the wet and warm *Pliocene* geological period gave way to the *Pleistocene* ice epoch, a grinding cycle of repeated dry ice ages, with alternating advances and retreats of African grassland lasting right up until the most recent glaciation. Soon after the start of this period, australopithecines were replaced in the African savannah by two diverging lines of walking apes, with larger brains. These two were the first humans (i.e. of the *Homo* genus) characterised by their stone tools, and *Paranthropus*, who developed larger jaws to cope

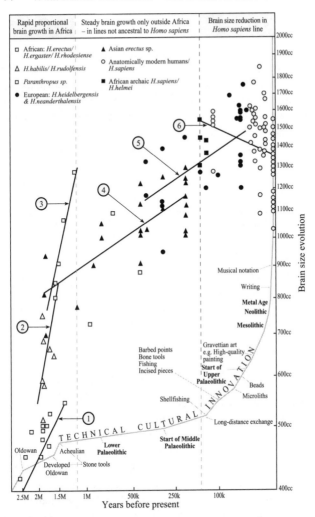

Figure 2 Brain size and cultural evolution. A graph of brain growth reveals three phases over the last 2.5 million years, as separated by vertical dashed lines. The curve below shows how rapid cultural acceleration occurred during brain size reduction. (Recognised cultural milestones given equal weighting. Log-log regression lines 1–6 relate to six closely related contemporary regional human types as shown by symbols in the key. (Figure from Oppenheimer, 2003)

with grinding up tough vegetable matter. Both groups developed larger brains.

Naturally, we are inclined to think of humans as being special and set apart from the other apes by brain size. Some even think that an increase in brain size led to or was selected for by tool-making, but this argument seems unlikely. Firstly most of our brain growth occurred over a period, when the types of tools were static in design. Secondly, while fashioning *stone* tools, unlike walking on two legs or manual dexterity, may be characteristic to humans and possibly *Paranthropus* as well (Elton et al., 2001), even chimpanzees make crude but effective tools out of stones and wood, and they have smaller brains and branched off much earlier than the walking apes. If chimp's common ancestor with australopithecines already made such tools, why did the tool habit not dramatically select for larger brains in either group?

One of the earliest human tool-makers, *Homo habilis*, had an average brain volume of 650 cm^3, but among the known *habilis* skulls is one at 1.9 million years old with a chimp-like brain volume of only 500 cm^3, which is at the top end of the range for the earlier australopithecines (Elton et al., 2001; Ruff et al., 1997). But they soon grew larger ones.

What did we grow big brains for?

The idea that we somehow grew a big brain first, then decided what it was for, is a negation of the principles of natural selection. New kinds of behaviour precede the physical adaptation that evolves to better exploit that behaviour. Well before 2 million years ago there must already have been some aspect of our behaviour – something to do with the way we faced the climatic challenge, perhaps – that gave large, energy-expensive brains survival value. The problem of finding food in an increasingly dry environment must have taxed our ancestors' resourcefulness and larger brains clearly helped them in some way. That behaviour, like our brains, must still be with us today, because over subsequent major glaciations during the past 2.5 million years, new human species with progressively larger brains and more skills appeared in Africa. By 1 million years ago, brain volumes of various human species living both within and outside Africa had increased from 400 to 1,000 cm^3 (McBrearty and Brooks, 2000) and even into the modern size range (Figure 2). In other words, human brains had grown to three-quarters of their modern size long before we came on the scene.

There have been various suggestions as to what the key behaviour selecting for big brains might have been. The ice ages forced Africa into extreme aridity but although we can argue the value of larger brains in such circumstances, why should *our* brains have grown, and not those of the other mammals living at the edge of the savannah? It has been suggested that we needed to eat meat in order to facilitate our brain growth (Aiello and Wheeler, 1995). Yet, meat-eating is more a means than a motive for brain enlargement. The parallel reduction in size of human intestines, as shown by an alteration of the shape of the ribcage in *Homo ergaster*, is used as evidence for a change to eating more meat, but this change in the ribcage happened before the dramatic brain growth.

Without more direct evidence, such arguments for the role of climate and meat-eating in the enhanced brain growth of early humans remain largely armchair speculation. We know that, at least in Africa, stone tools were used by *Homo erectus* to butcher meat (Elton et al., 2001), but to establish a link between meat-eating, worsening weather, and brain growth we would need a comparison with purely vegetarian primates in the same environment over the same period.

Measurements of brain size in fossil skulls from large primate species over the period roughly from 2.5 million years (the start of the cooling) to 1.5 million years ago, including the two main branches of hominids that diverged during that period, *Homo* and *Paranthropus*, provide just that comparison. Other control groups include several prehistoric species of large, grass-eating, baboon-like *Theropithecus* monkeys which occupied the same habitat over the same period. The results of the comparison are dramatic, showing that ancestry is more important than diet. The large vegetarian monkey species show no increase in brain size, but hominids from both the omnivorous *Homo* and the vegetarian *Paranthropus* branches do. Importantly, not only do successive new *Homo* and *Paranthropus* species appear with larger brains, but brain size increases specifically *within* each species of each genus (Elton et al., 2001). This gives strong evidence for a shared new behaviour selecting for larger brains held by the common ancestor of the *Homo* and *Paranthropus* branches, but not shared with other contemporary primates. Over the period from 2.5 to 1.5 million years ago, the average hominid brain size more than doubled, from 400 cm³ to 900 cm³.

If we compare this early era of phenomenal brain growth with more recent times in the human line, there is a clear discontinuity between ancient and modern. Between the earliest *Homo habilis* just under 2 million years ago and the first so-called *Homo rhodesiense* fossils of 1.1–1.3 million years ago, a period of roughly 700,000 years, brain volume increased by two and a half times. In the subsequent 1.2 million years, although there were modest trends in brain size increase in individual human types outside Africa, such as Asian *Homo erectus* and European Neanderthals, a net increase of only 6 per cent was required to reach the brain size of today's humans. Surprisingly, there has been an overall *decline* in brain volume in modern humans over the past 150,000 years (see Figure 2).

These results suggest that, irrespective of diet, the earliest period of increased climatic adversity starting from 2.5 million years ago selectively favoured brain growth in the new hominid species, but not in other primates sharing the same environment. What does this mean? First, it supports the view that all these hominids belonging to the *Paranthropus* and *Homo* branches, and by implication their common ancestor, possessed some new behaviour selectively favouring brain growth which they had shared from at least the beginning of the cool period. In other words, the behavioural seeds of our extraordinarily rapid brain development may already have been in place in walking apes 2.5 million years ago. Second, it puts the meat theory under some strain. Third, the selection for brain size seemed to have its greatest acceleration at the beginning of our genus, over 2 million years ago.

There is a further problem with the 'meat makes brainy hunters' theory. The effect is absent in cooperative carnivores like lions. Humans, by contrast, have always retained their physical and mental flexibility in exploiting food resources. We still eat vegetables – lots of them, including fruits, roots, leaves, seeds, nuts, and berries. Our hands and teeth have become more generalist and flexible rather than specialist. The only physical feature that has developed in relation to our hands, apart from the opposable thumb, is the part of the brain devoted to their manipulation. A remarkable number of the behavioural differences in dietary strategy that set us apart from the carnivores are in fact characteristics that we *share* with our nearest living primate relative, the chimpanzee: diverse, adaptive omnivory, with optional cooperative hunting thrown in.

We should be looking much more closely at the behaviour of our closest living relatives for the seeds of our success. The history of primates over the past 10 million years has not been of specialist ruminants who decided to stop eating vegetables and start eating vegetarians instead, and who in the process became much smarter. It is the history of an already intelligent, large-brained order of forest-based generalists who made a virtue of their flexibility, even when they changed habitat. They all preserved, even improved, the dexterity of their five-fingered hand and in most cases their teeth got smaller rather than larger. Neither chimps nor our ancestors ever gave up the flexibility and survival value of a diverse diet, nor the flexible social cooperation that they used to exploit their environment so well.

It was against this long-established background of flexibility and social cooperation that the unique new behaviour associated with rapid brain growth kicked in 2.5 million years ago as the weather got worse. This new behaviour offered the potential to cope with climatic adversity. That it was present 2.5 million years ago, before the first humans, is evidenced by the rapid brain growth shared by humans' sister genus *Paranthropus* who continued to just over a million years ago.

Ever newer models

If we take *Homo habilis* as the early prototype of those tool-makers, then *Homo erectus* was the line-defining human – the Model T Ford of the new genus. Spanning a greater brain growth than any other human type, they were just like us from the neck down and dominated the planet for a million and a half years – about eight times as long as the present crowd. They had stone tools – simple retouched pebbles at first, but later more sophisticated hand-axes. Their African progenitor *Homo ergaster* was the first human to leave Africa, 1.95 million years ago, to become the Asian *Homo erectus*. The latter were slightly smaller than ourselves, and rapidly spread to the Middle East, Russia, India, the Far East, and Southeast Asia, carrying with them their so-called 'pebble-tool' technology (Foley and Lahr 1997; Lahr and Foley 1998). *Homo habilis*, or something like it, probably also made this leap at the same time, a possible precursor to *Homo floresiensis*, although the position of latter on the tree remains a puzzle. There is better evidence, however, that all subsequent human species made it out of Africa at the first available interglacial warm-up between ice ages.

Homo erectus types then dominated the world for nearly a million years until another terrible series of ice ages dried up much of Africa over a million years ago (Rossignol-Strick et al., 1998) and brought about the emergence of a new human family with larger brains. One view (Stringer, 2002) is that this family formed one overall species, *Homo heidelbergensis*, ultimately including and giving rise to sub-types such as *Homo sapiens* and *Homo neanderthalis* in the west, and eastern variants found in India (Narmada) and China (Maba and Dali). The first African representative of this new model was *Homo rhodesiense*. The same size as us and with a brain volume of as much as 1,250 cm^3 (McBrearty and Brookes, 2000), they used a more sophisticated stone tool kit known as Acheulian, named after a village in France near where the style was first found. Acheulian tools included largish flat stones shaped on both sides to form teardrop-shaped pointed hand-axes. This new arrival first made it out of Africa to Europe, and possibly to China, during a brief warm-up about half a million years ago, and carried the Acheulian technology with them.

Then, 350,000 years ago, another severe ice age struck, perhaps forcing other large-brained human types onto the African stage around 300,000 years ago (Lahr and Foley, 1998). They are known to some as archaic *Homo sapiens* (McBrearty and Brooks, 2000), and to others as *Homo helmei* (Foley and Lahr, 1997). I shall use the latter name to avoid confusion. Beetle-browed, the same size as us, and with an average brain volume slightly larger than ours at 1,400 cm^3, they represented the plateau as far as dramatic brain growth was concerned. They were also associated with the start of one of the most important revolutions in human technology, known as the Middle Palaeolithic (Foley and Lahr, 1997). Some have gone so far as to suggest that if brought up in a modern family, these heavy-browed creatures might fit into our society.

A larger and longer out-of-Africa movement, during a warm period, saw *Homo helmei* spreading throughout Eurasia 250,000 years ago. *Homo helmei* may have given rise to *Homo neanderthalensis* (Lahr and Foley, 1998) in Europe and Asia and had several possible relatives in India and China from the same period. Irrespective of when Neanderthals' ancestor left, the source human family containing our own ancestors remained in Africa, for the time being, physically separate from their Neanderthal cousins in Europe (Stringer, 1996).

Our own species, *Homo sapiens*, was born around 200,000 years ago, out of what was nearly a human extinction in which the total population fell an estimated 10,000 in a mother of all ice ages (Takahata et al., 1995). Although *Homo sapiens* duly made it out of Africa to the Levant at the next interglacial, 120,000 years ago, the genetic evidence indicates that their descendants died out there without issue in the ice age after that. When modern humans finally spread out of Africa to the rest of the world around 70,000–80,000 years ago, Eurasia was still inhabited by several other human species. The European Neanderthals, and possibly the Southeast Asian *Homo erectus*, persisted until less than 30,000 years ago, but no specific genetic traces of them remain in living humans.

Significantly, both Neanderthals and those modern humans living before the last ice age 20,000–30,000 years ago had rather bigger brains than do people living today (Lahr and Foley, 1998). It seems that the magic brain-enlarging effect of ice ages had played itself out before the time of our birth as a subspecies of *Homo helmei*. Maybe the obstetric risks of large heads were limiting. Either that, or brain size was no longer the most important determinant of success, and something new that we were doing with our brains – some other behavioural or cultural innovation – had taken over.

Once we had left Africa, although our brains had stopped growing, the climate continued to dominate human expansions and inventions right up to the modern age. It may be no exaggeration to say that the forces driving the waves of human technical innovation advancing across Eurasia from 80,000 years ago were more a result of stress and relief than of any biological improvement in the human computer. For example, the spreads of new technologies labelled by archaeologists as Early, Middle, and Late Upper Palaeolithic, Mesolithic, and Neolithic all coincided with dramatic ameliorations of Europe's climate and population expansions into new territories. These events were mirrored in Southeast Asia with expansions and advances of boat-making and sailing in response to the flooding of continental shelf as the sea level rose and fell.

In summary, then, rapidly increasing brain size was a key feature that set humans apart from the walking apes that lived before 2.5 million years ago. Since then our brains have trebled in volume. This increase was not gradual and steady: most of it came as a doubling of volume in *Homo erectus* 2 million years ago. In other words, the greatest acceleration in relative brain size occurred before 1.5 million years ago, rather early in our genus, and then gradually slowed down. The paradox is that our apparent behavioural explosion is mostly recent and is accelerating.

Baldwin's idea

The resolution of the paradox of ancient brain growth versus the recent human cultural explosion is that human culture feeds into itself, thus generating its own exponentially accelerating tempo. The history of human cultural evolution is not a virtual copy of the biological tree, with each successive human species leaping in intelligence and immediately using much smarter tools. Far from our biological evolution driving our cultural innovations, it was always the other way round, and although our brains stopped growing a long time ago our culture continues to evolve. The coevolution of culture and genes underlies recent human evolution. Although a deceptively simple concept, it runs counter to all our ethnic and species prejudices.

The mechanisms by which behavioural innovations or 'new culture' drive evolution were first elaborated by American psychologist Mark Baldwin a century ago (Deacon, 1997). Baldwin gave a behavioural interpretation of Darwin's view of evolutionary phenomena even as simple as the giraffe growing a long neck to eat the top leaves on bushes and trees. He suggested that behavioural flexibility and learning could amplify and bias the course of natural selection. Once new, invented, or learnt habits had changed the context or habitat of a particular group of animals, natural selection could favour genetically determined behavioural and physical characteristics that best exploited that new environment. Known as 'coevolution' or 'genetic assimilation', this simple argument avoided the pitfall of Lamarck's discredited theory of inheritance of acquired characteristics, while allowing that new behaviour could affect physical evolution.

Invented culture in higher non-human primates is geographically localized and is seen particularly clearly among chimps. In chimp tribes, specific tool-making techniques are possessed by members of a particular group and by other nearby but unrelated groups. These techniques are culturally acquired and not genetically determined and are therefore not necessarily found farther afield. Such local culture has its own pace of evolution with a degree of independence from genetic evolution particularly in humans (Blackmore, 1999).

From this Baldwinian perspective, we can make one prediction and one observation. The prediction is that if complex deliberate communication requires a developed brain, then simple deliberate communication of some sort must have preceded the evolution of big brains. The observation is that the extraordinary invention and sophisticated flowering of writing happened 5,000 years ago, and the invention of musical notation much more recently. These two coded non-oral systems of communication unleashed, arguably, the highest peaks of human achievement, yet we do not invoke a new species of human with special genes and a new brain to account for each of them.

How did our brain grow, and why does size matter?

Much of the perceived difference between modern humans and other animals has been related to a large brain. Several things, however, need to be pointed out. Size is very important but it is not everything. Bigger may not necessarily be smarter. For instance, pigs, being big, have much larger brains than small, expert hunters such as wild cats. Humans who for medical reasons have had half their brain removed in childhood can enjoy near-normal human intellect and skills with the remaining 700 cm^3. Clearly, connections do count for something, and we definitely have more interconnections inside our brains than do other mammals; but how did this come about?

In general, larger bodies require larger brains. To put it crudely, this is because the larger organs and muscles of larger bodies need more brain to control them, or at least a minimum share of the attention the brain pays to the larger bulk of the body. This relationship between body and brain size, although predictable in most mammals, is not a simple ratio – if it were, then mice, for example, would have much smaller brains than they actually possess. The relationship becomes even less straightforward in the higher mammals since the body/brain size ratio has been distorted in several profound ways. Primates, for instance, have proportionately larger adult brains than do other mammals, because they have bodies that, from early life, grow more slowly for the same absolute rate of brain growth.

Humans also have a slower clock for brain maturation than do other apes. In all mammals, brain growth switches off before body growth in a way that matches the functional needs of the adult body size. Humans, however, differ from other primates in that their internal clock keeps their brains growing for longer than would be expected for their final body size as primates. The result of the prolongation of foetal and infant development stages is a brain size more appropriate for a 1,000 kg ape such as the extinct *Gigantopithecus* (Deacon, 1997). There is additionally a relative ballooning of the cerebral cortex in humans, which endows it with far more neural tissue than is required for the mundane tasks of keeping the rest of the body running. In other words, in humans (and to a lesser extent in modern apes) there is a huge volume of apparently redundant cortex without a civil service role (Deacon, 1997).

Most of this 'upsizing' happened long before we came along. Simple comparison of brain and body size in earlier humans shows that these changes moved into overdrive with the evolution of *Homo erectus*. So, with the knowledge that just a few genetic alterations brought about a huge growth of functional potential in the human brain, we come back again to the question of what new behaviour drove that rapid growth 2.5 million years ago?

While the ability to recognise and groom a large number of colleagues may be associated with a large brain (Dunbar, 1996), and language might have been an energetically cheap means of social grooming in this context (Aiello and Dunbar, 1993), I find it difficult to see such a networking effect fuelling each jump in human brain size over the past 2.5 million years. The large human brain is after all an energetically expensive organ to maintain and a major cause of maternal and foetal death due to obstructed labour. It is also difficult to conceive that complex spoken language – our own unique skill – evolved more as a tool for reciprocal grooming and gossip than as a means to extend our cooperation productively and to teach our offspring by transmitting practical information and planning food acquisition. Chimps that have been taught to communicate by sign language certainly concentrate much more on food issues in their communications than on social chit-chat. The same problem of energy 'cost/benefit' trade-off applies to the theory that human evolved culture (their 'meme complex') drove brain growth (Blackmore, this volume). How could this have occurred usefully before complex language itself had developed?

I would turn the argument the other way round. I think that *language* was that unique behaviour shared between the sister genera *Homo* and *Paranthropus* 2.5 million years ago that enabled them, cooperatively and flexibly, to survive the barren cycles of the Pleistocene ice epoch and thus drove their brain growth. According to Baldwin's 'new behaviour before adaptive physical change' (coevolution) theory, they must have had some form of language to start with. It would be hard to argue that the symbolic coded lexicon and syntax of complex language and the productive cooperation it unlocks should not benefit in a graded way from an increase in computing power. Language is the best candidate driver of brain size by analogy with computers. Put simply, it is much more likely that we were already communicating usefully and deliberately 2.5 million years ago, and that this drove our brain growth, *than* that our brain grew until some threshold size was reached and we miraculously discovered we could talk.

Symbolic thought and language: purely human abilities?

Deliberate communication of one form or another undoubtedly started a long time ago in animals. This includes singing for your mate and specific cross-species alarm calls. Complex vocal language (speech) is merely the most sophisticated form of animal communication, and has selected for a number of specialized physical changes in humans. Speech has special advantages over simple gesture language apart from its ability to convey complex ideas. We can communicate in the dark, through trees, and without looking at the person we are speaking to. It is much easier to con, deceive, and tell lies, and to hide our communication from strangers speaking other tongues. Children learn to lie around the age of four. Some have suggested that males' prowess at telling jokes, and making females laugh, might have been an element in sexual selection. Like all other aspects of culture, however, language was invented and has to be internally reinvented in every child learning to speak.

We modern humans justifiably differentiate ourselves from our other living primate relatives by our power of speech. Unfortunately we do not leave the qualitative comparisons there. In the same way that we exaggerate religious and ethnic variations among our own kind, we try to take perceived differences from other apes much further in order to establish an us/them framework. A recent and extreme manifestation of this habit of de-humanising exclusion between modern human groups was seen in the term *untermensch* (literally 'under-people' or 'less-than-human') used by the Nazis to describe the people they persecuted and murdered.

In the same exclusive vein, an old view of language is the idea that logical or rational thought is somehow dependent on words. This concept originated with Plato (Englefield, 1977) and was much in vogue in the nineteenth century with writers such as Jacob Grimm: "Animals do not speak because they do not think" (Grimm, 1851) and Max Müller: "Language is our Rubicon, and no brute will dare to cross it" and "... without speech, no reason, without reason, no speech" (Müller, 1891).

We have also credited ourselves with having multiple other unique intellectual and manipulative skills that fence us off from the rest of the animal kingdom. Trying to look through that fence is condemned as 'anthropomorphism'. In spite of this, since the beginning of the twentieth century our nearest living relative, the chimp, has surprised careful observers by charmingly picking the wicker from these hurdles one by one. Old myths of unique human skills have died hard. First, people maintained that humans were the only animals to use tools. When that idea lost credibility, the prejudice was refined to state that humans were the only animals to *modify* tools. When this was disproved, we had to content ourselves with the assertion that only humans were capable of inventing and making tools. Again, chimps proved us wrong.

Much of this simple information was available from Wolfgang Köhler's studies in the early 1920s of a chimp colony on the island of Tenerife. Köhler, a Gestalt psychologist, went much further than showing that chimps could solve problems. He elegantly demonstrated that they were capable of both abstract and rational thought (Englefield, 1977; Wells, 1999). Unfortunately, few humans were able to look at his experimental results rationally at the time. It took Jane Goodall and others with their patient observation and brilliant camera-work in the field to convert the scientists and the public to the implications of Köhler's results, much later in the twentieth century.

The big surprise in the second half of the twentieth century was to find that chimps, a non-speaking ape species separated from us by at least 5 million years on the evolutionary tree, have a nascent language ability. That some such an innate skill might be present in our common ancestor overcomes the problem inherent in a standard contemporary view that complex language resulted from a sudden leap rather than following gradualist Darwinian evolution. Chimps have been taught to communicate with humans. More impressively, they are able to take their new skill and use it to communicate with one another using symbolic and coded signs. The greatest star of this story is Kanzi, a bonobo (bonobos are close relatives of chimpanzees, with several behavioural traits reminiscent of ourselves). Kanzi learnt to communicate using a complex coded symbol language on a computer. He also spontaneously learnt to comprehend spoken English, correctly interpreting syntax. He seems to have picked up his skills spontaneously as an infant at his chimp foster mother's side, when his childlike learning ability was at its best. She was actually the intended target of the language teaching and, as an adult by contrast, was struggling to learn these new symbols (Savage-Rumbaugh and Lewin, 1994). Chimps have also been shown to demonstrate abstract, symbolic, and rational thought, as well as what is termed 'symbolic inference' and 'symbolic manipulation', although they are clearly not nearly as good at these skills as ourselves (Deacon, 1997). This is likely to be simply a matter of degree. As far as language is concerned, they are obviously hampered by lack of vocal control and either not disposed to or unable to see the value of extended non-verbal communication.

Surprisingly, the full implications of these experiments are still largely ignored by linguists. The view of language essentially as a series of inventions, was initiated by the eighteenth-century Enlightenment *philosophe* Étienne Bonnot de Condillac. He argued that spoken language had developed out of gesture language (*langage d'action*) and that both were inventions arising initially from simple association (Englefield, 1977; Wells, 1987,1999). The Condillac view anticipated the concept of cultural evolution (Blackmore, this volume) and, with some development, can be traced through Darwinism and a mid-twentieth-century thinker, Ronald Englefield (1977), right down to the present day with the work of New Zealand psychologist Michael Corballis (this volume) and others. The full theory sees gesture language as arising originally among apes, and then becoming conventional or coded as the new skill drove its own evolution. Subsequently, verbal signals, some already present in the 'innate' primate repertory, were co-opted and developed into deliberate coded communication. Evolutionary pressures then promoted the development of the vocal apparatus and also of part of the brain immediately next to that responsible for gestures. This speech centre is often called Broca's area.

The gradualist view of the acquisition of speech contrasts with the more popular view of a sudden event, occurring between 35,000 and 50,000 years ago amongst modern humans as a kind of 'big bang' speciation event. The notion of a great leap forward in the quality of human thinking is further reflected in a common interpretation of Upper Palaeolithic art in Europe. European cave paintings and carved figurines which have been dated to over 30,000 years ago are seen, according to this perspective, as the first stirrings of symbolic and abstract thought and also of language. Such a Eurocentric interpretation ignores the knowledge that Australians were already painting on rocks on the other side of the world at the same time as the early Europeans. It is absurd to suggest that they and the rest of the world had to learn their own speech and painting from Europeans. There is every reason, and much evidence, to suppose that our common African ancestor had already mastered the skills of speech, art, and symbolic representation long before leaving Africa 80,000 years ago (Oppenheimer, 2003).

Another problem with the creationist or 'big bang' view of modern humans' unique abilities is that there is evidence that Neanderthals had the same specialised vocal anatomy that we have. The possession of a similar hyoid bone, an enlarged thoracic spinal cord, and an enlarged orifice to carry the hypoglossal nerve to the tongue, are consistent with Neanderthals speaking. On Baldwin's hypothesis, these attributes also indicate that Neanderthals' (and our own) common ancestor *Homo heidelbergensis* was already speaking over half a million years ago. Since *Homo heidelbergensis* also had an equally enlarged nerve orifice and some other key anatomical features of speech, the argument could possibly be stretched back further to *Homo erectus*, who shows evidence of a lopsided brain (Steele, 1998; see also Deacon, 1997). The latter is thought to be an important associated phenomenon of language. *Homo habilis* is thought by some to show an impression, inside the skull, of Broca's area, consistent with the view that the process of specialised enlargement to adapt to speech had already begun 2 million years ago.

This anatomical speculation brings us back to the first humans and the dramatic sprint in brain enlargement in *Homo* and *Paranthropus*. If there ever was a big bang in the speciation of smart hominids, this was it. Tim Crow, a professor of psychiatry in Oxford, has argued that two important speciation events can be traced as two closely related mutations on the Y chromosome, sometime after the split between chimps and ourselves. There is some reason for supposing that one or both of these mutations might be associated with cerebral asymmetry, and possibly with language (Crow, 2000a and b). If so, then we might speculate that the first mutation occurred in the common ancestor of *Homo* and *Paranthropus* and the second in *Homo erectus*, since the latter shows the first evidence of cerebral asymmetry.

Consistent with the view that spoken language was ultimately a primate invention, like tool-making, which drove the biological evolution of the brain and vocal apparatus, like any cultural invention, it has also evolved separately outside our bodies within specific cultural communities. The unique combination of lexical and syntactic features of a language such as French are the cultural possessions of the French community, and clearly do not result from any conceivable biological aspect of being French.

Summary

In summary, of all the mental and practical skills that philosophers, biologists and theologians have put forward as qualitative differences between modern humans and chimps, the only one that remains is human speech. Clearly, there is a great quantitative difference in intellectual ability, but human intellect did not suddenly flower 35,000 years ago in the European Upper Palaeolithic – it had been evolving over the previous 4 million years. For the past 2 million years humans have been improving on the walking-ape model by using their brains, but they may have been aided in this by speech-driven coevolution in brain size.

Acknowledgement

I thank Professor Charles Pasternak for inviting me to contribute to this volume.

References

Acad. Sci. Paris, Sciences de la Terre et des planets – Series IIA – / *Earth and Planetary Sciences* **332**:137–144.

Aiello, L. and Dunbar, R. (1993) Neocortex size, group size and the evolution of language. *Current Antropology* **34**:184–93.

Aiello, L. C. and Wheeler, P. (1995) The expensive tissue hypothesis: The brain and the digestive system in human and primate evolution. *Current Anthropology* **36**:199–221.

Blackmore, S. (1999) *The Meme Machine*. Oxford, Oxford University Press.

Corballis, M. C. and Gentilucci, M. (2007) The Hominid that Talked (this volume).

Corballis, M. C. and Suddendorf, T. (2007) Memory, Time and Language (this volume).

Crow, T. J. (2000a) Did *Homo sapiens* speciate on the Y chromosome? *Psycoloquy* 11(001).

Crow, T. J. (2000b) Schizophrenia as the price that *Homo sapiens* pays for language: A resolution of the central paradox in the origin of the species. *Brain Research Reviews* **31**:118–29.

Deacon, T. (1997) *The Symbolic Species*. London, Penguin, pp. 322–34.

Dunbar, R. (1996) *Grooming, Gossip and the Evolution of Language*. London, Faber & Faber.

Elton, S., Bishop, L. C., and Wood, B. (2001) Comparative context of Plio-Pleistocene hominid brain evolution. *Journal of Human Evolution* **41**:1–27.

Englefield, R. (1977) *Language: Its Origin and Relation to Thought*. eds. G. A. Wells and D. R. Oppenheimer. London, Elek Pemberton.

Foley, R. and Lahr, M. M. (1997) Mode 3 technologies and the evolution of modern humans. *Cambridge Archaeological Journal* 7 (1):3–36.

Grimm J. (1851) *Über den Urschprung der Sprache in: Aus den kleineren Schriften von Jacob Grimm*. ed. L. Spiedel. Berlin, 1911.

Lahr, M. M. and Foley, R. (1998) Towards a theory of modern human origins: Geography, demography, and diversity in recent human evolution. *Yearbook of Physical Anthropology* **41**:137–76.

McBrearty, S. and Brooks, A. S. (2000) The revolution that wasn't: A new interpretation of the origin of modern human behavior. *Journal of Human Evolution* **39**:453–563.

Müller, F. M. (1891) *The Science of Language*. London.

Oppenheimer, S. (2003) *Out of Eden: the Peopling of the World*. London, Constable.

Rossignol-Strick, M., Paterne, M., Bassinot, F. C., Emeis, K.-C., and de

Lange, G. J. (1998) An unusual mid-Pleistocene monsoon period over Africa and Asia. *Nature* **392**:269–272.

Ruff, C. B., Trinkaus, E., and Holliday, T. W. (1997) Body mass and encephalization in Pleistocene *Homo*. *Nature* **387**:173–6.

Savage-Rumbaugh, E. S. and Lewin, R. (1994) *Kanzi: The Ape at the Brink of the Human Mind*. New York, John Wiley.

Senuta B., Pickford M., Gommery D., Mein P., Cheboi K., and Coppens Y. (2001) First hominid from the Miocene (Lukeino Formation, Kenya). *Earth and Planetary Sciences* **332**:137–44.

Steele, J. (1998) Cerebral asymmetry, cognitive laterality, and human evolution. *Current Psychology of Cognition* **17**:1202–1214.

Stringer, C. (1996) Current issues in modern human origins. In W. E. Meikle et al. (eds.) *Contemporary Issues in Human Evolution*. San Francisco, California Academy of Science, pp. 115–34.

Stringer, C. (2002) Modern human origins: progress and prospects. *Phil. Trans. R. Soc. Lond. B* **357**, 563–579.

Takahata, N., Satta, Y., and Klein, J. (1995) Divergence time and population size in the lineage leading to modern humans. *Theoretical Population Biology* **48**:198–21.

Wells, G. A. (1987) *The Origin of Language: Aspects of the Discussion from Condillac to Wundt*. Illinois, Open Court.

Wells, G. A. (1999) *The Origin of Language*. London, Rationalist Press Association.

Wheeler, P. E. (1993) Human ancestors walked tall, stayed cool. *Natural History* **102** (2): 65–7.

White, T. D., Suwa, G., and Asfaw, B. (1994) *Australopithecus ramidus*, a new species of early hominid from Aramis, Ethiopia. *Nature* **371**:306–12.

8: Curiosity and Quest

Charles Pasternak

Introduction

Aristotle considered that 'All men by nature desire to know'. In my view, this is one of the characteristics that make us human. Curiosity about the world we live in leads directly to exploration, to quest. Yet surely animals are likewise curious, and also quest: for food and water, for shelter and a mate. How, then, do curiosity and quest distinguish us from all other animals, and in particular from our nearest relative, the chimpanzee? In this essay I will show that searching is indeed fundamental to living organisms – to plants and microbes as well as to animals – but that humans are endowed with four attributes that enable them to search more avidly than any other creature. Man's quest has encompassed the entire surface of the earth; he has been to the moon and observed the most distant stars. The chimpanzee has not ventured beyond his environment. Man dominates the globe; the chimpanzee faces extinction.

Humans and the great apes have long been considered, at least by a select few, to be close relatives. Already by the middle of the eighteenth century, and therefore anticipating Charles Darwin by a hundred years, both Jean-Jacques Rousseau and the Swedish botanist Carl Linnaeus subscribed to that view. Rousseau went even further: in his opinion man and chimpanzee belong to the same species. Linnaeus was not so audacious. He placed humans into a separate category (genus) from chimpanzees and coined the appellation *Homo sapiens* (wise man), in order to distinguish man from the intellectually less able chimpanzee (of which we now recognise two species, *Pan troglodytes*, the common chimpanzee, and *Pan paniscus*, the pygmy chimpanzee or bonobo). Darwin had no reason to quibble with *Homo sapiens*, and only a century later did anthropologists begin to realise – as Rousseau had suggested – that the great apes are considerably more intelligent than had been thought. They too use simple tools: stones for breaking open nuts, leaves for wiping themselves clean, sticks for digging termites out of the ground; there is even a cultural element here, for chimpanzees of different tribes use sticks in slightly different ways. They, like humans, have the ability to reason and they display consciousness, self-awareness, and the feeling of misery or joy (see, for example, de Waal and Tyack, 2003; McGrew, 2004). They can even learn the rudiments of language (Rumbaugh et al., 1996). It is time to introduce *Homo quaerens*, searching man [from the Latin *quaerere*, to search, which gives us not only quest and inquisitiveness, but also conquest – a very human attribute].

The similarity between chimpanzee and man, to which I have just alluded, is confirmed at the molecular level also: our DNA differs from that of a chimpanzee by no more than 2 per cent (by the hybridisation technique); when indels – insertions and deletions – are included, the difference rises to 5 per cent (Britten, 2002). Even such relatively small disparities, however, might still reflect the existence of quite a number of genes that are characteristically either 'human' or 'chimpanzee-like'. I do not believe that such genes exist, and will present my arguments for this view.

What of the future? Is our ability to quest improving all the time? Might our tinkering with nature lead to our own destruction? Or is a new species of human perhaps likely to emerge?

These are the topics that I will address. Most have been considered earlier (Pasternak, 2003a). This review gives me an opportunity to update some of the evidence that lay behind the propositions I made then, and to present new data that have emerged over the last few years. These entirely confirm my earlier propositions.

All organisms search

Plants do not merely *use* the energy of the sun to synthesise important molecules like carbohydrate and fat, proteins and nucleic acids (RNA and DNA), they *seek* sunlight as avidly as any bather on a Mediterranean beach. Two mechanisms are involved: growth, so that the new shoots of plants, shrubs and trees extend in a direction away from the shade (phototropism), and for several plants, movement during the day, so that the maximum area of leaf always faces the sun (heliotropism).

Those microbes that are photosynthetic (using the energy of sunlight for the synthesis of constituent molecules, like plants) possess mechanisms that sense light and swim towards its source. Microbes like *Halobacterium salinarium*, that live in salty environments like the Great Salt Lake in Utah, or the Dead Sea between Israel and Jordan, are good examples. Other microbes use oxygen in the air to gain energy by turning foodstuffs like carbohydrates and proteins into carbon dioxide and water (the reverse process of photosynthesis), just like animals, including ourselves. They possess mechanisms that sense oxygen rather than light, and swim in the direction of its optimal concentration – not too high (for it can be toxic) and not too low. Such bacteria also swim towards food (chemotaxis; see, for example, Wadhams and Armitage, 2004): *Salmonella typhimurium*, a benign relative of the extremely pathogenic *Salmonella typhi*, for example, has been shown to move in the direction of a source of amino acids (the breakdown products of proteins), and away from noxious substances like carbolic acid. Avoidance is but the flip side of searching; negative searching, you might say. Other bacteria can sense the direction of the magnetic poles. More complicated microbes, such as various kinds of protozoa, exhibit similar mechanisms of moving towards beneficial stimuli, and away from dangerous ones.

The reader may accuse me of being anthropomorphic, and of confusing passive responses to the environment, with active decisions taken by questing animals. There are two answers to this. First, we know from physiological and biochemical studies that the mechanism underlying an active, or voluntary, response, like turning towards a prey (or a thief) and running after it, is very similar to the passive, or involuntary, response of a beating heart or a writhing intestine. Both involve the same type of nerve transmission, and depend on the same types of proteins. Second, the proteins that mediate all the responses of plants and microbes that I have just described are similar in structure to proteins that function in animals during processes like vision that are crucial to searching. To be precise, it is not the entire protein that is the same, but only a part of it: a stretch of some 270 specific amino acids, known as a PAS domain, that is found in all organisms from plants to man (see Fig. 1).

Found in proteins of:

Archaea	**e.g.** *Halobacterium salinarium*
Bacteria	**e.g.** *Escherichia coli*
Fungi	**e.g.** *Saccharomyces cerevisiae*
Plants	**e.g.** *Arabidopsis thaliana*
Nematodes	**e.g.** *Caenorhabditis elegans*
Insects	**e.g.** *Drosophila melanogaster*
Mammals	**e.g.** *mouse*
	human

Figure 1 PAS domains in proteins: sensors of light, oxygen and other stimuli. Reproduced from Pasternak (2003a) by permission of the publisher.

The continuity of molecular similarity is apparent not only across the entire spectrum of plants, microbes and animals, but across more than a billion years of evolution. For *Halobacterium salinarium* is the modern equivalent of one of the earliest types of microbe – indeed of life – that may have existed as long ago as 3 billion years. Searching by living creatures is as old, and as fundamental to their existence, as growth and reproduction.

Human search is especially intense

We search not only out of necessity, but out of sheer curiosity as well: we explore our environment, we seek scientific explanations for natural phenomena, we search to create works of art. There is no need to find the source of the Nile or to journey to the Moon, to comprehend the nature of fundamental particles or the structure of proteins, to compose *The Trout Quintet* or to paint *The Girl with the Pearl Earring*, to write *Hamlet* or *Madame Bovary*. We should not assume that animals aren't a bit curious too. Some years ago the explorer Wilfred Thesiger found a (dead) dog on the top of Mount Kilimanjaro (Thesiger, 1970). The animal had clearly died from exposure and lack of food, but what was it doing on the mountain? Animals do not normally venture beyond their known habitat. Had the dog's curiosity led it beyond its normal territory? The reason why no animal – be it dog or dolphin, gorilla or chimpanzee – has come close to humans in so far as gratification of innate curiosity is concerned is the lack of four attributes that humans have acquired over the past four million years or so.

The first is the upright gait. After the lineages leading to modern chimpanzees and humans diverged around 6 million years ago (Patterson et al., 2006), there emerged, in the Great Rift Valley of eastern Africa, apes that walked on their two legs alone, instead of on legs and knuckles. The best fossil remains of this new genus, termed *Australopithecus* (southern ape), were found in the Middle Awash region of Ethiopia's Afar Depression by a team of American anthropologists led by Donald Johanson in 1974. The skeleton proved to be that of a girl, whom they named 'Lucy', and dated to be around 3 million years old. There is good reason to believe that *Australopithecus* is a direct ancestor of *Homo* (Lovejoy, 2005). Several potential evolutionary advantages for an upright gait may be mentioned. First, it doubles the area of land surveyed and therefore gives earlier warning of an approaching predator or prey. Second, it frees the hands to carry offspring or food, and to feel for objects in the dark. On the other hand, the evolution of bipedalism may be due simply to sexual selection by females (Dawkins, 2005), as I have argued for the case of art (Pasternak, 2003a). *Australopithecus* females may have been attracted by the sight of their male counterparts standing upright, towering above them. Once they favoured males able to do this, the underlying genes would soon have begun to spread among the population.

Freeing the hands has an equally important consequence. It allowed the gradual appearance – over a million years or so – of a more delicate, flexible thumb. This enables the owner to use the precision grip with firmness, and it is this that allowed our first *Homo* ancestor (*H. habilis*, or 'handyman') to begin tool-making around 2 million years ago (Marzke, 1997). The importance of the human hand, not just for sharpening stone implements, for making music or for drawing pictures, but for the entire development of sophisticated technology over the last ten thousand years, cannot be stressed enough. For good reason did the eighteenth-century philosopher Immanuel Kant call the human hand 'the exterior brain of man'. The flexible thumb, leading to an agile hand, then, is the second human attribute that is key to human quest.

The third attribute is the human voice box (or larynx). Unlike the upright gait or the mobile thumb, it is difficult to put a date on the appearance of the human larynx. This is because there are no bones – just muscle and cartilage – associated with it. The vocal cords themselves are no more than infoldings of the larynx. They vibrate, like the strings of a violin, to produce a huge range of sounds in modern humans, but no more than grunts and cries in the chimpanzee. At death, muscle and cartilage soon decompose, whereas bones remain intact for centuries (and when fossilised by salty water seeping over them, for millions of years). So we do not know whether *H. habilis*, or descendants such as *H. erectus, H. ergaster* or *H. neanderthaliensis*, had the possibility of speech. The historian Steven Mithen thinks not. Even *H. neanderthaliensis* (Neanderthal Man), who coexisted with *H. sapiens* in northern Europe up to around 30,000 years ago (though not thought to be a direct ancestor of *H. sapiens*), he considers to have lacked the power of speech: they just sang, or rather hummed, to each other (Mithen, 2005). Failure to communicate as effectively as *H. sapiens* may have been one reason for their demise: like every species of *Homo* other than *H. sapiens*, they have become extinct. Speech leads directly to language, and hence to literature, without which humankind would be very much the poorer (though none of the Amerindian cultures, apart from the Maya, had a written script). The origins of language have been much debated. A decade ago, Robin Dunbar (1996) proposed an attractive hypothesis: language arose through gossiping among small groups of humans, which had gradually replaced the grooming typical of chimpanzees and other primates. Speech is useless without hearing. It has recently been suggested that the development of the human ear enabled it to pick up human speech better than the chimpanzee ear (Martinez et al., 2004). This appears to have happened by 350,000 years ago, according to fossils of human remains found in northern Spain. So it is possible that human hearing actually preceded human speech.

The fourth attribute that allows us to exercise our superior quality of quest is, of course, the brain. We have some three times as many cortical neurons (nerve cells in the outer layer of the brain, that actually makes up most of the human brain) as a chimpanzee. It is in the cortex that processes like thought and memory, reasoning and deduction, take place. Since the skull is made of bone, it fossilises and skulls dating back millions of years have been recovered. By measuring the internal volume (with water or sand, for example), a rough indication of the number of nerve cells that it originally contained can be made. Brain size actually varies very much from one human to another (for reasons that are not clear; Einstein's brain was *not* particularly large): between 1,000 and 2,000 cc or ml, with an average of 1350 cc. Today's chimpanzees typically have a brain size of around 450 cc, which is probably similar to that of the common ancestor of chimpanzees and humans, living 6 million years ago. *Australopithecus afarensis*, that lived between 4 and 2.5 million years ago, had a brain size of 400–500 cc, *H. habilis*, living between 2.3 and 1.6 million years ago, had a brain of 500–800 cc, and *H. erectus*, living between 1.9 and 0.3 million years ago, had a brain size of 750–1250 cc (figures taken from Pinker, 1997; see Corballis and Suddendorf, this volume pp. 17–26, for slightly different values).

It is easy to see why an increased brain size, and therefore superior mental function, should have an evolutionary advantage. Of course the argument for sexual selection by females can be applied to all three attributes – the mobile thumb ('man the toolmaker'), the voice-box ('man the talker') and the brain ('man the clever one') – as much as to the upright gait. But why did this happen in the lineage leading to modern humans and not in that leading to modern chimpanzees? If one favours sexual selection as the driving force, we should note that with chimpanzees, it isn't the females who do the choosing. Bruce Lahn and his team in Chicago have another hypothesis. They have discovered that certain genes involved in the development of the nervous system have a higher rate of mutation in primates than in other animals, and a higher rate of mutation in humans than in chimpanzees (e.g. Dorus et al., 2004; Evans et al., 2006). In other words, once the two lineages began to diverge 6 million years ago, that leading to humans began to acquire mutations, that proved beneficial, at a faster rate than that leading to chimpanzees. The result is that three to four times as many genes are expressed in the human brain than in the chimpanzee brain (whereas the expression of genes in tissues like liver or blood has remained the same (Normile, 2001). Another study (Donaldson and Gottgens, 2006) has pinpointed a difference between genes coding for proteins that regulate the expression of particular stretches of DNA (i.e. other genes) in chimpanzees and humans. Clearly this is a very active area of research – especially since the entire genome (i.e. totality of DNA) in chimpanzees and humans has been sequenced, and comparisons can now be made – and it is likely that much interesting work will be published between the writing of this chapter (July 2006) and its publication (summer 2007).

I would like to stress that I do not consider any of the attributes I have mentioned – especially the agile thumb, the voice box and the larger number of cortical neurons – to underlie the essential difference between humans and chimpanzees on its own. Rather it is the combination of all three – hand, speech and brain – that allows humans to search more avidly than other creatures. The linkage between the three attributes can be appreciated if the different parts of the human body are scaled according to the number of neurons in the brain that control each part (see Fig. 2). It is clear that hands and mouth are controlled by far more brain cells than other parts of the body. I find that a remark that the biologist Peter Medawar made in relation to the immune system has resonance here: "One individual differs from all others not because he has unique endowments but because he has a unique *combination* of endowments" (Medawar, 1981). In so far as human development is concerned, the actions of thumb, speech and brain are synergistic.

Figure 2 Cartoon of the human body according to number of brain cells that control each part. Donated by Susan Greenfield (see Susan Greenfield, *The Human Brain: A Guided Tour*, Weidenfeld & Nicolson, 1997).

The exploratory drive of humans, their search for new lands on earth, is particularly striking. Whether out of mere curiosity, or out of need, or from harassment of one sort or another, successive species of *Homo* (the most recent being *H. sapiens*) wandered out of Africa and into Eurasia between 1.9 million and 100,000 years ago (e.g. Templeton, 2005). This was followed by *H. sapiens* taking to the seas of southeast Asia in simple boats more than 50,000 years ago, to finish up in Australia. Others roamed across the frozen north from Siberia into Alaska some 12,000–16,000 years ago. These migrations, especially those across water, must have taken a lot of courage. The journeys outdo by far the quest of Christopher Columbus to reach the Indies by going west instead of east in 1492. Do humans really prefer to gather new information – exploration – rather than using existing knowledge – exploitation? A group of scientists from London and Pasadena have begun to investigate this question (Daw et al., 2006). They show that certain regions of the brain are preferentially activated during decisions to explore (essentially to gamble), whereas other regions are activated during safer, but potentially less rewarding, decisions based on previous knowledge. An interesting feature of their work is that the 'exploratory' regions seem to be larger in humans than in other primates (Nathaniel Daw, personal communication).

Specifically 'human' genes do not exist

I have referred to the surprising ability of chimpanzees to enact tasks previously thought to be restricted to humans: the use of tools, the ability to reason, the comprehension of language, for example. If one plots the relative ability of chimpanzees and humans at any of these accomplishments one obtains a bell-shaped curve for each (see Fig. 3).

This reflects the fact that not everyone (whether chimpanzee or human) is equally proficient: some are at the left-hand edge of the curve (the dullards, the incapacitated), some at the right-hand edge (the bright, the gifted), with the majority in the middle. But there is an overlap between the two curves, which indicates that the difference between chimpanzee and human is merely quantitative, not qualitative. Chimpanzees, for example, can acquire a vocabulary of perhaps a thousand words if taught from birth. It is the same for a young child of three or four. Thereafter, a child continues to acquire words and

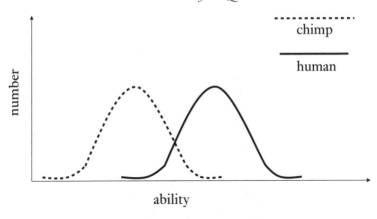

Figure 3 The spread of abilities in chimpanzees and humans.

phrases; a chimpanzee does not. Of course the chimpanzee curve is not always to the left of that for humans: if I had taken the ability to climb trees, the order of the two curves would be reversed.

There is a similar overlap if one analyses the four attributes of humans to which I referred above. Chimpanzees *can* stand upright for short periods of time (though not to walk any distance); they *can* grasp objects with the precision grip (though more clumsily, and with much less force, than a human); they *can* utter a variety of sounds – enough, when coupled with gestures, for meaningful communication between themselves; and they *can* carry out cognitive tasks (though limited in extent compared to humans). The anatomical differences between chimpanzees and humans are likewise relatively minor (see Figs. 4–7), and not indicative of a qualitative dissimilarity. Indeed, the voice box at birth of a chimpanzee resembles that of a human baby quite closely (each can swallow and breathe at the same time). Thereafter the human larynx develops somewhat differently, allowing a child to utter distinctive words around two years of age (but no longer able to swallow and breathe simultaneously). Hence the difference between chimpanzee and human is really one of relative growth and development, and the same is true for the other three attributes (see Robin Dunbar, pp. 37–48 of this volume, in regard to certain cerebral abilities).

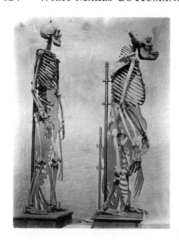

Figure 4 Skeleton of human compared with that of a gorilla. The skeleton of the gorilla has been deliberately propped upright for comparison [the author could not find a similar juxtaposition between human and chimpanzee]. Reproduced from Pasternak (2003a) by permission of the publisher.

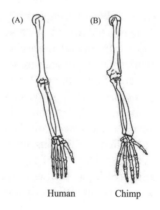

Figure 5 Skeleton of human hand compared with that of a chimpanzee. The altered position of the (longer) human thumb is to be noted. The dimensions for the chimpanzee, which actually has a longer arm, have been reduced for better comparison of fingers and thumb. Reproduced from Pasternak (2003a) by permission of the publisher.

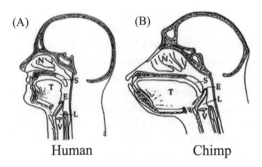

(A)   (B)

Human   Chimp

Figure 6 Voice box of human and chimpanzee. E = epiglottis; L = larynx; N = nasal cavity; S = soft palate; T = tongue; T = vocal cord. The larynx extends downwards to the lungs. The pharynx (not marked), that leads to the oesophagus and thence to the stomach, is behind the larynx. Reproduced from Pasternak (2003a) by permission of the publisher.

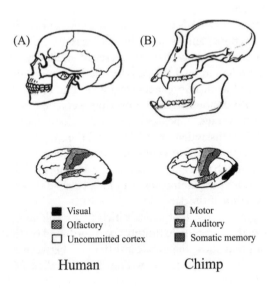

(A)   (B)

■ Visual   ▨ Motor
▨ Olfactory   ▨ Auditory
□ Uncommitted cortex ▨ Somatic memory

Human   Chimp

Figure 7 Brain of human and chimpanzee. The greater volume of human neocortex, that is part of the 'uncommitted cortex' in the lower diagram, cannot easily be appreciated from this two-dimensional representation. Reproduced from Pasternak (2003a) by permission of the publisher.

Every aspect of a living creature – its shape and size, appearance and movement, growth and reproduction – results from the action of its constituent proteins. This is as true of a conifer or a hellebore, *Clostridium* or *Halobacterium*, clam or heron, as it is of a chimpanzee or a human. But it is not proteins that are passed from generation to generation, and that become modified through the aeons to produce the variety of creatures which inhabit the earth today: it is DNA. That molecule specifies the kind of proteins that an organism makes. Genes are simply stretches of DNA. What, then, of the genes that underlie all the differences between chimpanzee and human? If we take the figure of 95 per cent similarity quoted earlier, two interpretations are possible (Fig. 8). On the one hand, the 5 per cent dissimilarity might indicate that some 5 per cent of genes are specifically 'human' or 'chimpanzee-like'. Since there are thought to be about 25,000 genes in chimpanzee and human, 125 of these might be specific for one or the other species. (Theoretically, *all* the genes might be specific, because we know that in primates less than 5 per cent of the total DNA – rather confusingly called the genome – functions as genes. The significance of the majority of DNA is unkown; it may represent vestiges of virus or other infections, and is sometimes referred to simply as 'junk' DNA. However we know that the degree of similarity between two species, that refers to total DNA, is by and large reflected in genetic regions as well as in non-genetic regions). The other explanation, which virtually follows from the previous sentence, is that *all* the genes are, on average, 5 per cent dissimilar: some more, some less (see Fig. 8). The dissimilarity reflects not different genes, but merely different mutations within genes that are common to ape and man (such mutations change amino acids at specific sites within a protein: an asparagine for a threonine, for example). I consider this to be a better interpretation of the data.

You might suppose that genes which play a role in the development of upright gait, mobile thumb, vocal cords and cortical neurons are the ones that show the greatest difference between chimpanzee and human. But you would be wrong. A gene called *FOXP2*, that appears to be involved in speech and language acquisition (Fisher and Marcus, 2006), differs by less than 0.1 per cent between chimpanzee and human. Genes that specify proteins of identical function, such as insulin or haemoglobin, differ by more; (the mutations are in regions of the proteins that do not affect their activity). The conclusion to be

DNA of related organisms: 95% similarity

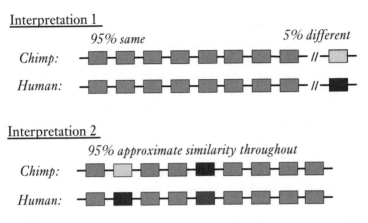

435 CAP

Figure 8 Interpretations of 95 per cent similarity between DNA of chimpanzees and humans. Reproduced from Pasternak (2003a) by permission of the publisher.

drawn is that the 5 per cent difference in DNA, that has arisen over the 6 million years since the lineages leading to humans and modern chimpanzees diverged, reflects mainly 'silent' mutations: irrelevant mutations, that have no effect on function. It is a much smaller number of relevant mutations, some of which do not alter the *structure* of a protein at all, but merely the *amount* that is synthesised (Donaldson and Gottgens, 2006), which appear to have been critical in the evolution of humans. Other mutations (which likewise occur not within protein-coding genes) affect particularly proteins made in the brain (Smith, 2006), which reinforces the importance of brain neurons (see Fig. 2) in contributing to the essential difference between man and chimpanzee. As mentioned earlier, the human brain has increased some three-fold over the last 2 million years; the size of the chimpanzee brain has remained pretty constant for 6 million years.

Extinction or survival of *Homo quaerens*?

Before considering such long-term scenarios, I would like to make a point regarding human behaviour over the next few decades. This is far too short a period for any genetic changes to become apparent. Indeed, even two thousand years is too short. The ancient Greeks were, on average, no cleverer and no more stupid than we are today. The curves of Fig. 3 for humans then and now would be superimposable. Focussing on the right hand end, the intellectual ability of Socrates or Plato was no less than that of Ludwig Wittgenstein or Albert Einstein; Aristotle's insight was the equal of Francis Crick's; the experimental genius of Archimedes matched that of Fred Sanger. Two thousand years ago people searched, on average, as avidly as they do today. But cultural, non-genetic, changes also affect our way of life (see Susan Blackmore, pp. 1–16 of this volume). The current trend to 'dumb down' in education and art, that is apparent in the USA, the UK and other western European nations, means that curiosity and competition among the young is being eroded: lethargy is taking over from quest (Pasternak, 2003b). Let me illustrate what I mean with a few English newspaper headlines taken at random: 'One diploma may replace school exams' (2003), 'English test pass marks lowered for third year running' (2004), 'Failed at school? No, it was merely a "deferred success"' (2005), '"Spoon-fed" pupils can't cope at college' (2006). The competitive edge that the west had over the rest of the world is gradually being eroded. The east – China and India in particular – will regain the supremacy that they once enjoyed thousands of years ago. Nothing wrong in that, of course, but political analysts should be aware of it.

In the longer term, the prospect of man's ingenuity getting the better of him and finally destroying him is being proposed by some, who also draw attention to our possible extinction by microbes or meteors (e.g. Rees, 2003). I do not take so pessimistic a view. First, the possibility of man's weaponry going out of hand is not that probable. The stand-off between the Soviet Union and the United States during thirty years of Cold War led to no nuclear disaster: pragmatism in the end prevailed. Second, if any creature is likely to escape some global epidemic, it is surely *Homo quaerens*. Our quest to understand the threat of diseases like HIV, SARS or bird flu, and to find measures to combat them, means that we are the species least likely to succumb.

The consequences of global warming may lose lives in areas where no action is taken to protect the coast line against rising sea levels, but it will not lead to man's extinction. On the contrary, it will delay the onset of the next ice age that is on the way. Furthermore, burying green-house gases like carbon dioxide underground could be made feasible (Socolow, 2005). Third, as for the possibility of the next major asteroid destroying life on earth, it may prove possible, for the first time in four billion years, to deflect it: questing man is already working on it (Schweickart et al., 2003).

It is unlikely that a new species of *Homo* will emerge in the future. Of course our genes are changing very slightly and extremely slowly all the time, and mutations that confer a selective advantage on their possessor, such as resistance to HIV or other pathogenic agent, are likely to spread within a population. But most species arise by allopatric speciation. That is, by geographical separation between two emerging species. Darwin's observations on the dissimilar finches that live on the different islands of the Galapagos, are a key example. His hypothesis, that contributed to *The Origin of Species*, went roughly as follows (I am simplifying). Originally there was one kind of finch, living on a single Galapagos land-mass. As this broke up into several separate islands, the finches on them gradually evolved into separate species: finches with one type of beak, that was particularly effective for capturing prey on that island, gradually out-bred all other types. The same was happening on a second island (different types of prey, different types of beak), and so forth. [The extent to which a particular gene is expressed has recently been shown to underlie the formation of the different species-specific beaks (Patel, 2006).] The reason that distinct species arose is that the finches could not fly from one island to another, and therefore could not inter-breed. Humans, on the other hand, now inter-breed with each other more and more; eventually we will all – Africans, Asians, Europeans, and so forth – come to resemble each other. No new species is likely to arise.

Conclusion

I believe that what makes us human is our innate curiosity and our never-ceasing quest: for beauty and novelty in art (more novelty and less beauty these days), for understanding the inside of our brain and the outside of our solar system, for ways to produce offspring without sex and then educating them without learning, for the means to avoid pain (ours) and the design of weaponry to end lives (theirs), for faster travel and slower ageing. Sometimes we even pause and search for ways to help the underprivileged of Africa with meaningful deeds instead of empty words. Our ability for actions that elude the cleverest chimpanzee is the result of inheriting a unique combination of characteristics: an upright gait, a mobile thumb, a voice box capable of speech, and a brain that contains three times as many neurons as that of a chimpanzee. Other contributors to this volume address several of these traits in greater detail (e.g. Corballis and Suddendorf, pp. 17–26, Corballis and Gentilucci, pp. 49–70, and Dunbar, pp. 37–48, on speech and brain; Wolpert, pp. 164–181, and Wrangham, pp. 182–203, on thumb (the manufacture of tools, and the ability to light a fire for cooking, respectively); and practically everyone on the cognitive capabilities arising out of our larger brain).

I began this chapter with a quotation from Aristotle, and end it with a twentieth-century warning to those of our elder readers who are contemplating a narrative about their life: 'Only when one has lost all curiosity about the future has one reached the age to write an auto-biography' (Waugh, 1964).

Acknowledgements

I am grateful to Kasia Lewis for help in the preparation of this article, and to the Trustees of the Oxford International Biomedical Centre for allowing me the time to speculate on what makes us human.

References

Britten, R. J. (2002). Divergence between samples of chimpanzee and human DNA sequences is 5%, counting indels. *Proc Nat Acad Sci USA* **99**: 13,633–5.

Daw, N. D., O'Doherty, J. P., Dayan, Peter, et al. (2006). Cortical substrates for exploratory decisions in humans. *Nature* **441**: 876–879.

Dawkins, Richard (2005). *The Ancestor's Tale. A Pilgrimage to the Dawn of Life.* (Phoenix paperback, London, pp. 276–278; first published by Weidenfeld & Nicolson, London, 2004).

Donaldson, I. J. and Gottgens, B. (2006). Evolution of candidate transcriptional regulatory motifs since the human–chimpanzee divergence. *Genome Biol* 7: R52.

Dorus, S., Vallender, E. J., Evans, P. D. et al. (2004). Accelerated evolution of nervous system genes in the origin of *Homo sapiens*. *Cell* 119: 1027–40.

Dunbar, R. (1996). *Grooming, Gossip and the Evolution of Language* (Faber & Faber, London).

Evans, P. D., Vallender, E. J. and Lahn, B. T. (2006). Molecular evolution of the brain size regulator genes CDK5RAP2 and CENPJ. *Gene* 375: 75–9.

Fisher, S. E., and Marcus, G. F. (2006). The eloquent ape: genes, brains and the evolution of language. *Nature Rev Gen* 7: 9–20.

Lovejoy, C. O. (2005). The natural history of human gait and posture. Part 1. Spine and pelvis. *Gait Posture* 21: 95–112.

Martinez, I., Rosa, M., Arsuaga, J. L., Jarabo, P., Quam, R., Lorenzo, C., Gracia, A., Carretero, J. M., Bermudez de Castro, J. M., and Carbonell, E. (2004). Auditory capacities in Middle Pleistocene humans from the Sierra de Atapuerca in Spain. *Proc Nat Acad Sci, USA* 101: 9976–9981

Marzke, M. W. (1997). Precision grips, hand morphology, and tools. *Am J Phys Anthropol* 102: 91–110.

McGrew, W. (2004). *The Cultured Chimpanzee: Reflections on Cultural Primatology* (Cambridge University Press, Cambridge, UK).

Medawar, P. (1981). *The Uniqueness of the Individual* (Dover Publications, New York; 2nd edn), p. 134.

Mithen, S. (2005). *The Singing Neanderthals: The Origins of Music, Language, Mind and Body* (Weidenfeld & Nicolson, London).

Normile, D. (2001). Gene expression differs in human and chimp brains. *Science* 292: 44–45.

Pasternak, C. (2003a). *Quest: The Essence of Humanity* (John Wiley, Chichester).

Pasternak, C. (2003b). Curiosity made us great, but it's waning in the west. *Times Higher Educational Supplement*, August 8.

Patterson, N., Richter, D. J., Gnerre, S., et al (2006). Genetic evidence for complex speciation of humans and chimpanzees. *Nature* 441: 1103–8.

Patel, N. H. (2006). How to build a longer beak. *Nature* 442: 515–516.

Pinker, S. (1997). *How the Mind Works* (Penguin, Harmondsworth), p. 198.

Rees, M. (2003). *Our Final Century* (Heineman, London); published in the USA as *Our Final Hour* (Basic Books).

Rumbaugh, D. M., Savage-Rumbaugh, E. S. and Washburn, D. A. (1996). Toward a new outlook on primate learning and behavior: complex learning and emergent processes in comparative perspective (review). *Japanese Psychol Res* 38: 113–25.

Schweikhart, R. L., Lu, E. T., Hut, P., and Chapman, C. R. (2003). The asteroid tugboat. *Scientific American* **289** (November): 34–41.

Smith, K. (2006). Homing in on the genes for humanity. *Nature* **442**: 725.

Socolow, R. H. (2005). Can we bury global warming? *Scientific American* **239** (July): 30–45.

Templeton, A. R. (2005). Haplotype trees and modern human origins. *Am J Phys Anthropol* Suppl **41**: 33–59.

Thesiger, W. (1970). Wild dog at 5894m. *East African Wildlife Journal* **8**: 202. And note that Ernest Hemingway's *The Snows of Kilimanjaro* (1936) is written around the finding of a frozen leopard on the mountain by a local missionary in 1926.

de Waal, Frans B. M. and Tyack, Peter L. (2003). *Animal Social Complexity. Intelligence, Culture, and Individualised Societies* (Harvard University Press, Cambridge, MA).

Wadhams, G. H. and Armitage, J. P. (2004). Making sense of it all: bacterial chemotaxis. *Nature Reviews Mol Cell Biol* **5**: 1024–37.

Waugh, E. (1964). *A Little Learning* (Chapman & Hall, London).

9: Human Evolution and the Human Condition

Ian Tattersall

Human uniqueness

Just what is it about we human beings that makes us feel ourselves to be so *different* from the rest of the living world? Quite evidently, we have a whole host of physical peculiarities, mostly related to our large brains, small faces, and upright postures, that clearly distinguish us from our closest living relatives, the great apes. But without any doubt, the differences that most *significantly* differentiate us from them are the cognitive ones – although the behavioural gulf that separates us from the apes seems to be steadily narrowing, as these complex creatures are discovered to indulge in ever more activities that we had formerly thought to be unique to ourselves. The latest revelation of this kind is that apes can consciously plan future activities, as demonstrated by the reservation of tools for later use (Mulcahy and Call, 2006). Still, we obviously relate to the world around us in a significantly more complex manner than they do; and even though it is impossible for us to imagine just how apes subjectively experience their lives – and therefore to know the degree to which the quality of their experience resembles ours – there are clearly major differences between apes and humans in our ways of processing information about the environment and about each other. To put this complex and difficult matter in a nutshell, we are *symbolic* creatures (Pribram, 1971; Lock and Peters, 1996); they are not. Only human beings, as far as we know, mentally divide up the world around them into discrete entities to which names are given. And once we have generated mental symbols of this kind – whether they represent concrete objects or abstractions – we can put them together in new combinations, and ask questions like "what if?" In other words, we can and do constantly remake the world in our heads; and it is in this mentally reconstructed world that we human beings live, rather than in the world as presented directly by Nature – which is the one in which, to the best of our knowledge, all other living creatures live.

Still, especially with the recent popularity of evolutionary psychology, in which the basic trick is to choose some aspect of human behaviour (the more bizarre the better) and then to blame it on adaptation to a long-gone "environment of evolutionary adaptedness" (e.g. Barkow et al., 1992; Wright, 1994), it has become a popular pastime to compile lists – even book-length lists (Brown, 1991) – of those features of human behaviour that make us unique. Such features include: abstraction in speech and thought, actions under self-control distinguished from those not under control, aesthetics, affection expressed and felt, ambivalence, anthropomorphization, art, baby talk, belief in the supernatural and religion ... all the way down the alphabet to violence, visiting, weapons, and world view. The problem with such lists, of course, is that they can never be complete; there's always something else to add. Some examples that I haven't seen widely cited yet include the human propensities to play bingo, hang-glide, and wear tattoos. And none of these features in itself specifies anything about the human condition; we simply can't know which of them, if any, is the "key" human attribute, the one that was targeted by past natural selection.

The human mind

From all this it seems justifiable to conclude that, while it is obviously entertaining for members of an egocentric species like ours to tell each other stories about all those very many things that make us different from every other creature, trying to identify what makes us different by selecting particular behaviours to dwell upon doesn't really get us very far. And the reason for this is, of course, that all of those behaviours are effects, not causes. They are products of the human mind and of conscious choice; they are not determinants of what makes us human. As a result, if we want to know just what it is that makes us cognitively unique we have to turn to the human mind itself, rather than merely to its expressions. The human mind is, of course, in turn the product of the physical brain. And if we could say just what it is about the human brain that makes it function in a different manner from anatomically not-too-dissimilar structures in other species, then we could truly specify, in physical terms, just what it is that makes us cognitively human. But at present, although new techniques of brain-imaging are teaching us more each day about which parts of the human brain are active in performing which behavioral functions, we still have no idea at all about how a mass of electro-chemical signals in the human brain – and apparently in ours alone – give rise to what each of us subjectively experiences as his or her peculiarly human form of consciousness. Given this fact – and its own structural basis may very well in the end be the very last biological problem left for the human intellect to solve – we are left with the investigation of the mind, and of how we acquired it, as the most profitable avenue toward specifying just what it is that makes us cognitively unique.

Some scientists prefer a mechanistic approach to this problem. Evolutionary psychologists have argued that human cognition is modular, composed of numerous discrete functional units with independent histories of acquisition (see contributions and references in Barkow et al., 1992). For example, with acknowledgement to the American evolutionary psychologist Leda Cosmides for the metaphor, the English prehistorian Steven Mithen (1996: 43) has likened the human mind and its many proposed modules to a Swiss Army knife with many different blades, each module likely possessing "its own specific form of memory and reasoning process." In the evolutionary psychological construct, Darwinian natural selection has led step-by-step to the gradual emergence of the modern human mind via the gradual accretion of new, discrete, and increasingly specialized aspects of intelligence. But while this formulation might be immediately attractive to the undeniably reductionist human mind – for we are indeed a story-telling species, and evolutionary psychologists tell good stories – there are difficulties with the notion of classical natural selection as the inexorable propulsive force behind increasing human intelligence. To substantiate this, it's necessary to digress for a moment into the nature of natural selection itself.

Evolutionary process(es)

Individuals in all populations vary in their physical features, and they inherit many of those variations from their parents. The basic idea behind evolution by natural selection is that, since in every generation more offspring are produced than will survive to reproduce themselves, randomly arising novel features (essentially, genetic copying errors) that enhance reproductive success will become commoner within populations, changing their complexion over time. On the face of it, the notion that populations will become better adapted because favoured individuals will have more offspring looks not only plausible, but inevitable. Some individuals are, indeed, more successful reproductively than others. But a moment's thought will tell you that the leap from the reproductive success of individuals to the fine-tuning of their features only works when, in effect, we forget about the entire individual and think of particular beneficial characteristics as the targets of natural selection. And this involves considering individual features as existing and evolving in isolation from others (Tattersall, 2002). However, the reality is that, while we can use our cognitive powers to recognize numerous individual characteristics in each organism, every individual is first and foremost an integrated whole: a whole in which most heritable characteristics are controlled by multiple genes, and in which nearly every gene influences multiple characters. You can be reproductively successful for a lot of different reasons, most of which will involve the products of different groups of genes; and in any case natural selection can, by its very nature, affect the reproductive success only of the whole organism, and therefore of its entire genotype (collection of genes). Under most circumstances – although probably not all: exceptions are particularly likely among features that are directly related to the reproductive process itself – it cannot operate on the individual features of an organism, still less on particular genes. Yet this is the assumption that underlies the modular notion of brain/mind evolution, which dissects intellectual function into particulate components with independent histories. And it is an assumption that is profoundly flawed; we cannot proceed as if each attribute under consideration somehow exists separately from the entire organism in which it is embedded, and as if each attribute has had an evolutionary history independent not only of its possessors, but also of the other traits that together make up the functioning whole. The larger patterns we see in the evolutionary histories of organisms are almost certainly determined at least as much by events affecting entire populations, or even species, as by the reproductive winnowing of individuals; it is, after all, of very little use in the long run to be the most prolific and hence "best adapted" individual of your species if that entire species is being outcompeted into extinction.

The human evolutionary record

All of this suggests that, in our search for what makes us unique and how we got to be that way, we would do better to step back a little, and to pose the question a little differently. One way of doing this is to ask exactly what we know about the actual historical patterns of innovation in potential markers for cognitive advance among our predecessors. The archive of past hominid behaviours is the archaeological record, while the fossil record is the register of physical change in our lineage. Do we see in those records a signal of gradual accretionary improvement in hominid structure and function – a pattern that would indeed suggest a slow process of fine-tuning? Or do we see something else? Well, if we look at the available evidence, as we'll briefly do below, it turns out that the structuring of innovation in hominid evolution – and particularly of technological evolution, which we can take at some level to be a reflection of cognitive complexity – was episodic, with long periods of non-change interspersed with the sudden appearance of major novelties (Tattersall, 1998a and b). This is actually a pretty routine evolutionary phenomenon in the biological record, and in the case of the human family it applies equally to patterns of physical change and of technological/ behavioural innovation. Interestingly, though, while the patterns are similar the two records are distinctly out of synch: biological and technological change did not proceed hand-in-hand. Still, while perhaps counterintuitive this lack of coordination is hardly surprising if you think about it a little, because obviously every change, technological as well as biological, has to originate *within* a species – for there is nowhere else that it can happen (Tattersall, 2004).

The hominid behavioural record begins essentially with the invention of crude stone tools – small sharp flakes chipped off a cobble held in one hand using a hammer stone held in the other – at around two and a half million years ago (Schick and Toth, 1993). Whoever the makers were, and this is not certainly known, they do not seem to have differed significantly from their nontechnological predecessors, small-bodied creatures with short legs and brains of not much better than ape size. Indeed, the creatures who represented the hominid family for the first few million years of its existence are often referred to as "bipedal apes". In the million years or so following the introduction of stone tools average hominid brain sizes may have crept up a little, but there was no radical improvement in stone working technology (Klein, 1999). Indeed, even after tall hominids with substantially modern body proportions and at least some increase in brain size had made their unanticipated appearance at some time after two million years ago, stone tools of the early style continued to be made for several hundred thousand years.

Still, the appearance in Africa of the new kind of hominid, often called *Homo ergaster*, did usher in the period of human evolution during which average brain sizes increased fairly consistently – in a pattern that is not yet clearly evident – from around 650 cc, not much larger than a modern ape's, to the modern human 1400 cc or so (Holloway, 2000). However, there is no clear evidence that this was a linear increase, and indeed it more plausibly reflects the differential success of larger-brained species within the family than a process of gradual enlargement within a single lineage. In any event, it was not until about one and a half million years ago that a new kind of stoneworking was finally introduced in Africa (Klein, 1999). A larger piece of stone, typically around eight inches long, was carefully fashioned on both sides to a symmetrical teardrop shape, producing what is known as a "handaxe". At last, toolmakers seem to have been shaping stone to a "mental template" that they had in mind before knapping began, rather than like their predecessors simply going after an attribute – a sharp cutting edge – regardless of what the resulting implement looked like. Surely a cognitive leap, but apparently not one that was initially taken by a new kind of hominid, and one that may or not have been accompanied by wider behavioral changes: the record simply doesn't tell us.

At about 600,000 years ago, in Africa, we begin to find evidence of a hominid, often known as *Homo heidelbergensis*, that had a significantly enlarged brain, around 1250 cc in volume (Clark et al., 1994; Conroy et al., 2000). By about half a million years ago this species was present in Europe, where it seems to have been implicated in some significant technological advances, including the building of the first documented artificial shelters (de Lumley and Boone, 1976) and the domestication of fire in hearths (the first good but isolated evidence for which comes from a site in Israel some 790,000 years old: Goren-Inbar et al., 2004). However, in Africa the first *Homo heidelbergensis* fossils are associated with tools of the early tradition; and this is also true at least of the first members of the species in Europe, emphasizing the disconnect between toolmaking styles and particular hominid species. Only about 300,000 years ago was a significantly new stone working technology introduced (Klein, 1999). This was the "prepared core" technique, whereby a stone was fashioned with numerous blows, often from a "soft" hammer of bone or suchlike, until a final blow would detach a flake that took little modification into a finished tool. This is surely evidence of an advance in the ability to envisage the potential offered by stone as a material; but the wider ramifications of this cognitive advance remain entirely conjectural. The best-known practitioner of the prepared-core technique was *Homo neanderthalensis*, an endemic European species that flourished in isolation between about 200,000 and 30,000 years ago. The Neanderthals, as members of this species are popularly known, were fine craftsmen in stone, invented the burial of the dead, ground ochre, and looked after their kin (Stringer and Gamble, 1995); but although they left behind themselves an abundant material record of their lives, there is essentially nothing in that record that convincingly suggests that they possessed symbolic behaviours: claimed examples of Neanderthal art, decoration or notation are few at best, and all are arguable (Mellars, 1996). This is also true for all other extinct species of hominids.

But it is emphatically not true of the *Homo sapiens* – the Cro-Magnons – who entered Europe at about 40,000 years ago, and in a mere ten millennia drove them to extinction. The lives of the Cro-Magnons were thoroughly permeated by symbol (R. White, 1986). Not only were these people making spectacular animal art on the walls of caves well over 30,000 years ago, but they were producing elegant carvings and engravings, making notations on bone plaques, decorating utilitarian objects, and making music on vulture-bone flutes – an activity for which vulture bones, evidently possessing some deep symbolic meaning for the flute-makers, were entirely reserved. And if they made music, surely they sang and danced as well. Soon the

Cro-Magnons were baking figurines in kilns and sewing tailored garments with the finest of eyed bone needles. These people, in other words, were *us*, possessed of language and of a sensibility entirely equivalent to our own (White, 1986). It is important to note, however, that they were not the first humans to show *any* material evidence of the modern symbolic sensibility – hints of this show up in Africa (the ultimate place of origin of the Cro-Magnons) as long ago as 75,000 years (Henshilwood et al., 2002) – but no other early people has left us such a dramatic material document of lives governed by symbol.

Yet the first human beings who *looked* exactly like us apparently did not behave in this way. The earliest putative *Homo sapiens* fossils in Africa show up in the 160–200,000 year range (T. White et al., 2003; McDougall et al., 2005) and are associated with quite crude stone tools, and nothing else. And around 100,000 years ago in Israel, we have good evidence that humans who were entirely modern in their bony skeletons were producing a material culture that was virtually indistinguishable from that of the Neanderthals with whom they shared their territory in some way for several tens of thousands of years at least (Vandermeersch, 1981; Valladas et al., 1988). This was not in itself anything remarkable; hominid species had coexisted from the beginning (Tattersall, 2000), and as we've seen we cannot tie particular hominid species to particular technologies. But in the light of the later achievements of *Homo sapiens* it looks, perhaps, a little strange.

The emergence of human uniqueness

What, then, happened to change things? It has been beguilingly suggested that at around 50,000 years ago a human species with the same bony structure as us acquired a genetic neural novelty that enabled symbolic mental activity, and that through enormous adaptive advantage the population with this gene spread very rapidly and replaced the more archaic form Old World-wide (Klein and Edgar, 2002). More plausible, though, is the notion that the neural *potential* for symbolic thought arose as a by-product of the major developmental reorganization that signalled the emergence of *Homo sapiens* as a (highly) distinctive physical entity in the period between about 200,000 and 150,000 years ago. That biological potential then lay fallow, as it were, until it was released by a cultural stimulus of some sort (Tattersall,

1998a and b). In evolutionary terms this would have been an entirely routine event: birds, for example, used feathers as body insulation for many millions of years before co-opting them for flight. Indeed, there is an argument to be made for the idea that *any* innovation has to arise not as an adaption but as an *exaptation*, i.e. independently of the function to which it will eventually be put.

In the human case, what might the cultural innovation have been? Most plausibly, it was the invention of language, which has the advantage in this connection of being a communal possession rather than a purely personal one (unless, of course, the essential function of language is, instead of communication, to be a conduit to thought). Language is the ultimate symbolic activity; indeed, at least from our modern perspective, symbolic thought seems impossible in its absence. Like thought itself, language involves forming mental symbols and combining and recombining them to come up with an infinity of new meanings and associations. And (at least within a linguistic milieu) languages are apparently spontaneously invented with relative ease (Kegl, 2002). But whatever exactly it was that allowed human beings to discover their symbolic potential, it evidently followed some considerable time after the acquisition of the potential itself. But, once the horse was out of the stable, the rules of the game changed and the cultural history of humankind has subsequently been dominated by the discovery of new ways in which to use that potential (Tattersall, 2004). It has been argued that the early appearance in Africa – sometimes very early, as in the case of long, thin stone "blades" a quarter of a million years ago – of elements that in later times were associated with the Cro-Magnons, implies that the human symbolic capacity was acquired slowly, over a long period of time, and that the "human revolution" that we see with the arrival of *Homo sapiens* in Europe was thus illusory, created by what might be seen as an artificial contrast between the dazzling record left by the invading Cro-Magnons and that of the nonsymbolic resident Neanderthals (McBrearty and Brooks, 2000). But all of those early African intimations of "modern" behaviours – pigment grinding, long-distance exchange of materials, shellfishing, flint mining – are technological manifestations, rather than directly symbolic ones, and there is some doubt about how far symbolism can be read into technological expressions. Thus, the Neanderthals were exquisite craftsmen in stone; yet everything we know about them suggests that their intelligence, while doubtless impressive, was almost certainly intuitive rather than symbolic.

Capability and intelligence are of course intangible qualities, and leave no direct trace. As a result, it is virtually impossible to establish the former existence of symbolic intelligence in the absence of clearly symbolic objects which were the products of that intelligence. But while absence of evidence is certainly not evidence of absence, neither does it suggest presence. In Africa, the first firm intimations of symbolic behaviours – engraved ochre plaques, pierced shell beads – only show up at about 75,000 years ago (Henshilwood et al., 2002), admittedly a bit later than the first suggested symbolic organization of living space (Deacon and Deacon, 1999). And, following these early inklings, similar evidence is thin indeed on the ground for a very long time. Doubtless, some degree of sampling error has affected the record we have; but what seems most plausibly to have been the case is that, while the initial discovery of the human symbolic potential may (or may not) have taken place at a single point in time, that discovery simply marked the beginning of an ongoing process. Indeed, it is a process that continues today, as we busily explore new ways to exploit our remarkable symbolic capacities.

Whatever the exact case, what is evident is that the human capacity was not predicted by anything that preceded it. It does not represent an incremental improvement upon what went before, but rather something truly new. Average human brain sizes had certainly increased, at a remarkable rate, in the two million years that preceded the appearance on Earth of *Homo sapiens*. And doubtless this means that over this period hominids were – on average – becoming smarter. Certainly, we see in the lithic record an improvement in technology, albeit an episodic and stepwise one. By themselves even the stone tools of the Cro-Magnons could be regarded as representing yet another stepwise improvement. But the Cro-Magnons also left an unambiguously symbolic record: and as far as the admittedly incomplete material record is concerned, symbolic intelligence was entirely unanticipated. Once it had acquired symbolism, *Homo sapiens* was no longer doing business as before, but a little better. Symbolic *Homo sapiens* was and is an entity of a totally new kind. And this fact alone takes the appearance of this new sensibility out of the domain of polishing over the eons by natural selection, and into the realm of emergence, the process whereby a chance addition to an existing substrate can produce something entirely unexpected (Tattersall, 2004).

The fact that it did not come about via fine-tuning by natural selection not only clarifies why the cognitive mechanism that underpins our behavioural uniqueness is a generalized rather than a specialized one; it also explains a lot about the kinds of creatures we are. Which is something that undoubtedly needs explaining, for human beings are bizarre animals indeed, certainly in the sense that you can (probably fairly easily) find a member of our species to illustrate both pairs of any set of behavioural antitheses you could think of: cruel, kind; greedy, generous; boring, fascinating; and on and on. What, then, is our condition? How do we describe our species in behavioural terms? As symbolically mediated, certainly; but after that, all bets are off. Odd as it may seem, the only animal that, so far as we know, agonizes about its condition is the only one that doesn't have one, or that at any rate has the condition which is most impossibly hard to characterize. If evolution had fine-tuned us for anything, surely it would be a great deal easier for us to specify the kind of creature we are. As it is, we are simultaneously many kinds of creatures: we all have a fish brain inside us, and a reptile brain, and a primitive mammal brain and probably nearly all of a chimpanzee brain too (Allman, 1999). But we have something else: an extra overlayering that makes symbolic thoughts possible – but symbolic thoughts that are also mediated by a lot of very ancient brain centres indeed. It is our combination of ancient emotional and intuitive brain processes with this additional symbolic element that makes us what we are; and the result is a structure, with an almost infinite range of potentialities, that no engineer would ever have dreamed of designing. This it is that gives us our free will – and the responsibility that goes with it.

Acknowledgment

I thank Professor Charles Pasternak for inviting me to contribute to this fascinating volume.

References

Allman J. M. 1999. *Evolving Brains*. New York: Scientific American Library.
Barkow J. H., Cosmides L., Tooby J. (eds.). 1992. *The Adapted Mind*. New York: Oxford University Press.

Brown D. E. 1991. *Human Universals*. New York City: McGraw-Hill.

Clark J. D., deHeinzelin J., Schick K. D., Hart W. K., White T., Wolde-Gabriel G., Walter R. C., Suwa G., Asfaw B., Vrba E., and Hale-Selassie J. 1994. African *Homo erectus*: Old radiometric ages and young Oldowan assemblages in the Middle Awash valley, Ethiopia. *Science* 264: 1907–1910.

Conroy G., Weber G. W., Sedler H., Recheis W., zur Nedden D., and Jara H. M. 2000. Endocranial capacity of the Bodo cranium as determined from three-dimensional computed tomography. *Amer. Jour. Phys. Anthropol.* 113: 111–118.

Deacon H. and Deacon J. 1999. *Human Beginnings in South Africa: Uncovering the Secrets of the Stone Age*. Cape Town: David Philip.

Goren-Inbar N., Alperson N., Kislev M. E., Simchoni O., Melamed Y., Ben-Nun A., and Werker E. 2004. Evidence of hominin control of fire at Gesher Benot Ya'aquov, Israel. *Science* 304: 725–727.

Henshilwood C., d'Errico F., Yates R., Jacobs Z., Tribolo C., Duller G. A., Mercier N., Sealy J. C., Valladas H., Watts I. and Wintle A. G. 2002. Emergence of modern human behavior: Middle Stone Age engravings from South Africa. *Science* 295, 1278–1280.

Holloway R. 2000. Brain. In Delson E., Tattersall I., Van Couvering J. A., and Brooks A., *Encyclopedia of Human Evolution and Prehistory*, 2nd edn. New York: Garland Publishing, pp. 141–149.

Kegl J. 2002. Language Emergence in a Language-Ready Brain: Acquisition Issues. In Morgan G. and Woll B., *Language Acquisition in Signed Languages*. Cambridge: Cambridge University Press, pp. 207–254.

Klein R. 1999. *The Human Career*. Chicago: University of Chicago Press.

Klein R. and Edgar B. 2002. *The Dawn of Human Culture*. New York: Wiley.

Lock A. and Peters C. R. 1996. *Handbook of Human Symbolic Evolution*. Oxford: Clarendon Press.

Lumley H. de and Boone, Y. 1976. Les structures d'habitat au Paléolithique inférieur. In Lumley, H. de (ed.), *La Préhistoire Francaise*, vol. 1. Paris: CNRS, pp. 625–643.

McBrearty S. and Brooks A. S. 2000. The revolution that wasn't: A new interpretation of the origin of modern human behavior. *Jour. Hum. Evol.* 39: 453–563.

McDougall I., Brown F. H., and Fleagle J. G. 2005. Stratigraphic placement and age of modern humans from Kibish, Ethiopia. *Nature* 433: 733–736.

Mellars P. 1996. *The Neanderthal Legacy*. Princeton, NJ: Princeton University Press.

Mithen S. 1996. *The Prehistory of the Mind*. London: Thames and Hudson.

Mulcahy N. J. and Call J. 2006. Apes save tools for future use. *Science* 312: 1038–1040.

Pribram K. 1971. *What Makes Man Human*. New York: American Museum of Natural History (James Arthur Lecture Series).

Schick K. and Toth N. 1993. *Making Silent Stones Speak: Human Evolution and the Dawn of Technology*. New York: Simon and Schuster.

Stringer C. B. and Gamble C. 1995. *In Search of the Neanderthals*. London: Thames and Hudson.

Tattersall I. 1998a. *Becoming Human: Evolution and Human Uniqueness*. New York: Harcourt Brace.

Tattersall I. 1998b. *Origin of the Human Capacity*. New York City: American Museum of Natural History (James Arthur Lecture Series).

Tattersall I. 2000. Once we were not alone. *Scientific American* 282 (1): 56–62.

Tattersall I. 2002. Adaptation: The unifying myth of biological anthropology. *Teaching Anthropology*: SACC Notes 9 (1): 9–11, 39.

Tattersall I. 2004. What happened in the origin of human consciousness? *Anat. Rec. (New Anat.)* 267B: 19–26.

Valladas H., Reyss J. L., Joron J. L., Valladas G., Bar-Yosef O., and Vandermeersch B. 1988. Thermoluminescence dating of Mousterian "Proto-Cro-Magnon" remains from Israel and the origin of modern man. *Nature* 331: 614–616.

Vandermeersch B. 1981. *Les Hommes Fossiles de Qafzeh (Israel)*. Paris: CNRS.

White R. 1986. *Dark Caves, Bright Visions: Life in Ice Age Europe*. New York: American Museum of Natural History/WW Norton.

White T. D., Asfaw B., DeGusta D., Gilbert H., Richards G. D., Suwa G., and Howell F. C. 2003. Pleistocene *Homo sapiens* from Middle Awash, Ethiopia. *Nature* 423: 742–747.

Wright R. 1994. *The Moral Animal*. New York: Random House.

10: The Place of "Deep Social Mind" in the Evolution of Human Nature

Andrew Whiten

(Reproduced from an article published by the Royal Society of Edinburgh in 2006, with permission)

Synopsis

Establishing the "nature" of any species has traditionally been an essentially descriptive exercise aiming to delineate ever more clearly what it is to be a member of that species. Since Darwin, however, we can think of the nature of a species in additional ways; from an evolutionary perspective, we can ask (for example) what differentiates the nature of a species such as our own from its closest living relatives, and how the difference arose from common origins. I take each approach in turn, examining what I have called "deep social mind". At a descriptive level, the claim is that human beings are not merely the cleverest species, but also the most social, in the depth of their cognitive interpenetration. Different aspects of this are found in the phenomena of culture, theory of mind ("mind-reading"), cooperation, and language. I outline how the evolutionary ancestry of these can be systematically examined and propose that their precursors formed an adaptive complex through which our ancestors survived an evolutionary bottleneck. They did so by refining an extraordinary pattern of hunting-and-gathering in the face of competition from numerous "professional" predatory species. Understanding how this was achieved may be of fundamental importance in explaining the "nature" of human nature.

Introduction: Stalking "human nature"

We can mean one of two rather different things when we talk of the "nature" of either a characteristic or a species (Whiten, 2000a). First, in trying to weigh up the nature of a particular species such as *H. sapiens*, we might try to define the essence, or perhaps the scope or limits, of what it is to be a member of that species. In the case of human nature, then, one is aiming to set out just what it is to be human. For centuries, perhaps millennia, this is what it has meant to attempt to characterize the nature of humans, or indeed, the nature of any other kind of creature. This, I think, is at least the broad objective – the "common denominator" shared by contributors to this volume and the meeting that gave rise to it. Let's call this the descriptive approach, since its ambition is essentially to give an increasingly comprehensive account of being human.

Since the discoveries of Darwin and Wallace, however, we have had available a new perspective: to understand human nature as a part and a product of "nature" as a whole. Accepting that humans share ancestors with other living species leads us to a cluster of new questions such as:

- What is distinctive about human nature in comparison with those components of the rest of nature, from which we have diverged (e.g. the genus most similar to ourselves, and sharing the most recent common ancestor, the chimpanzee)?
- Conversely, what aspects of our nature exist by virtue of that common ancestry (and will thus be shared with other species)?
- What explains why our nature and that of our living relatives have diverged from the ancestral one?
- What is the legacy we inherit from this particular evolutionary history?

These questions probe "the nature of human nature" within an explicit evolutionary framework. However, note that the clause with which the first of the four questions above begins is also a perfectly valid way to approach the more general descriptive goal outlined in my opening paragraph; that is to say, even without an evolutionary perspective, it can be a useful device to delineate the nature of one species in comparison to others, particularly that which is most like it. Indeed, that is the way in which I shall shortly introduce what I mean by "deep social mind", because one claim I want to make is that we are not only much smarter than other animals (as our essential distinctiveness is so often characterized), but we are actually more social than any species on earth, in a very interesting way.

However, this is only the first step because I also want to address evolutionary questions intimately linked to this claim about our social minds. In fact, I will propose that a diversity of kinds of evidence points to the evolution of a special social mentality as critical in the success with which our ancestors survived certain novel evolutionary bottlenecks – a success that can be fairly described as miraculous in the circumstances, but that may be crucial in understanding why human nature is as it is. Before I explain more fully what I mean by this, I need to indicate how we know any of these things about our past.

Reconstructing the creation of human nature

The past century and a half has witnessed an extraordinary set of advances in scientific knowledge about our past. The sources of this knowledge are extremely diverse, generated by very different and specialized sub-disciplines. There is space here to do little other than list some by way of illustration, leaving to one side the various methodological riders and cautions which are necessary for their interpretation (e.g. see Whiten, 1999; Boyd and Silk, 2000; Ingold, 2006). At their core is the "hard" evidence provided by the sciences of excavation, including palaeontology and archaeology, which recover the fossils of our ancestors and other materials like tools. Refinements such as high-resolution analysis of wear patterns on teeth and tools are amongst the advances which allow increasing confidence about past behaviour. Analysis of contemporary large molecules such as DNA itself, in conjunction with the more fragmentary fossil record, permits the construction of comprehensive genealogies. Using the framework so generated, comparative studies of non-human primates have been used to infer the behavioural and mental characteristics of pre-hominid ancestors, such as the common ancestor of ourselves and chimpanzees. Similarly, because the historical evidence is that a vast era of hunting-and-gathering subsistence preceded our mere ten millennia of agriculture, studies of contemporary hunter-gatherers have been used to generate inferences about behavioural correlates of that way of life. We shall consider findings produced by these approaches below.

In the context of the Royal Society of Edinburgh's millennial celebration, it seems appropriate to recognize just how fortunate has been the recent convergence of the varied scientific achievements which have taught us so much about how we became human. For example, the discovery of evolution by selection in the nineteenth century provided a crucial rationale for the extensive primate and hunter-gatherer studies which were at last completed in the second half of the twentieth century, in what now looks like a small window of opportunity that is presently being closed as these subjects of study literally disappear. Imagine if instead the Darwinian insight had been delayed and followed the closing of that window of opportunity! If we add in the totality of what has come together, from carbon dating to coevolutionary theory, from taphonomy to socioecology and so on, we must see ourselves as standing at a uniquely privileged scientific vantage point with respect to understanding the creation of human nature. Let us consider some of the findings undreamed of a century ago, which will lead us back to the topic of deep social mind.

The scientific study of a miracle: the survival of *Homo*

We now know much about the main stages of hominid evolution and its ecological context (e.g. Foley, 1995; Potts, 1996; and see Berry, 2006). When we put all the information together, it is, on the face of it, highly improbable that our ancestors should have survived the evolutionary obstacle course they were forced to run; and the solution through which they did so – the beginnings of the trajectory that led to present human nature – is no less a miraculous oddity in the context of the rest of nature.

The key findings that substantiate this rather expansive statement are as follows. First, the fossil record shows that the origin of the speciation that led to the creation of chimpanzees and humans occurred at a time of drastic environmental change in Africa (Potts, 1996). Forests which had supported several species of ape shrank towards the Congo basin, and were increasingly replaced by a broad arc of more thinly wooded grasslands. These provided for very large biomasses of grazing and browsing mammals. By contrast, primates were strongly adapted to arboreal habitats, and the ancestors of chimpanzees (and gorillas) remained restricted to the dwindling forested areas. Contrasting with this conservative response, our own ancestors adapted to the new, open environment. As apes, they were not initially suited to do so and had somehow to carve a new ecological niche in competition with a multitude of savannah-adapted species. In short, they had to become very peculiar apes – and they did. By 4 million years ago (Mya), some were already the first bipedal mammals.

This was already a peculiar innovation, but the real miracle was in the method of subsistence that was adopted. Hominids became serious carnivores and hunters, qualitatively and quantitatively different from anything seen amongst other primates. By 1.8 Mya, cut marks were being left on bones (Potts, 1992), and by 400 thousand years ago (Kya), long, straight spears were being made with a weight distribution as sophisticated as that of a modern javelin (Thieme, 1997). What makes this so strange an evolutionary innovation is that this subsistence style was forged in competition with over a dozen species of formidable predators like the big cats – the "professional predators". By contrast with the claws, teeth and other adaptations of these animals, the small ancestral ape was physically an unlikely candidate for a savannah hunter. A vulnerable prey for these predators, our ancestors' generation of a niche that also involved outmanoeuvring them, in successfully competing with them at their own game, was a highly improbable scenario. Yet it is what happened.

How was the miracle worked? What each such adaptively evolving new species has to do is find a new ecological "niche" – a gap, as it were, within the plethora of existing or coevolving subsistence strategies of animals inhabiting the savannahs. In the case of the early hominids, it has been suggested, the bodily limitations were countered by exploiting a "cognitive niche" (Tooby and DeVore, 1987). Essentially, there was selection for intelligence, with hominids becoming able to outwit prey (and perhaps other predators) sufficiently well to hold their own against competitors whose hunting success relied on other kinds of adaptation. In Tooby and DeVore's (1987) words, hominids became increasingly skilled in mounting "evolutionary surprise attacks" on prey. Normally, predator and prey are engaged in a long-term evolutionary "arms race", in which the prey develop better protective strategies (e.g. escape speed), the predators are accordingly further refined (e.g. pursuit speed and ambush), and so on. But if new hunting tactics are generated by intelligence, in relatively rapid time-frames, counter-adaptations resting on genetic change in the prey will not be able to keep up so well. Thus, the invention of traps and weapons represents particular refinements in the "cognitive niche".

I do not want to deny the cognitive niche account; indeed, it seems not only consistent with all the evidence about our past, but perhaps an inescapable inference from it. However, I want to argue that this niche is not adequately described in terms of intellectual engagement only with the physical world of hunting, gathering and early technology. What is missing is a suite of adaptations in the way the mind operated socially that were no less critical to early hominids' "miraculous" transition in subsistence style. These adaptations included forms of cultural transmission, mental coordination and cooperation which allowed the group to act as one large, super-intelligent forager/hunter, exploiting what would be better described as a distinctive "socio–cognitive niche".

To introduce the main elements of the deep social mind which this hypothesis refers to, I shall next temporarily put this evolutionary perspective to one side and concentrate on the more basic approach to human nature I outlined at the outset: that of describing what is distinctive about our present human nature in contrast with that of other species. Of course, this does not in itself imply a specific account of the evolutionary events which generated our current state. Nevertheless, it does delineate major features of human social nature, each of which must represent the end point of a substantial evolutionary construction process, and we shall return to the evolutionary perspective further below.

"Deep social mind"

The concept of deep social mind (Whiten, 1999) addresses both of the two main senses of human nature outlined above, but with respect to the purely descriptive approach, it does so in the explicit comparative fashion that I highlighted. Put most boldly, the claim is that humans are more social – more deeply social – than any other species on earth, our closest primate relatives not excepted. This may immediately strike the zoologist as unlikely: what about such species as ants which reach extraordinary heights of sociality? Surely in the size, density, intimacy and social structuring of their communities (including castes prepared to sacrifice their lives for their fellows) ants are truly "more social" than us? In these senses of "social", I suspect they are.

However, by "deep" I am referring additionally to a special degree of cognitive or mental penetration between individuals. This is best explained in relation to each of four main elements which together make up deep social mind. Some of these have long been vaunted as the distinguishing marks of human nature, others (and the synergy between them that is an important part of the concept at stake) are of note only through more recent research. The elements can only be sketched here; for more details see Whiten (1999).

"Mind-reading"

This term refers not to telepathy, but to the evidence that adult humans are mentalists rather than behaviourists, predicting and explaining others' actions in relation to a complex system of "every-day psychology", key constructs in which are states of mind such as thinking, wanting and believing (Wellman, 1990; Whiten and Perner, 1991). Much of what we know of mind-reading (also referred to as "theory of mind") has been discovered in research on the development of the ability in children, mostly during the 1990s (e.g. Carruthers and Smith, 1996; Whiten, 1998). Research on other facets of the capacity in humans is only now beginning to be systematically addressed (e.g. Sperber, 2000). Nevertheless, even if we were to restrict ourselves to the now well-charted mentalism of preschool children, the sense in which this represents a facet of deep social mind will be clear. Children of this age achieve deep penetration into the minds of others, extending to recognizing when others will be guided by beliefs which do not correspond with reality, and indeed, intentionally creating such beliefs themselves through acts of deception. Similarly deep mental interpenetration also occurs in more friendly interactions, such as that between teacher and novice. Things get more complex as third parties attempt to read what is going on in such exchanges, as when "Jane suspects that John wants Jill to think Jane doesn't believe her" (Kinderman et al., 1998). The web of such multiple mental interpenetrations in a human community makes it deeply social in a sense unprecedented in the natural world.

Culture

By contrast with the recency of what we have learned through the research effort on mind-reading, human cultural variations and their transmission have long received massive attention in disciplines as diverse as cultural anthropology (see Ingold, 2006), and the study of language acquisition (e.g. McShane, 1980; Tomasello, 1999). What this work tells us is that the contents of mature human minds are massively shaped by cultural acquisitions – even the most extensive of the regional variations in traditions found amongst animals cannot really be compared on the same scale (Whiten and Boesch, 2001). Thus, human minds are again unprecedentedly deeply social, in that vast amounts of the knowledge they accumulate (both "knowing how" and "knowing that") are acquired socially, from other minds. Sperber (1996) described human culture as an "epidemic of representations", highlighting the way in which mental representations leap and multiply between one brain and those that thus acquire it. Therefore, an important link between how cultural transmission and mind-reading each instantiate deep social mind should be clear: Sperber's "epidemic" refers to how the contents of one mind are read into another (or in the case of teaching or indoctrination, we should instead perhaps say "written" into another). Sperber (1996) noted that, of course, this does not equate to any kind of straightforward "photocopying" process, since each mind-to-mind leap entails a process of interpretation and mental reconstruction, with scope for all manner of modifications in relation to the original mental representation. The same is true of every act of mind-reading (Whiten, 2000b).

Language and communication

Like the phenomenon of culture, language is a long-standing candidate for what makes human nature distinctive (e.g. Burling, 1993; Berry, 2006). I do not want to quarrel with this, but instead emphasize that the function language serves so well, in comparison with forms of communication found commonly in the animal kingdom, is to permit "what one has in mind" (e.g. intentions, ideas and knowledge) to be transmitted to another mind. Some of these transmissions will form the basis for cultural transmission. Thus, although language is often presented as the primary, distinctive human capacity, it may make as much sense to see it as a tool through which the two deeply social functions already described – mind-reading and cultural transmission – operate particularly powerfully. Either way, language allows our minds to interconnect in intimate ways which count as deeply social in the sense I have been outlining.

Cooperation

In my initial exploration of the idea of deep social mind (Whiten, 1999), I distinguished two different (although related) aspects of cooperation, each of which takes distinctive forms in humans. The first is essentially the coordination of which human groups are capable, such that the group as a whole acts in the manner of a well coordinated organism. Individuals' minds here operate in a deeply social manner to the extent that they are subjugated to, and organized towards, achieving overarching group goals. Pack-hunting mammals may show elementary forms of such coordination, but it is perhaps the ants we must return to, to refine any such claim to human distinctiveness. An ant colony has often been compared to a giant organism, with individuals playing the parts of organs, each with their differentiated, yet coordinated, roles directed at the well-being of the colony as a whole (e.g. Wilson, 1975). The difference between ant and human in how such deep sociality is played out must appeal to the level of mental operation involved, as discussed in the preceding sections.

A second aspect of human cooperation is related to that of coordination, but worth distinguishing from it; it refers to capacities which emerge in certain social contexts to act in egalitarian ways, such as distributing resources and power relations in an equitable way (Erdal and Whiten, 1994). Again, this reflects a "submerging" of individual social minds in relation to group-level processes, achieved in a unique, human mental fashion.

The evolution of deep social mind

It is one thing to describe these components of deep social mind within the state of human nature we see today. What I have said so far about each of the elements above is, I hope, fairly uncontroversial – a description of how our species is distinctive in these respects, with the concept of "deep social mind" essentially an attempt at a supervening description of the shared consequences of these elements for the nature of humans.

However, our deep social mind is so elaborate that there must be a complex story to tell of its evolution too. We are not interested in a "just-so" story, of course, but one based on relevant data, of the several different kinds I alluded to earlier. Fortunately, such data are available concerning all the elements I have discussed, although the evidence varies in quantity and kind across them. There seems to be least in the case of language, and in the space available here, I shall focus on the other three elements. For these three, we can have confidence that there is an evolutionary story to tell because there are primitive forms of culture, mind-reading and cooperation in our closest relatives (Whiten, 1999), and thus, by inference, these characteristics have an ancestry that extends far into the evolutionary past.

I want to do more than attempt to outline this past for each characteristic, however. My hypothesis is that the combination of them represents what biologists describe as an adaptive complex, i.e. the functional significance of each characteristic is amplified by the others, natural selection thus favouring their combined effect. Therefore, although I am certainly not proposing that we should think of deep social mind as a unitary "thing" at the psychological or neural levels, the proposing of "adaptive complex" status for it implies that the term is more than just a loose label for characteristics which happen to share certain features. I suggest that the functional significance of the complex may have been critical in our ancestors' success in carving a viable niche within the inhospitable African environment sketched earlier. I will return to this hypothesis at the end of the chapter, having first addressed each of the three main characteristics in turn. For expository purposes, I will deal with them in a different sequence to that used above to introduce them, devoting the majority of my limited space to the first as an illustration of how we approach such apparent evolutionary intangibles scientifically.

Cooperation

There is little to be gleaned directly from the fossil record about cooperation or indeed any aspect of social behaviour, although inferences have long been made (e.g. Isaac, 1978). A richer set of inferences can be made through the following strategy. First, we can extract what the fossil record maximally tells us about past ways of life; critical for our purposes are the findings about an ancient ancestry for hunting, noted earlier. Secondly, we can exploit the fact that, until recently (and in some cases, even now), a number of human groups continue to subsist on hunting, not having made the transition to horticulture/agriculture/herding that most human populations have during the past ten millennia or so. We can then study these hunting groups to discover what kinds of social behaviour are associated with that way of life. One of the principal discoveries of such work has been that, in the tropics (i.e. the hominid evolutionary context), hunting is typically part of a more complex subsistence pattern in which gathering wild foods plays a part (often a greater one, and usually achieved mostly by women, whilst men tend to be the hunters). The obvious inference from this has been that our ancestral subsistence pattern is best described as a hunting-and-gathering way of life. A third step in the reconstruction strategy is to exploit comparative studies of non-human primates to draw inferences about shared ancestral behaviours; for example, characteristics shared with chimpanzees are likely a result of inheritance from our common ancestor of 5–6 Mya.

This multipart strategy is prone to numerous kinds of pitfalls. These are noted in the case of hunter-gatherer studies by Ingold (2006), and a series of earlier critics (e.g. Solway and Lee, 1990). Erdal and Whiten (1996) and Whiten (1999) discussed several of these thorny issues, but were not convinced that we should forsake the information about our past that is potentially available through the serendipitous existence of contemporary hunter-gatherers. To the contrary, Erdal and Whiten (1996) adopted a conservative strategy to reach the most reliable inferences; rather than utilizing one or a few hunter-gatherer societies as "referential models" of the past, we surveyed a wide array of 24 such societies across four continents and extracted patterns of sociality which were common to them. These, we inferred, were fundamental social correlates of this way of life, and thus, likely attributes of our ancestors. Since the brains of early *Homo sapiens* about 400 Kya were similarly sized to our own and the fossil evidence noted earlier indicates a hunting past of several (perhaps many) hundreds of millennia ago (by contrast with a mere 10–12 recent millennia of horticulture, for example), our inferences about hunter-gatherer sociality are likely to be relevant to quite ancient ancestors. This is not to deny that there will have been important behavioural changes during this long period, of course, but our inferences are specified only at quite broad levels. We focus on summarizing two here (for details, see Erdal and Whiten, 1996, especially Table 1).

(a) *Egalitarianism*. One of the most striking patterns that recurs in hunter-gatherers round the world is egalitarianism, defined by social equality. This is expressed in a number of ways. First, there is food sharing; gathered food, and particularly the meat gained by hunting, is typically shared through the whole group according to need. Thus, the mental state is one in which these foods are considered group resources. Secondly, monogamy is also typical, with the consequence for equality lying in reproductive output, contrasting with the variation that can occur in great apes and the many polygamous non-hunting-gathering human societies, where some (males in particular) may gain great reproductive superiority. A third aspect of egalitarianism is that social status tends also to express equality; formal leaders are rare. The equality is often held in place by the concerted efforts of the rest of the group to resist any tendencies towards leadership or self-aggrandisement, a social tactic referred to as reverse dominance (Boehm, 1993, 1999) or counter-dominance (Erdal and Whiten, 1996). This multifaceted egalitarianism is unusual, whether contrasted with the societies of great apes or with humans not living in hunting-gathering bands. Therefore, Knauft (1991) proposed that a "U-shaped curve" describes hominid social evolution, beginning with non-egalitarian apes, shifting to hunting-gathering egalitarianism and then becoming very hierarchical again in many modern societies during the past 10,000 years of settlement.

(b) *Coordination*. Hunter-gatherers also cooperate by coordinating actions at many different levels, in ways unprecedented amongst the great apes. Examples occur within hunting bands, where at several junctures in a hunt there is communication and negotiation in interpreting tracks and signs, using differing roles in ambushes, and in butchery and retrieval of carcasses; but coordination is also important at the highest levels of organization of group activities, such as in sharing relevant information between hunters and gatherers, and pooling the resources gained by a variety of foragers and foraging practices.

The combined effect of the many different manifestations of egalitarianism and coordination is that a hunting-gathering group acts like one great forager, formidable in the way it scours its range for a variety of food types subjected to "evolutionary surprise attacks". This, it seems, is a viable niche even in the midst of professional carnivorous competitors like lions.

Culture

Present-day hunter-gatherers can also offer an insight into the role of culture in human evolution, and other inferences derive from the tools and other artefacts recovered within the fossil record (Whiten, 1999). Here, to pursue my central theme, I shall simply highlight the way in which culture reinforces the social-cognitive niche that is human hunting-and-gathering. Hunter-gatherers often have few material possessions, only those which can be carried by individuals living an intermittently nomadic lifestyle. Nevertheless, the tools and weapons they do have are important aspects of the way in which evolutionary surprise attacks are executed, and the techniques involved in both manufacture and use represent the outcome of generations of invention, social transmission of knowledge and incorporation of refinements in a continual "ratcheting-up" process of cultural evolution (Tomasello, 1999; see also Ayala, 2006). There is also much social transmission of wisdom and knowledge about non-technological aspects of hunting-gathering ways, like prey-tracking. Thus, the mind that operates hunting strategies or gathering strategies is as sophisticated as it is, and survives as well as it does in its competitive environment, very much because of the depth of its assimilation of socially transmitted information. That this has relevance for our past is implied by the sophistication of the javelin-like spears mentioned above, and indeed, of the Acheulian stone tools a million years older.

Mind-reading

The enormous literature on mind-reading that grew in the 1990s has unfortunately scarcely touched the (dwindling) hunter-gatherer peoples, except for a demonstration by Avis and Harris (1991) that Baka children come to recognize the ways in which false beliefs can influence behaviour much as do the children so extensively studied in the USA and Europe. Although aspects of adult theories of mind may vary culturally (Lillard, 1998), that expected of any individual who attributes false belief (and presumably much more, at maturity) is likely to include the recognition of varied states of perception, knowledge, desire, and intention, as well as a model of how these interact to explain and predict behaviour (Wellman, 1990). Although its specific role in hunting-and-gathering remains to be formally studied, it is not too ambitious a speculation that such a theory of mind will have profound effects on the sophistication with which such socially mediated activities as hunting-and-gathering can be carried out, as well as those associated patterns of egalitarianism, coordination and culture outlined above.

Inferences about such mental operations in our evolutionary past are necessarily yet more speculative. However, that such processes operated in the distant past is supported by evidence for more primitive forms of mind-reading (of states of seeing, and perhaps of knowledge) in chimpanzees (Hare et al., 2001; Whiten, 2001), and thus, presumably in our common ancestor. One can similarly point to primitive versions in chimpanzees of the sharing, counter-dominance, coordination, and cultural phenomena outlined above (Whiten, 1999) which make a similar point about the credence of a long evolutionary history to the fashioning of these aspects of human nature.

Synergy: an adaptive complex?

The proposal was outlined earlier that the aspects of social mind described above act together as an adaptive complex (aptly labelled

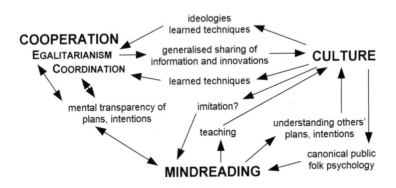

Figure 1 Hypothesized reinforcing effects amongst three components of deep social mind. Each arrow indicates the nature of such effects. For example, culture is proposed to support egalitarianism through publicly recognized ideologies of social equality and sharing. Mind-reading and co-operation are proposed to be subject to reciprocal effects: mind-reading supports the mental transparency that permits better coordination, and egalitarianism makes such transparency more viable.

"deep social mind"), and that the ways their precursors did so during hominid evolution were critical to the novel form of hunting-and-gathering that managed to survive and prosper amongst its superficially better-equipped competitors. Having described each of the main elements, ways in which they might be plausibly interact are now suggested in Figure 1. Such effects existing in the past would have had the potential to create positive feedback loops favoured by natural selection, refining the underlying mental capacities to shape an important socio-cognitive component of what is now human nature.

Omissions

The above is a necessarily potted account of one particular segment of the evolution of human nature. Readers are encouraged to consult the key references cited for supporting detail.

It is also important to finish by emphasizing that focusing only on social mind necessarily leaves out factors which are important in any full account of the human evolution. Berry (2006) provides a helpful overview of some of these; examples include such heterochronous processes as neoteny and recapitulation, which, in different forms, may each have played critical roles in making human nature what it is (Gould, 1978; Parker and McKinney, 1999).

Closer to the phenomena of social mind is the whole issue of sexual selection, which Miller (2000) has argued – I think quite persuasively – may be a key part of the explanation for the hyper-expansion of human brain power that accompanied our creation. This is but one of many relevant factors which cannot be treated in any appropriate depth here; I mention this one to underline that our topic is so big, that whole swathes of potentially important factors have perforce to be temporarily left aside.

References

Avis, J. and Harris, P. L. (1991) Belief-desire reasoning among Baka children: evidence for a universal conception of mind. *Child Development* 62, 460–467.

Ayala, F. J. (2006) Biological evolution and human nature. In Jeeves, M., Steel, M., Byrne, R., Torrance, A., Whiten, A., and Myers, D. (eds) *Human Nature*, pp. 46–64. Edinburgh: Royal Society of Edinburgh.

Berry, R. J. (2006) Natural selection could not have done it all. In Jeeves, M., Steel, M., Byrne, R., Torrance, A., Whiten, A., and Myers, D. (eds) *Human Nature*, pp. 65–83. Edinburgh: Royal Society of Edinburgh.

Boehm, C. (1993) Egalitarian behaviour and reverse dominance hierarchy. *Current Anthropology* 34, 227–254.

Boehm, C. (1999) *Hierarchy in the Forest: The Evolution of Egalitarian Behaviour*. Cambridge, MA: Harvard University Press.

Boyd, R. and Silk, J. (2000) *How Humans Evolved*, 2nd edn. New York: Norton.

Burling, R. (1993) Primate calls, human language and non-verbal communication. *Current Anthropology* 34, 25–53.

Carruthers, P. and Smith, P. K. (1996) *Theories of Theories of Mind*. Cambridge: Cambridge University Press.

Erdal, D. and Whiten, A. (1994) On human egalitarianism: an evolutionary product of Machiavellian status escalation? *Current Anthropology* 35, 175–183.

Erdal, D. and Whiten, A. (1996) Egalitarianism and Machiavellian intelligence in human evolution. In Mellars, P. and Gibson, K. (eds) *Modelling the Early Human Mind*, pp. 139–150. Cambridge: McDonald Institute Monographs.

Foley, R. (1995) *Humans Before Humanity: An Evolutionary Perspective*. Oxford: Blackwell.

Gould, S. J. (1978) *Ontogeny and Phylogeny*. Cambridge, MA: Harvard University Press.

Hare, B., Call, J., and Tomasello, M. (2001) Do chimpanzees know what conspecifics know? *Animal Behaviour* 61, 139–151.

Ingold, T. (2006) Against human nature. In Jeeves, M., Steel, M., Byrne, R., Torrance, A., Whiten, A., and Myers, D. (eds) *Human Nature*, pp. 106–131. Edinburgh: Royal Society of Edinburgh.

Isaac, G. (1978) The food-sharing behaviour of protohuman hominids. *Scientific American* 238, 90–108.

Kinderman, P., Dunbar, R., and Bentall, R. P. (1998) Theory-of-mind deficits and causal attributions. *British Journal of Psychology* 89, 191–204.

Knauft, B. M. (1991) Violence and sociality in human evolution. *Current Anthropology* 32, 391–428.

Lillard, A. (1998) Ethnopsychologies: cultural variations in theories of mind. *Psychological Bulletin* 123, 3–32.

McShane, J. (1980) *Learning to Talk*. Cambridge: Cambridge University Press.

Miller, G. (2000) *The Mating Mind: How Sexual Choice Shaped the Evolution of Human Nature*. London: Heinemann.

Parker, S. T. and McKinney, M. L. (1999) *Origins of Intelligence: The*

Evolution of Cognitive Development in Monkeys, Apes and Humans. Baltimore, MD: Johns Hopkins University Press.

Potts, R. (1992) The hominid way of life. In Jones, S., Martin, R., and Pilbeam, D. (eds) *The Cambridge Encyclopaedia of Human Evolution*, pp. 325–334. Cambridge: Cambridge University Press.

Potts, R. (1996) *Humanity's Descent: The Consequences of Ecological Instability.* New York: Avon Books.

Solway, J. S. and Lee, R. B. (1990) Foragers, genuine or spurious? Situating the Kalahari San in history. *Current Anthropology* 31(2), 109–146.

Sperber, D. (1996) *Explaining Culture: A Naturalistic Approach.* Oxford: Blackwell.

Sperber, D. (ed.) (2000) *Metarepresentations: A Multidisciplinary Perspective.* Oxford: Oxford University Press.

Thieme, H. (1997) Lower Palaeolithic hunting spears from Germany. *Nature* 385, 807–810.

Tomasello, M. (1999) *The Cultural Origins of Human Cognition.* Cambridge, MA: Harvard University Press.

Tooby, J. and DeVore, I. (1987) The reconstruction of hominid behavioral evolution through strategic modelling. In Kinzey, W. G. (ed.) *The Evolution of Human Behavior: Primate Models*, pp. 183–227. New York: SUNY Press.

Wellman, H. M. (1990) *The Child's Theory of Mind.* Cambridge, MA: Bradford Books.

Whiten, A. (1998) Evolutionary and developmental origins of the mind-reading system. In Langer, J. and Killen, M. (eds) *Piaget, Evolution and Development*, pp. 73–99. Englewood Cliffs, NJ: Lawrence Erlbaum Associates.

Whiten, A. (1999) The evolution of deep social mind in humans. In Corballis, M. and Lea, S. E. G. (eds) *The Descent of Mind*, pp. 155–175. Oxford: Oxford University Press.

Whiten, A. (2000a) Social complexity and social intelligence. In *The Nature of Intelligence* No. 233 Foundatio Novartis Foundation Symposium, pp. 185–201. Chichester: John Wiley & Sons.

Whiten, A. (2000b) Chimpanzee cognition and the question of mental re-representation. In Sperber, D. (ed.) *Metarepresentations*, pp. 139–167. Oxford: Oxford University Press.

Whiten, A. (2001) Theory of mind in non-verbal apes? Conceptual issues and the critical experiments. In Walsh, D. (ed.) *Philosophy Supplement No. 49: Naturalism, Evolution and Mind*, pp. 199–223. Cambridge: Cambridge University Press

Whiten, A. and Boesch, C. (2001) The cultures of chimpanzees. *Scientific American* 284, 48–55.

Whiten, A. and Perner, J. (1991) Fundamental issues in the multidisciplinary study of mindreading. In Whiten, A. (ed.) *Natural Theories of Mind: Evolution, Development and Simulation of Everyday Mindreading*, pp. 1–17. Oxford: Basil Blackwell.

Wilson, E. O. (1975) *Sociobiology: The New Synthesis*. Cambridge, MA: Harvard University Press.

11: Causal Belief Makes Us Human

Lewis Wolpert

Abstract

The primary function of the brain is to control movement and inter-action with the environment. Humans, unlike other primates, have a belief in physical cause and effect which enables the acquisition of new interactions, and led to technology. Human children have causal beliefs as a developmental primitive, and these can be demonstrated even in infants. By contrast, behavioural studies requiring simple manipulations of the environment show that chimpanzees do not have such concepts. It is proposed that the evolution of causal thinking was essential for the development of tool use as it is not possible to make a complex tool without understanding cause and effect. The evolution of language may have been linked to the same process. It has been technology that resulted from causal beliefs that has made us human, not social interaction.

Introduction

The word 'belief' is not easy to define (Schacter and Scarry, 2000). Nei-ther philosophers nor scientists have succeeded. Distinguishing belief from knowledge is not easy. One does not believe that this is a page in a book – it is knowledge about the world. In general, belief is about things that affect our lives. Belief is essential for making sense of the world and explaining the causes of events that are important for us. It is also about moral issues, good and evil actions and people. A characteristic of belief, unlike common knowledge is that it is always graded with respect to our confidence in it: it has a true and false value, how right or wrong it is.

One can think of causal belief as an explanatory tool for understanding the physical world. Humans cannot tolerate not knowing the causes of important events like death, illness, and climate change.

Belief is a property of the brain but what is the ultimate function of the brain itself? Just one, to control movement, so this must be at the core of any attempt to understand the origins of causal belief. Movement was present in the cells which gave rise to multicellular organisms some three thousand million years ago. A key point is that the protein molecules that produced these movements are the precursors of all muscle cells. Muscle-like cells are found in all animals including primitive ones like hydra, a small fresh water creature with just two layers of cells arranged in the form of a tube which uses the movement of its tentacles to capture prey. In higher forms like flatworms and molluscs, muscles are well developed and the ability to move is a characteristic of almost all animals. Again this ability to move is fundamental to animal life – not just finding food and shelter but the ability to escape from enemies. And this is where brains come from. Getting the muscles to contract in the right order was a critical evolutionary advance and required the evolution of nerves. Here we find the nerve circuits that excite muscles in the right order and are the precursors of brains.

The first advantage of the ability to move was probably dispersal and access to new habitats. Further advantages then opened up, such as finding food and avoiding danger. For the first time it became necessary to perceive the nature of the environment in order to decide when and where to move. There was a need for senses. Light-sensitive cells are present among single cell organisms so it is not too difficult to imagine light coming to control movement. Later came the eye, and other sensory systems that detected touch, sound, temperature, and odour. All these had and have but one function, to control movement. Organisms were thereby enabled to begin altering their immediate environment, for example by building nests. Emotions developed to help ready the organism for appropriate motor responses like flight or attack. And that is why plants do not have brains. Plants are very successful but they do not need brains for they neither move significantly nor, more importantly, do they exert significant forces on their environment.

Thus I propose that consciousness (in the sense that we have an internal model of what we are doing and can decide how to behave) has only one ultimate function, and that is to control movement. There is no human or animal emotion that is not ultimately expressed as movement. In fact the argument is almost a truism: for what else is human behaviour? Sense organs have but one function, to help decide how to move. The evolution of the brain that gave us beliefs is no more than an expansion of the original circuits that controlled movement in our ancient animal ancestors. Once the brain developed it took on other functions such as those related to homeostasis, like hormonal release and temperature regulation.

The evolution of causal belief opened up a completely new set of movements that were the basis of technology and understanding the environment (Oakley, 1949). Technology is a fundamental characteristic of humans, the ability to deliberately manipulate the environment to improve chances of survival. Early technology owed nothing to science, and science only began to have an influence as recently as the late eighteenth century (Wolpert, 1993). Technology was the result largely of imaginative trial and error. In order to practise technology a belief in cause and effect was absolutely essential, and how this belief arose is a fundamental step in human evolution.

Causal belief in children

Causal belief is regarded by developmental psychologists as a developmental primitive – it is a fundamental feature of children's development and behaviour (Corrigan and Denton, 1996; Schlottmann, 2001; Gopnik et al., 1999). An explanatory drive is at the core of a child's development and is as important as the drive for sex or food. They want to understand what is happening in the world around them. This drive consumes children in their first three years. There is a gap of some eight months in the developing infant's ability to go from understanding that an object can be retrieved by pulling on the cloth on which it is resting, to retrieving the object with a stick; the former develops at around ten months. At this early stage they do not use a hooked stick to get a toy unless it is already placed on the hook. At eighteen months they manage it well. They have moved from believing that two objects must have just a point of contact between them in order for the one to move the other, to using their knowledge to put the tool in the appropriate contact with the object (Baillargeon et al., 1996); they will use a 'tool', a rake, to pull a toy out of reach towards them.

Leslie (1996) has proposed that infants just a few months old already perceive the world as composed of cohesive solid bodies that keep much the same form when stationary or moving. In addition they have a special system in their brains – a module perhaps – for mapping the "energy" of these objects, some measure of their mechanical properties which can be likened to the concept of force. This concept gradually develops and is consistently present at two to three years. At this age, children know that a moving object – a ball – can make another move on impact. It is this concept of mechanics which may be the key brain property that originally evolved in early humans.

Studying young children's causal beliefs makes use of the standard habituation and dishabituation technique. This technique uses the fact that babies like novelty and will look longer at new things: the same thing over and over again causes them to habituate and lose interest, while a new thing causes them to regain their interest, to dishabituate. This technique is widely used to test babies' beliefs: they look longer at novel or surprising events involving objects that go against normal causes – like a box at the edge of a shelf not falling down, or an animal passing across a window without being seen. Babies already apparently have clear concepts about physical causality. They perceive physical events according to three principles which may be genetically determined: moving objects maintain both connectedness and cohesion, they do not break up or fuse; they move continuously and do not disappear and appear again without other objects in the way; they move together or interact only if they touch. There are many experiments to support this – for example, they clearly expect that for a moving block to make another one move, it must make contact with it.

Young children thus perceive that certain objects have causal properties with a renewable source of energy or force, and this is a most sophisticated idea unique to humans. These special objects, or agents, can act in pursuit of goals. They also have a concept of 'force' which is a primitive mechanical notion – not the same as the scientific concept of force. The basic idea is that when bodies move they possess a force and this can, on impact, be transmitted to other objects which can receive or resist. Infants expect a stationary object to be displaced when hit by a moving object and by six months can reliably estimate how far it should move. It is likely that these key principles are learned. They know a glass pan would break if dropped, but a metal one would not. They are also already aware that the size of an object affects whether it can pass through a gap. They also have an appreciation of gravity and if a falling ball suddenly stops in mid-air they are puzzled, and they also expect a toy car rolling down a slope to increase its speed.

Young children already distinguish between people and inanimate objects and are sensitive to the differences between human action and the motion of objects. They know that two inanimate objects have to contact each other if a causal event is to take place, but that with people and animals, a causal event does not require physical contact. The key is that animate objects can cause themselves to move or change their form, whereas inanimate ones cannot. Understanding that distinction requires a concept of cause.

Animals

Causal understanding is unique to humans – the weight of a falling rock clearly 'forces' the log to splinter. How did this ability to have causal beliefs evolve, for animals do not have such beliefs? There are of course cognitive similarities between human and mammalian and especially primate cognition: primates remember their local environment, take novel detours, follow object movement, recognise similarities and have some insight into problem solving. They also recognise individuals, predict their behaviour, and form alliances. However, they have little understanding of the causal relationships between inanimate objects. They do not view the world in terms of underlying 'forces' that are fundamental to human thinking. They do not understand the world in intentional or causal terms (Povinelli, 2000; Tomasello, 1999). Non-human primates do not understand the causal relation between their acts and the outcomes they experience. Apes, for example, cannot select an appropriate tool for a simple physical manipulation without extensive teaching. Yet gorillas eat thistle and other awkward plants which require skilled manual manipulation.

Povinelli (2000), whose work is a bit controversial, shows us that while many humans' and other primates' abilities to perceive and move are similar, primates like chimpanzees do not have concepts of variable causes to explain interaction between objects. One might have thought that Wolfgang Kohler's experiments with chimpanzees showed just the opposite. His chimpanzees, some eighty years ago, could sometimes, perhaps with some training, stack boxes on top of each other to get a banana nailed to the ceiling. But Kohler himself acknowledged that the chimpanzees had no knowledge of the forces involved. For example, they would try to place one box on another along its diagonal edge; and if stones were placed on the ground so that the box toppled over, they never removed the stones.

In an experiment by Povinelli's group, apes could choose one of two rake tools to obtain a food reward. The choice was between dragging food along a solid surface, or dragging it over a large hole into which the food would fall. Only one of six apes was successful and this solitary success may have been due to chance at the first trial, although the apes did eventually learn by trial and error. They also did badly with an inverted two-prong rake that could not move the food, and on tests with flimsy tools. Again, when required to get a banana by pulling on a rope they could not distinguish between a rope just lying on, or merely very close to the banana, and a rope that was actually tied to the banana. They showed no appreciation of physical connection as distinct from mere contact.

In another series of key experiments, primates were set the task of using a stick to push food out of a clear tube. The tools were of various sizes, some being too short, too thick, or too flexible. An understanding of basic forces should enable an individual to choose the right tool. Apes can do it, but only after much trial and error. In another test, there was a small trap under part of the tube and to get the food the subject needed to push the food from that end of the tube that avoided the trap. Chimpanzees failed to do better than just chance over seventy trials. Then, eventually, when the animals had learned to do it the tube was rotated through 180 degrees and so the trap was not on top and had no effect on getting the food. But they continued to push the food away from the trap. By contrast, two- to three-year-old children understood what to do from the earliest trials. Again male macaques, separated by a wire fence from apples, prodded the apples with sticks, but had great difficulty appreciating that the touch must result in moving the apple nearer. They required fifty 30-minute sessions. Young children did it almost at once.

However the chimpanzee Kanzi, a bonobo ape, showed remarkable skills. It learned to create and use stone tools to gain access to food to cut a rope and it could make stone flakes and evaluate them after observing a human striking two rocks together. On its own it created flakes by throwing one rock on to another on the ground, suggesting that he may indeed have a concept of force. It is not clear whether apes poking sticks into termite mounds and so extracting them is by imitation or learned by trial and error.

It is not that chimpanzees lack visual imagination or are unable to learn quite complex tasks by trial and error, but they do not reason about things. They have, for example, no concept of force, and even worse, no concept of causality. They do appreciate that contact is necessary in using a tool to get food, but will focus only on the contact and not the force it generates on the target object. A hook at the end of the stick is not perceived as a means to get the reward. One may illustrate the differences in chimpanzee and human thinking with the claim that an ape seeing the wind blowing and shaking a branch till the fruit falls would never learn from this to shake the branch to get the fruit.

In the tropical forests of West Africa, chimpanzees have been observed spending hours using stone or wooden hammers to break open the shells of nuts by first placing them on a stone, the anvil. Moreover this behaviour is ancient. These sites show no evidence of real tool making, or the selection of stones with respect to the material of which they are composed; only the weight of the stone appears to have been selected. However it has been observed that the stone on which the nuts were being cracked, the anvil, was made level by inserting a stone under it at the low end. This is an example of a physical causal understanding. The nut cracking technique of the Tai chimpanzee requires about ten years of practice to master in the wild.

New Caledonian crows manufacture and use several types of tools for extractive foraging of invertebrates, including straight and hooked sticks, and complex stepped-cut flat tools made from leaves (Chappell and Kacelnik, 2002). These tools have some of the hallmarks of complex tool manufacture; form is imposed on the raw material with control of various shapes. A skilled tool-making technique is involved, and there is even standardisation of the shape of the finished tools. They show evidence of causal belief.

Chimpanzees and apes are thus at the edge of causal understanding as shown by their use of simple tools, such as trimming a grass reed to get out ants. But in no case of stone tool use is there evidence of modifying the structure of the stone to improve its function. All the above evidence makes clear that while primates and some birds use simple tools there is an almost total absence of causal beliefs in animals other than humans. In no case of stone tool use is there evidence that individual animals modified the structure of the stone in order to improve the tool's function, though a few cases of anvil stabilisation have in fact been observed. Crows have created tools with a specific form, but we don't know how they think about such processes and to what extent they have a concept of cause and effect. So while animals like crows and monkeys have some understanding of tool use, they have a very limited capacity for refining and combining objects to make better tools. The tools chimpanzees use have a narrow range of functions and there is little evidence that they can think up new functions for the same tool. Compare this with the way humans use a knife for a whole variety of purposes. Another important difference is that chimpanzees are slow to pick up skills from other animals. In essence, chimpanzees lack the technical intelligence needed for manipulating and transforming physical objects. The general consensus seems to be that primates lack causal beliefs.

Tools

What served as the prime mover in the evolution of the human brain? – technology or social behaviour? – and what were the adaptive advantages that led to the evolution of causal beliefs? A key issue is the relationship between causal beliefs, tool use and language; there may have been a mutual positive synergy between all three, possibly linked by the development of tool use (Gibson and Ingold, 1993). A distinguishing feature of hominid tool use, compared to that by apes, is the use of secondary tools, i.e. tools that were made by the use of another tool. Thus even simple stone tools require a hammer stone. It may be that stone hammers, like those used by chimpanzees to break hard-shelled fruits or nuts, were then used to shape rocks into cutting tools.

The evolutionary advantage of causal beliefs, obvious even in young children as well as all adults, may be related to the making of complex tools. I suggest the key factor is that one cannot make a complex tool without a concept of cause and effect. By complex I mean a tool that has a well characterised form for the use to which it will be put and, even more importantly, any tool made out of two pieces put together like a spear with a stone head. It is only with causal beliefs that technology became possible, and it was technology – the ability to physically interact with the environment – that made life easier. Just consider things as simple as the basket and the wheel.

Darwin was insistent on the continuity of mental skills as observed in chimpanzees, in using sticks to get ants, for example. But he was forced to concede to the Duke of Argyll who claimed that "the fashioning of an implement for a special purpose is absolutely peculiar to humans". This is fundamental to my ideas about beliefs and their origins. "It is the technological path that we humans took that has separated us most profoundly from our primate ancestry and from our extant primate relatives. Our technological adaptation has been shaping our evolutionary trajectory in crucial ways for the past several million years." (Schick and Toth, 1993). Note how this view, to which I am committed, differs from those who put the emphasis on social relationships. Julian Huxley in 1941 claimed that there is no essential difference between man's conscious use of a chipped flint as an implement and his design of the most elaborate machine. How right he is. Tool use was probably the most important adaptation in human evolution. There is even evidence that specific regions of the human brain are associated with tool use.

Tomasello (1999) believes that the normal processes of biological evolution – genetic variation and natural selection – could have created one by one each of the cognitive skills necessary for complex tool use, language and complex social organisation. Is 250,000 years not enough? He believes the answer lies in cultural transmission. This applies in particular to tool use and language, and so the key, in his view, is the evolution of a new form of social cognition. Humans identify with other humans more than apes do with other apes.

Contrary to the emphasis I and others have given to tool use in human evolution, there is a quite widely held view that primate brain evolution has been driven principally by the demands of the social world rather than by the demands of interacting with the physical environment. Robin Dunbar (1996, 2006) claims that there is a growing consensus that primate brain evolution has been driven principally by the demands of the social world, interactions with the environment and particularly with other members of the group. He argues that human brain growth, language, and intelligent behaviour were evolutionary changes related to the increasing social complexity of hominid community life. This argument is partly based on the increase in size of that part of the brain, the neocortex, which correlates with social skills such as mating behaviour, grooming and social play. Dunbar found that changes in the size of the neocortex correlate with changes in social variables, such as group size, rather than changes in the physical environment. There is also some evidence that neocortex size correlates with some measures of social skills such as mating behaviour. For Dunbar, the evolution of language is intimately linked to its ability to facilitate the bonding of larger groups and cooperation within them. But without causal thinking about interactions of objects I find it hard to see how improved social understanding could have been a real advantage, or how it could have led to technology.

Even though human ancestors were on two feet and with free hands some four million years ago, tool use is usually assumed to only go back two to three million years. The tools were used for both butchery and plant preparation, and show a clear understanding of the mechanical properties and geometry of the materials. In order to detach sharp–edged flakes, the core must be struck obliquely with some skill.

Manual dexterity required sensory and motor changes in the brain. The modern human brain must have evolved in relation to the skill involved in tool use. That very slow improvement over some one million years in tool making abilities may have been related to the necessity for further adaptive changes in the brain. The earliest primitive human appeared about 1.8 million years ago with a brain size of 600 cc to 200 cc more than an ape. *Homo sapiens*, modern humans like us, only emerged 100,000 years ago with a brain that had increased from about 600 cc to 1,300 cc. Brains of modern humans are three times larger than other primates, and 75 per cent of the growth occurs after birth, while the corresponding figure in the chimpanzee is 40 per cent. Increase in brain size has costs. Neural tissue of the brain has the greatest nutritional requirement in the body, and so increase in brain size is a major metabolic burden which could require new and improved technology to acquire food.

Both manual and vocal skills depend on programmed sequences in the brain. It has been the areas of motor control, control of hand and body movements, that have undergone considerable expansion. Areas of the frontal lobes linked with association and motor control, like the premotor area, have increased in size compared to other primates. It is in the premotor area that the commands for motor activity are elaborated. Frontal lobe damage can lead to compulsive grasping or the inability to use a tool even while understanding its function. Specific regions of our brains are associated with tool use (Johnson-Frey, 2003). Chimpanzees do have basic motor skills and can be taught to trace complex patterns. Aimed throws are rare among monkeys, though chimpanzees and capuchins can do it.

But what about the hand itself? Sir Charles Bell in 1833 published his treatise on 'The Hand, Its Mechanism and Vital Endorsements, as Evincing Design'. He used it to support his religious faith, for who else but God could have designed so amazing a machine? For him, the hand was central to human life. And E. O. Wilson, more than 150 years later, again argues that any theory of intelligence – and this must include belief though he does not say so – must put at the fore the interdependence of brain and hand function. The human hand differs from apes in that it has a longer thumb and less curved finger bones. It is capable of both a power grip and a precision one – it can be used to wield a club or thread a needle. The early hominid hand had a short thumb and the gorilla has one very similar to the human, but rarely uses tools. Apes do have a thumb that can be brought into contact with the index finger, but have great difficulty bringing it right across the hand, which we humans do with ease each time we grasp a handle of a hammer. Of course, freeing the hands from walking with the evolution of bipedalism was a crucial step. It is also important to recognise that it is not just the shape of hands that matters, but the ability of the brain to control their complex movements. Human manipulative skills are much greater than those of apes, and this is genetically determined because it is an intrinsic property of the brain. It has been suggested that opposability of the thumb, and the associated wondrous dexterity, completely transformed our ancestor's relationship with external objects. This relationship could have promoted human consciousness as manipulation of objects became a self-conscious activity; once the individual becomes an agent operating on external objects in numerous different ways causal beliefs are involved.

Tool-making ancestors had to be competent field geologists in recognising which rocks were suitable for toolmaking. Some two million years ago humans had acquired the not inconsiderable skill of making stone tools. Even for a modern human, it requires several hours to become proficient at making such tools. A carefully controlled sharp glancing blow is required to initiate a fracture in making the tool. To achieve the symmetry and form of the hand axe, a concept of cause and effect was certainly necessary and present. Great care has to be taken in the initial selection of the stone and detaching the flakes.

A key feature of hominid tools is the use of secondary tools, that is objects used as tools in order to make another tool. Thus even simple stone tools require a hammer stone. It may be that stone hammers, like those used by chimpanzees to break hard-shelled fruits or nuts, were then used to shape rocks for cutting tools. Our tool-making ancestors also had to be competent field geologists in recognising which rocks were suitable for tool-making. Some two million years ago, humans had acquired the not inconsiderable skill needed to make stone tools, yet even for a modern human it requires several hours to master. A carefully controlled sharp glancing blow is required to initiate a fracture in making the tool.

Progress in tool making was very slow, and may have required further evolution of the brain to give improved causal understanding. It took at least a million years to go from the stone axes to other and more complex tools. The oldest wood tools are well made javelin-like spears found in Germany and dating back some 400,000 years. By 300,000 years ago, tool making skills had accelerated and by the Middle Stone Age there is clear evidence of hafted tools, that is composites, with the components joined together. This was a major advance and I wish to argue that one clearly cannot make such a tool – joining quite different pieces together – without having a very clear concept of cause and effect. One would have to understand that the two pieces serve different purposes, and imagine how the tool could be used. One could not discover such a composite tool by chance. It was a fundamental advance in the technological revolution that actually makes us human, and then drove human evolution.

This technology, unlike making the simpler stone tools by flaking, which is essentially repetitive in nature, is complex and the technologies are non-repetitive and require fine hand motor control to fit the components together. It is not quite clear to what extent human tool use was socially cooperative.

As already noted progress with this technology was slow, and slivers of flint used as blades date back only 100,000 years. Bone artefacts for harpoons are of a similar age. Over the last 40,000 years, bone, antler and ivory were fashioned as tools, particularly for making pointed tools such as spears and harpoons. About 20,000 years ago, bows and arrows make their appearance, together with needles and sewing. The tools of the Upper Palaeolithic suggest a possible division of labour for tools which were more difficult to make. Blades as distinct from flakes were now common, as were composite tools, and the use of a variety of materials like bone. Such techniques took time to master. Moreover some of the tools were no longer merely extensions of common bodily movements. A hammer is essentially a weighted fist. By contrast, using a saw involves recognising a quite new principle, and this is again true of the needle, which was of such importance to people surviving the last ice age.

The use of fire was a major 'invention'. Fire, and how to spark it, presents a severe problem. Just how long ago humans began using fire is not clear and estimates vary from 300,000 years to 1.5 million years. Use of fire requires clear causal beliefs about how to ignite a fire and keep it going. The ability to ignite a fire may have evolved over many generations. Striking two flints against each other, or rubbing wood together to give a spark, would most likely have occurred by chance. It was the recognition that this would ignite a fire that was crucial. Before the discovery of ignition, fire had to be borrowed from natural sources. This probably involved significant organisation of those who brought the fire and those who kept it going. In a way this might have been one of the origins of market exchange, and may have led to the advantage of humans knowing about numbers – they could then bargain and trade in a reliable and fair manner.

Abundant artefacts are associated with the fully modern skeletons of 40,000 years ago. They had not only stone tools but tools of bone which were suitable for shaping into, for example, fishhooks. They had mastered the invention of sewing, and making rope and baskets. The tools used by these ancestors are rather complex. Anthropologists tried to make these tools and found it required a five-step sequence, as well as the initial selection of the right materials. Making such tools could not be done by imitation alone; instruction was most likely involved.

No animal uses a container to carry food or water, though a captive chimp has been reported to use a coconut shell to carry water. Pots and bags are totally human. There have been many solutions as to how to interact with the environment in useful and quite simple ways, all of which require a concept of cause and effect. Consider, for, example 'simple' tools like digging sticks that humans use in a complex way. Humans also spend hours tracking game which clearly requires causal thinking. Planning ahead is essential, and trackers also needed an understanding of the environment they lived in, both animals and plants.

Language

What then was the crucial change in evolution that led to causal thinking and the ability to make tools and to interact with environment – effectively the origin of technology? The relationship in evolution between tool using, causal thinking and language is an interesting but very difficult problem; one might have served to haul along the others. It is striking that tool use and language both appear in children at about eighteen months. All three involve what Calvin (1993, 2003) has referred to as stringing things together. Most theories see language as a help to learning how tools are used and made. But it is recognised that tools and language share some critical features – rule-governed behaviour and common sequencing neurology. Human technology involves co-operation with others – individuals do not make tools alone. This is true today of the Aborigines. Calvin proposes an interesting possibility related to throwing. He examines the idea that throwing evolved to capture game. It provided action at a distance, and improved accuracy and distance would have been adaptive evolutionary steps. There could have been a transition from sticks to stones to a fast hand axe which might spin and inflict serious damage. Throwing required improved control of arm movements for accuracy, and throwing for hunting became linked to pointing, a key early gesture. Then pointing could have become associated with vocal grunts. Moreover, movements of the arm could distinguish predator from prey. Language may have had its origins in motor control. Evolution cannot invent something quite new but can only tinker with what is already there. As has been argued, the neurological basis of motor control has very similar features to the syntax of language. Just consider how the same muscles – 'words' – can be activated in an astonishing variety of movements – 'sentences' (Lieberman, 2000).

Both manual and vocal skills depend on programmed sequences in the brain. It has been the areas of motor control, control of hand and body movements, that have undergone considerable expansion. Areas of the frontal lobes linked with association and motor control, like the premotor area, have increased in size compared to other primates. It is in the premotor area that the commands for motor activity are elaborated. Frontal lobe damage can lead to compulsive grasping or the inability to use a tool even while understanding its function. Chimpanzees do have basic motor skills and can be taught to trace complex patterns. Aimed throws are rare among monkeys, though chimpanzees and capuchins can do it.

It is language that, in addition to causal beliefs, marks humans off from other species and its role in human evolution and its relationship to tool use and causal beliefs is a central problem. Alarm calls by animals communicate but contain no really factual information; and while bees do communicate information they do not use a language. Unlike human language, animals have closed communication systems. People use language, not just to signal emotional states or territorial claims, but to shape each other's minds. Gestures may have been involved in the origin of language but on their own they are not a language. Gorillas have been observed to make some thirty different gestures such as raising an arm before charging, putting hands on those of another, sucking their lower lip and then backing away, and poking another's body. Most involve some response. Even so, the gestures never involve a third object, or point to objects distant from themselves. By contrast, their vocalisations are much less complex.

In what way could language be related to the making and use of tools? Most theories see language helping in how tools are made and used. A few consider that it is tool use that actually led to language, or at least helped to lead to it. But it is recognised that tools and language share some critical features: tool use is sequential – motor actions strung together – and in this it resembles speech, which consists of a sequence of utterances. It is formally analogous to grammatical language. Both speech and composite tool manufacture involve sequences of non-repetitive fine motor control. While making a composite tool is a bit like making a sentence, describing how to make one is almost a short story. From an evolutionary point of view, language could not arise out of nothing. It had to evolve out of neural structures or cognitive abilities already present; motor control is an obvious possibility. But another possible origin relates to tool use and to having causal beliefs. It helps in thinking about causality if one has language, but having language itself requires causal thinking for that is what, for example, many verbs relate to.

Language has many metaphors, but two that are most commonly used relate to location in space, and cause and force. The equivalent of 'force' in causal belief may, in language, be a 'causal' or a 'doing' word, a verb. This relationship between verbs and causal thinking is an argument for believing that the evolution of language requires causal thinking. Many verbs would not have any meaning unless the individuals using them had beliefs in causes and effects. Verbs ranging from 'go', to 'hit', to 'throw', require causal thinking. Thus causal thinking preceded and was an essential prerequisite for language development. So we are back to the importance of tools being the driving force. Perhaps the slow progress in tool complexity is related to the evolution of language some 100,000 years ago. Language would help enormously with the construction and use of new tools, both in terms of co-operation and imaginative thinking.

Merlin Donald (1991) has argued that language emerged from the programming of the movements used to make tools and throw them. The actions used in making tools could have come to represent the tools themselves, and hunting and tool use could have been mimed. Note that children point before they speak. Note too, that signed language is very easily learned by children. Michael Corballis (2002) argues that human language arose from gesture rather than primate vocalisation. It is not a new view, and has its origins in the eighteenth century when Darwin recognised its possible significance. Gestures could have been the forerunners of spoken language but may have interfered with the tool making process, thus giving vocal language a distinct advantage. Children simultaneously develop hierarchical representations for both language and the manipulation of objects; they combine words into phrases at the same age as that at which they combine objects such as nuts and bolts. Moreover both are dependent on a region of the brain known as Broca's area. Constructing objects is rather similar to language, and it raises the question whether construction of either involves a similar set of beliefs.

But does the ability to make complex tools in fact require language? In an experiment, students were divided into two groups and one was told verbally how to make a stone tool together with a practical demonstration, while the other group was taught by silent example alone. Both groups found it quite tough, but those taught in silence did just as well as the other group. Imitation may have initially been sufficient. Tool-making and learning may not have been initially dependent on language. But it would have been difficult for early humans to acquire new beliefs from others without language. Trust about the reliability of such beliefs would have been an important issue, and could have helped establish the role of rulers and specialists.

Conclusions

A strong case can be made that a key step in human evolution that made *Homo sapiens* different from other primates was the acquisition of causal beliefs. Without such beliefs it would not have been possible for technology, which is the main driver of human evolution, to develop. Causal beliefs are essential for making complex tools and planning ahead, and all other mammals, including non-human primates, lack these abilities. That infants and children develop causal beliefs during their infancy shows that it has a strong genetic basis, though the neurological mechanisms involved are not yet known. The relationship between causal beliefs and the evolution of language, and changes in cognition and brain structure remains a tantalising problem.

References

Baillargeon, R., Kotovsky, L., and Needham, A. 1996. The acquisition of physical knowledge in infancy. In *Causal cognition*, pp. 79–116. Ed. D. Sperber et al. Oxford: Clarendon Press.

Calvin, W. H. 1993. The unitary hypothesis: A common neural circuitry for novel manipulations, language, plan ahead, and throwing. In *Tools, language, and cognition in human evolution*, pp. 230–250. Eds. K. R. Gibson and T. Ingold. Cambridge: Cambridge University Press.

Calvin, W. H. 2003. *A brief history of the mind: from apes to intellect and beyond.* Oxford: Oxford University Press.

Chappell, J. and Kacelnik, A. 2002. Tool selectivity in a non-primate, the New Caledonian crow (*Corvus moneduloides*). *Animal Cognition* 5, 71–78.

Corballis, M. C. 2002. *From hand to mouth – the origins of language.* Princeton NJ: Princeton University Press.

Corrigan, R. and Denton, P. 1996. Causal understanding as a developmental primitive. *Dev. Rev.* 16, 162–202.

Dunbar, R. 1996. *Grooming, gossip and the evolution of language.* London: Faber.

Dunbar, R. 2004. *The human story.* London: Faber.

Donald, M. 1991. *The origins of the modern mind.* Cambridge, MA: Harvard University Press.

Gibson, K. R. and Ingold, T. 1993. *Tools, language, and cognition in human evolution.* Cambridge: Cambridge University Press.

Gopnik, A. et al. 1999. *How babies think.* London: Weidenfeld.

Johnson-Frey, S. H. 2003. The neural basis of complex tool use in humans. *Trends. Cog. Sci.* 8, 71–78.

Leslie, A. M. 1996. A theory of agency. In *Causal cognition,* pp. 121–141. Ed. D. Sperber et al. Oxford: Clarendon Press.

Lieberman, P. 2000. *Human language and our reptilian brain.* Cambridge, MA: Harvard University Press.

Oakley, K. 1949. *Man the tool-maker.* London: British Museum Press.

Povinelli, D. J. 2000. *Folk Physics for Apes.* Oxford: Oxford University Press.

Schacter, D. L. and Scarry, E. (eds.) 2000. *Memory, brain, and belief.* Cambridge, MA: Harvard University Press.

Schick, K. D. and Toth, N. 1993. *Making silent stones speak.* London: Weidenfeld and Nicolson.

Schlottmann, A. 2001. Perception versus knowledge of cause-and-effect in children: When seeing is believing. *Current Directions in Psychological Science* 10, 111–115.

Sperber, D. et al. 1996. *Causal cognition.* Oxford: Clarendon Press.

Tomasello, M. 1999. *The cultural origins of human cognition.* Cambridge, MA: Harvard University Press.

Wolpert, L. 1993. *The unnatural nature of science.* London: Faber.

12: The Cooking Enigma

Richard Wrangham

This chapter considers the role of cooking in the evolution of human diet. People in every culture know how to make fire, and everywhere they use it to improve their food (Tylor, 1878; Gott, 2002; Wrangham and Conklin-Brittain, 2003; see fig. 1). But "no beast is a cook," as Boswell (1773) asserted. This difference between humans and other animals has long been appreciated, and some have even used it to define us: Boswell (1773) called humans the "cooking animal". But while cooking is indisputably unique to humans, its evolutionary significance is a matter of debate. There are two contrasting views.

The first, which is conventional wisdom, sees cooking as merely one of many extra-oral food-processing techniques (such as pounding, grinding, or drying) that can raise food quality. According to this view, cooking may be valuable in facilitating meal preparation but it is not important for understanding human adaptation. For example, it would not be considered to have led to fundamental changes in the human digestive system. In line with this idea, the ecological effect of human diet choice and foraging strategies is often discussed without considering the influence of cooking (e.g. Kaplan et al., 2000). Similarly, studies of the evolution of human feeding behavior often focus on dietary composition without considering extra-oral food-processing in general or cooking in particular (e.g. Eaton and Konner, 1985; Ungar and Teaford, 2002). The essential implication is that human biological evolution was not influenced in any major ways by the adoption of cooking and that evolutionists can therefore ignore it.

Figure 1 A baboon on a Hadza fire. © Frank Marlowe.

The radical alternative is that cooking is a core human adaptation that has importantly directed our evolution, or as Coon (1954) wrote, that cooking was "the decisive factor in leading man from a primarily animal existence into one that was more fully human." This perspective suggests that for humans, unlike the other 308 species, cooked food is a need rather than an option. Accordingly, our reliance on cooking results from certain features of human biology that have evolved in response to the control of fire, such as our small guts, small teeth, and slow life histories (Wrangham and Conklin-Brittain, 2003). From a dietary perspective, it means that humans are distinguished as much by what we do with our food as by the food sources themselves (whether meat, roots or grasses, for example). In short, this view sees Boswell's characterization of humans as the "cooking animal" as not only biologically but also evolutionarily significant (Wrangham et al., 1999; Ulijaszek, 2002).

A few authors take an intermediate position. Notably, Brace (1995) has argued that cooking is an important option that has led to limited evolutionary effects, particularly a reduction in tooth size.

In this chapter, I present arguments relevant to resolving this debate.

Why cooking is expected to have evolutionary effects

The contrasting views on the role of cooking agree in at least one respect. Both acknowledge that cooking improves food. Some benefits vary across food types, such as reducing physical barriers, changing molecular structure, reducing toxin loads, and defrosting (Stahl, 1984; Brace, 1995; Wrangham and Conklin-Brittain, 2003). Others appear to be consistent. For example, cooking leads to bursting of cells, making food molecules more available. It also tenderizes meat and softens plant foods, thereby making chewing easier. In addition, it reduces water content and increases the proportion of edible material (Wrangham and Conklin-Brittain, 2003).

Exactly how these benefits translate into fitness has not been well established. However, current data suggest that they may lead to significant energetic savings. Thus, the cost of digestion is a high proportion of total energy expenditure in all animals. In humans it has been measured at around 5–15 per cent of energy expenditure (Westerterp, 2004). In other animals, the cost may be higher, for example, up to 43 per cent of energy intake in snakes (Secor and Faulkner, 2002). But the cost of digestion varies not only between species but also with food quality. For instance, high-protein diets increase the cost of digestion by about 30 per cent compared with high-fat diets (Westerterp-Plantenga et al., 1999). Relevant to cooking, large meals that are physically hard cost more (e.g. a 50–100 per cent increase in cost of digestion in toads; Secor and Faulkner, 2002).

By softening food and reducing meal size, therefore, cooking can be expected to reduce the cost of digestion, for example, by accelerating the digestive process. One measure of the rate at which foods are digested is the glycemic index, which assesses the rate of appearance of glucose in the blood following ingestion. As expected, the glycemic index is indeed consistently increased by cooking (Brand et al., 1985; Bjorck et al., 2000). Experiments are needed to test the hypothesis that proteins and lipids are also digested and absorbed more rapidly in cooked than raw foods. If so, cooked food may prove to offer consistent energy savings across all food types. Possible avenues for cost-saving include reduced energetic cost per gram of food, reduced time for the gut to be metabolically active, and a reduced size of gut needed to digest the food.

Evidence that cooking consistently improves food quality is suggestive in the context of evolution because even a small change in food quality can have very important effects. Among Galápagos finches, for example, a brief period of ecological constraint that causes a shift in diet can lead to the rapid evolution of larger or smaller beaks by natural selection (Boag and Grant, 1981; Grant and Grant, 2002). Such evolutionary changes in digestive anatomy then constrain future diet choices. Even minor changes in dietary adaptations, in their turn, are known to have widespread effects on various aspects of species biology.

Chimpanzees (*Pan troglodytes*) and gorillas (*Gorilla gorilla*) offer an instructive example of this process. These two species have closely similar diets. Both choose ripe fruits when they are available, being almost equally frugivorous (Tutin and Fernandez, 1985; Remis, 1997; Wrangham et al., 1998). When ripe fruits are scarce, both species also supplement their diets with fibrous foods such as piths and leaves. Despite this strong overall dietary similarity, there is one important difference that emerges from multiple field studies of the two species (gorillas, 11 sites; chimpanzees, 12 sites; Wrangham, 2005). In habitats with little or no fruit, gorillas can survive by eating fibrous foods for 100 per cent of their feeding time (Doran et al., 2002). Chimpanzees never do so (Basabose, 2002). This contrast is attributable to differences in digestive adaptation between the two species, probably including both dental traits and features of gut anatomy and dynamics. Thus, gorilla molars have long shearing edges compared with those of chimpanzees, and gut passage rates in gorillas are longer than in chimpanzees, allowing more opportunity for fermentation of plant fiber (Milton, 1999; Remis et al., 2001; Remis and Dierenfeld, 2004).

The relative ability of these two apes to rely on the foliar component of the diet might at first glance appear to be a trivial matter. But many consequences appear to follow from it, even aside from digestive adaptations. There are differences in distributional range for example. Gorillas successfully occupy high-altitude forests without fruits, where they live at high density with excellent survival and reproduction (Robbins et al., 2001). Chimpanzees, by contrast, continue to be selective frugivores when living at high altitudes. As a result they are limited to habitats below 2,600 m altitude, unlike gorillas, and at high altitudes they live in small, scattered groups (Yamagiwa et al., 1996; Basabose, 2002).

Life history differences also appear to be influenced by the dietary shift. In contrast to expectations from their being larger than chimpanzees, gorillas have a shorter and faster life history pattern compared with chimpanzees (Tutin, 1994). For example gorillas mature earlier, have an earlier first birth (gorillas around nine years; chimpanzees around fourteen years), and have a shorter interbirth interval (gorillas 3.9 years; chimpanzees 5.0–6.2 years; Knott, 2001). While the reasons for the accelerated schedule of growth and reproduction in gorillas are debated (Knott, 2001), they conform precisely to life history differences that are found between folivorous and nonfolivorous primates in general (Leigh, 1994). The ability to digest a leaf diet may demand rapid development of digestive abilities and is thought to allow a sufficiently predictable food regime that it permits the evolution of rapid rates of growth and reproduction (Janson and van Schaik, 1993; Leigh, 1994; Knott, 2001).

Finally, there is a striking species difference in grouping patterns. During periods with temporary fruit scarcity chimpanzees experience intense scramble competition for fruits, such that they then tend to travel in small groups or alone (Wrangham, 2000). But when fruit is scarce in gorilla habitats, groups of gorillas respond by eating more terrestrial foliage, with little tendency for groups to fragment (Goldsmith, 1999). Because this foliage is distributed homogeneously compared with the widely separated fruit trees required by chimpanzees, it apparently allows gorillas to remain in more stable groups than chimpanzees. The difference in grouping patterns, in turn, is probably responsible for other important contrasts between the species, such as in sexual behavior, the degree of sexual dimorphism, and aggression (Wrangham, 1979; Yamagiwa, 1999).

The comparison of chimpanzees and gorillas thus illustrates how a relatively small change in diet (an ability to survive on foliage without fruits) implies substantial effects on biogeography, life history and social behavior. Because cooking is universal and has many effects on the diet, it can reasonably be expected to have effects at least as large. For example, it should increase the range of edible foods and therefore allow extension into new biogeographical zones. Other things being equal, it should also provide a more predictable food supply during periods of scarcity because it enables a range of otherwise inedible items to be used. It should have further effects by softening food. For example, it should lead to a greater ability of adults to provision infants, whose dentition is too immature to allow hard chewing, other than by giving milk. It should likewise cause a substantial drop in the amount of time that individuals spend chewing, with large consequences for the species activity budgets (Wrangham and Conklin-Brittain, 2003).

In addition to raising food quality, cooking also radically changes the nature of food distribution. Thus a species that cooks is obliged to assemble food items into a location (onto or next to a fire) that is fixed for at least the time that it takes to cook. Unlike the ordinary feeding pattern of any nonhuman ape, therefore, this means that a cooking population is exposed to intragroup competition over a valuable accumulated food pile of food. Among other animals, including primates, the distribution of food is considered to be a key variable that sculpts social relationships. For example, among chimpanzees by far the most valuable type of concentrated food supply is meat. A successful hunt therefore commonly leads to intense competition, including direct aggression and various complex forms of social manipulation (Goodall, 1986).

In short, the adoption of cooking is expected to be accompanied by a series of large influences on various important biological systems, such as foraging behavior, digestive strategy, infant development, geographical range, and the regulation of social competition. The fact that cooking is a human universal, therefore, ought to be intensely provocative for students of human evolution because it raises the question of whether the practice of cooking has indeed influenced these and other systems.

Why cooking appears not to have had important evolutionary effects

Cooking was once considered to be an important influence on human evolution. In 1871, Charles Darwin considered "the art of making fire" as "probably the greatest [discovery], excepting language, ever made by man." He specifically cited the process "by which hard and stringy roots can be rendered digestible, and poisonous roots or herbs innocuous" (Dar in, 1871, 1:132). Likewise Frazer (1930, p. 1) similarly suggested th t "Of all human inventions the discovery of the method of kindling fire has probably been the most momentous and far-reaching," and he discussed the importance of cooking in this respect.

But in the second half of the twentieth century, such ideas largely disappeared. The main reason appears to have been the pattern that has crystallized in archaeological data. Data showed that fire was controlled in several sites in southern Europe during the Middle Paleolithic back to at least 250,000 years ago, and probably as early as 300,000–500,000 years ago (James, 1989; Straus, 1989; Gamble, 1993; Monnier et al., 1994; Brace, 1995). This evidence has been widely regarded as so much stronger than any indications of the control of fire in earlier times that the Middle Paleolithic is now conventionally interpreted as the first time that humans used fire. There is admittedly scattered evidence for earlier control of fire, but none of it is sufficiently convincing to persuade the skeptics (see table 1). In addition,

Table 1 Suggestive Evidence of the Control of Fire Before 400,000 Years Ago

Site	Mya	Evidence	Reference
Gesher-Benet, Ya'aqov, Israel	0.8	Burnt seeds, wood, flint hearthlike pattern	Goren-Inbar, 2004
Chesowanja, Baringo, Kenya	>1.4	Burnt clay + stone tools; low disturbance; 600° C temperature; hearthlike pattern	Gowlett et al., 1981; Gowlett, 1999
Middle Awash, Ethiopia	>1.42	Red patches, phytoliths	Clark and Harris, 1985
Gadeb, Ethiopia	0.7–1.4	Thermomagnetism	Clark and Kurashina 1980; Clark and Harris, 1985
Swartkrans, South Africa	1.5	Burned bones, 600° C temperature	Brain, 1993
Olduvai (+ Turkana), Tanzania	1.6	"Pot-lid" burning of basalt/quartz tools	Ludwig, 2000
Koobi Fora, Turkana, Kenya	1.6	Red patches ($n = 20$); archaeomagnetic; thermoluminescence; palynology	Barbetti, 1986; Bellomo, 1991; Rowlett, 2000

there are some well-known sites dated earlier than 500,000 years that show no evidence for control of fire. For example, the *Homo antecessor* site of Atapuerca, Spain, is dated at 800,000 years and has been examined sufficiently carefully to suggest that the hominids there did not use fire (Arsuaga et al., 1997; de Castro et al., 1997). To those who regard absence of evidence as evidence of absence, these facts suggest that the Middle Paleolithic was the first time when humans controlled fire (e.g. Carbonell, 1999).

According to such evidence, therefore, *Homo* must have relied on raw food before the Middle Paleolithic. In that case, if the adoption of cooking strongly influenced human biology, a suite of changes should be visible in our ancestors' evolutionary anatomy around 300,000–500,000 years ago. In fact, however, the evolutionary changes in anatomy that are recorded around that time were trivial. In Europe *Homo neanderthalensis* evolved from *Homo heidelbergensis*, while in Africa *H. heidelbergensis* (*rhodesiensis*) continued with little change until the origin of *Homo sapiens* around 200,000 years ago. This evolutionary quiescence implies that if fire was indeed first controlled in the Middle Paleolithic, cooking had little impact on human evolution.

The cooking enigma

These facts constitute a profound puzzle. On the one hand, cooking is absent among animals, universal in humans, and rich in potent biological consequences. It is therefore expected to have a strong impact on evolutionary biology. On the other hand, archaeological data place the acquisition of cooking at a time when nothing dramatic was happening in human evolution. The cooking enigma, therefore, is how cooking became a human universal without having visible effects on our evolutionary biology.

Three kinds of solution have been suggested. I label them here by the time when they conclude that cooking became a human universal. The first two ("Late" and "Sneak") are both based on the assumption that cooking has done little or nothing to influence our biology.

The Late solution

The Late solution suggests that cooking has been adopted too recently to have had time to influence our evolutionary biology.

Milton (2002, p. 112) suggested this idea: "Relatively recent changes in certain features of the modern human diet (e.g. cooking of most foods ...) may, in an evolutionary sense, have occurred so rapidly and so recently that human biology has not yet had time to adapt to them." Since speciation can occur in less than 25,000 years (Gould, 2002), the Late solution implies that if cooking has not had the time to affect our species' biology, it must have been adopted very recently indeed (e.g. less than 25,000 years ago). To be reconciled with the Middle Paleolithic evidence for the control of fire, this hypothesis would have to suggest that fire was controlled for a long period without leading to cooking. That solution is hard to imagine. Even wild chimpanzees take advantage of natural fires to eat foods that have been cooked by chance (Brewer, 1978).

The Sneak solution

The Sneak solution accepts the idea that cooking was adopted during the Middle Paleolithic and therefore concludes that it did little to affect human evolution or biology beyond eventually causing a reduction in tooth size (beginning around 100,000 years ago; Brace, 1995). In other words, cooking "sneaked" into human culture with minimal effect. In its favor, the Sneak solution provides a logical interpretation of the Middle Paleolithic archaeological evidence. Furthermore, it is compatible with the idea that cooking has only trivial nutritional effects, which was suggested by Lévi-Strauss (1969) and has not been completely abandoned. Against it lies the challenge of explaining why the apparently important results of adopting cooking, including a large improvement in the diet and a major change in the way in which it was distributed, did little or nothing to influence the course of human evolution. A possible solution is that previous food-processing techniques (such as pounding) closely mimicked the effects of cooking (Wrangham, 2006). However, such ideas have not been extensively developed.

The Basal solution

The Basal solution is the radical hypothesis that cooking was adopted around the origin of *Homo erectus* and was responsible for many of the features that characterize human evolutionary changes from australopithecines. It was proposed on the basis that many of the evolutionary changes that accompany hominization are easily explicable as responses to cooking, such as the reduced jaw and teeth, evidence of smaller gut, and yet higher energy expenditure (Wrangham et al., 1999). This solution faces the challenge of explaining why evidence of the control of fire is scarce before about 400,000 years ago. It must also be reconciled with the traditional idea that meat eating was the prime dietary mover of the evolution of the genus *Homo*.

I now consider evidence relevant to each of the three solutions.

The known

It is known that all human populations cook their food and that cooking consistently increases the palatability of food. It is also known that a diet of raw plant food creates substantial energetic problems for humans under even the best conditions. The implication is that humans are adapted to eating cooked food.

First, under subsistence conditions, there is no evidence of any population of humans, or even any individual, having lived off raw wild foods for more than a few days at a time. The longest period that I have found was Helena Valero's report of living alone in the 1930s for some seven months in the forests of Venezuela and Brazil, after escaping from Yanomamö Indians (Valero and Biocca, 1970). She began her adventure carrying a firebrand wrapped in leaves. After a few days a heavy rain put out her only fire. Not daring to steal fire from the villages, she was close to starvation until she found an abandoned banana plantation. She survived by eating raw bananas. This exceptional case illustrates that there is nothing specifically impossible about living off raw food, but the fact that the food was domesticated means that it tells us nothing about the capacity of humans to survive off wild foods.

Likewise, people often eat particular items raw (including various fruits or roots, or choice animal products such as blood or the fat in the tail of a fat-tailed sheep). But such items are normally part of a diet that also includes cooked food. Diets that are restricted to raw items are rare in all societies. They appear to be recorded most often among religious extremists and warriors on the march, who benefit by not using fires but are delighted when they can revert to cooking (Fernández-Armesto, 2002).

Thus there appear to be no cases of long-term survival on raw food in the wild.

Second, even under the most favorable conditions people who attempt to restrict their diets to raw food do not thrive. The most extreme examples are members of modern raw-food movements, who tend to live under urban conditions in which activity levels are low and the diet consists of domesticated agricultural plants, with high-quality items available year-round. Much of the food that these devotees eat is actually processed: methods include sprouting, pressing, and even drying up to 60° C (i.e., the temperature at which enzymes are supposedly killed), which under some definition would be scored as cooking.

Even under such benign conditions, people experience low caloric intake. There have been few attempts to calculate caloric intake, but in one energy assessment of a "raw-foodist" diet (for 141 vegans), daily caloric intake was 1,460 kcal and 1,830 kcal for women and men, respectively (Donaldson, 2001). This is less than needed for modern humans or predicted for *H. erectus* (Aiello and Wells, 2002). In addition, female reproductive function is seriously impaired on a raw-foodist diet. Thus, approximately 50 per cent of German women on a 100 per cent raw-foodist diet were amenorrheic, and more could be assumed to be subfecund (Koebnick et al., 1999). In sum, the sparse current evidence suggests that raw-food diets produce inadequate energy for humans even under excellent conditions, at least when the diet is dominated by plant items. Therefore, the implication is that in the wild, they could not thrive.

Third, even the most committed raw-foodists find it difficult to keep to their régime because they are consistently hungry even when they eat as much as possible. Some reduce this problem by including small amounts of cooked food in their diets, for example, up to 30 per cent of the diet (e.g. Koebnick et al., 1999).

These studies of raw-food diets are largely of vegetarians. They therefore do not resolve the question of whether humans can live off a raw diet that contains sufficient meat. However, they are still illuminating because they show that human digestion is incapable of the performance of a chimpanzee or gorilla.

Both chimpanzees and gorillas, by contrast to humans, would undoubtedly perform excellently on human raw-foodist diets, given that human raw-food diets offer superabundant access to foods with substantially lower-fiber concentrations than those in the diets of wild apes. We can therefore confidently conclude that digestion is adapted differently in humans from chimpanzees and that humans in subsistence society need cooked food under many and possibly all practical circumstances.

The unknown

Humans are not known to be able to survive on raw food, which suggests that during our evolution, we became physiologically committed to eating foods of such high quality that in most circumstances they had to be cooked. However, important gaps in our knowledge concern whether humans can survive on a raw diet with sufficient meat, whether human guts are better adapted to raw meat or to cooked food, what effects cooking has on food quality, and the conditions under which cooking can be recognized archaeologically.

First, although raw plant food is evidently a poor diet for humans, a sufficient inclusion of raw meat might, in theory, create an energetically adequate diet. The diets of Arctic foragers included a substantial component of raw meat, for example. Experiments are therefore needed to assess the optimal balance of meat and plants for humans to maximize caloric intake on a raw diet.

The theoretical reasons why a raw-food diet (at least when dominated by plant items even of the highest quality) is expected to be difficult for humans have not yet been elaborated. However, two obvious possibilities are that the plant component is bulky and that it would take a long time for humans to chew enough raw wild meat to satisfy requirements (Wrangham and Conklin-Brittain, 2003). The problem of excessive bulk comes from the fact that humans not only have small guts in total, and small hindguts in particular, in comparison to great apes, but they also have fast rates of gut passage. Small fermenting volumes (such as hindguts) and fast-gut passage rates are generally associated with diets having low levels of plant fiber and high density of calories because they do not allow adequate time or volume for retention of digesta, or for fermentation of fiber to volatile fatty acids (Milton, 1999; Lambert, 2002; Remis and Dierenfeld, 2004). Raw plant diets of chimpanzees have fiber levels averaging 32 per cent NDF in one study, far higher than the values in modern human diets (around 10 per cent; Conklin-Brittain et al., 1998; Conklin-Brittain et al., 2002).

Second, although the small and distinctive guts of humans appear well adapted to eating cooked food, the traditional conclusion from studies of gut anatomy and function is that the signals of adaptation to low-fiber foods of high caloric density reflect adaptation to a diet containing large amounts of high-quality raw food. For example, following Chivers and Hladik (1980), MacLarnon et al. (1986), Milton (1987), and others compared human gut proportions to other animals eating principally fauna, fruit, or insects. Milton (1987, p. 103) noted that human gut proportions were similar to those of *Cebus* and *Papio*, species that eat many insects and process their food with their hands. She concluded that the similarity represented "similar adaptive trends in gut morphology in response to diets made up of unusually high-quality dietary items that are capable of being digested and absorbed primarily in the small intestine."

The "unusually high-quality dietary items" to which humans are evidently adapted are normally considered to be meat and high-quality plant items such as fruits and seeds. But because researchers in this tradition have rarely considered whether cooked food provides a more reasonable explanation for the human digestive characteristics, the hypothesis that human guts are more closely adapted to cooked food than to raw meat remains to be tested. It should take into account that if the adaptation was to raw meat, plants had also to be eaten raw or not at all. This makes the fact that the human gut is poorly adapted to eating raw plant food puzzling.

There is therefore an obvious case for cooked food as the cause of the distinctive human guts. Human adaptation to a meat diet is certainly not as complete as in carnivores. Thus human teeth show little evidence of adaptation for carnivory, despite evidence of a slight shift toward long shearing edges in early hominids (Ungar, 2004). However, small teeth, as characterized by *Homo* compared to australopithecines, appear to be well adapted for eating cooked food (Lieberman et al., 2004; Lucas, 2004). Likewise, although the human digestive system does not appear to have been compared systematically with those of carnivores, it is clear that gut kinetics are radically different. Important, for example, is that although gut passage rates are similar between humans and dogs, dogs retain food in their stomachs for much longer (around four to twelve hours) than humans (around one to two hours; Ragir et al., 2000). In addition, humans show little evidence of being able to survive purely on meat diets, even when cooked (Speth and Spielmann, 1983).

Third, the nutritional effects of cooking are not well understood.

For example, it is often suggested that cooking might increase digestibility. But if digestibility means "the proportion (by dry weight) of a food item that can be digested," which is the standard usage, it is not necessarily an important variable. For example, the digestibility of a piece of pure meat appears to be close to 100 per cent regardless of whether it is cooked.

But even if the digestibility of meat is not affected by cooking, we can expect its nutritional value of meat to be increased as a result of cooking's effect in making it tender. Tenderizing should lead to a shorter time for a given weight of meat to be chewed and/or for it to be subsequently digested. By accelerating the digestive process, it can likewise be expected to increase the rate of gastric emptying and therefore to allow a shorter intermeal interval between meals (Petring and Blake, 1993; Pera et al., 2002).

Such effects of cooking should affect both meat and plant foods. A major effect of cooking, accordingly, may be that by tenderizing or softening food, it shortens the digestive process and therefore both reduces the energetic costs of digestion and increases the rate at which total calories can be absorbed (if the individual maximizes the rate of ingestion). This prediction conforms to evidence that merely by eating a softer diet animals have such reduced energetic costs of digestion that they have significantly higher energy gain (Oka et al., 2003; Wrangham, 2006).

Fourth, it is too early to be confident that the Middle Paleolithic marked the first control of fire, given the persistence of evidence from earlier times (see table 1). The recent claim for control of fire at 790,000 years at the Benot Ya'aqov site in Israel is supported by burned flints, seeds, and wood of six species found in hearthlike spatial patterns (Goren-Inbar et al., 2004). If further evidence for control of fire is found around this time but not earlier, it will support the notion that the first fire-using species was *H. heidelbergensis*, as Foley (2002) suggested. This would not solve the cooking enigma, however, because the anatomical changes from *H. erectus* to *H. heidelbergensis* were rather small.

Further back, a series of campfire-sized red patches of fossilized earth at Koobi Fora in Kenya from 1.6 million years ago has been subjected to extensive analysis. Archaeomagnetic and thermoluminescent analysis appear to rule out these patches as products of bushfires, burning tree stumps, or lightning strikes. Fossilized phytoliths suggest that the putative fires were burned with palm wood. To Rowlett (1999) such studies

> have removed all doubt that even early *H. erectus* had the technological capability of cooking foodstuffs ... These researches make it clear that *H. erectus*... at Koobi Fora not only controlled fires but probably could create them and had food closely associated with the fireplaces. They clearly had the technological capability of cooking tubers and other foodstuffs.

In line with the idea that sites before 500,000 years ago had hearths that rarely left evidence, the accepted Middle Paleolithic sites, such as Pech de l'Azé, include elaborate fire systems suggestive of substantial accumulated traditions, including elementary hearths, paved hearths, and dugout hearths with draft channels (Straus, 1989). Fires tend to be found in caves, so that a possible explanation for the Middle Paleolithic "fire explosion" is that at this time, humans increased their cave habitation as a response to glaciation (Brace, 1995).

There are many other unknowns, of course; several of which are likely to be knowable eventually. We know nothing about the genetic differences between *Pan* and *Homo* relevant to adaptation to a cooked diet, or when the relevant genes spread in the human lineage. We have no developed theory of how the change in food distribution resulting from eating at cooking fires would have influenced the regulation of social competition, social norms, group size, or cognition. Also, scant thought has been given to how the more predictable and energy-rich diet offered by cooking would have affected life histories. It is intriguing to speculate that it would have allowed more investment in the immune system and therefore in longer lives.

The unknowable

Current data give us little hope of knowing much about the detailed origins of cooking. For example, how was fire first controlled? How long was it used without being made? How long was it controlled without being used for cooking? And what methods of food preparation were used by humans before cooking? There are no obvious ways to answer these questions. As a result, even when the archaeological evidence can more clearly distinguish between possible and definite sites for the control of fire, we may still be uncertain whether a given population of fire users cooked their food.

Summary

Evidence from raw-foodists indicate that under subsistence conditions humans would not survive long term on the kinds of raw foods that are available in the wild. This implies that, as indicated by our digestive systems, humans are adapted to dietary items of unusually high quality compared with other species and that humans' high diet quality normally comes from the food being cooked. Therefore, given that humans currently depend on cooking for their high-quality food, a key question is how long we have done so. There are three types of solution, each with its own puzzle.

The Late solution suggests that cooking is recent, that is, probably less than 25,000 years ago. This has the merit of explaining why the advent of cooking did little to influence the course of human evolution. It faces the considerable difficulty, however, of explaining how humans could have exerted sophisticated control of fire for at least 250,000 years without using it to cook their food. The Late solution is therefore highly improbable.

The Sneak solution suggests that cooking has been practiced for at least 250,000 years without causing any dramatic changes in human body size, sexual dimorphism, tooth size, or gross morphology. This response to the archaeological evidence leaves unanswered the puzzle of how an adaptive change in diet with large apparent consequences for various biological systems occurred without leaving its mark on human anatomy. Although the Sneak solution is the standard answer to the cooking enigma, no serious attempts have been made to explain why cooking apparently had such small effects on human evolution.

The Basal solution suggests that cooking has been practiced since the origin of *H. erectus* and was responsible for many of the morphological changes associated with the evolution of *H. erectus*. This fits the many indications that early *Homo* had an unusually high-quality diet (such as small teeth and jaws and long-distance locomotion). It faces the challenge, however, of understanding why archaeological sites before 500,000 years ago show no evidence of the control of fire that is sufficient to convince skeptics.

References

Aiello, L. C., and Wells, J. C. K. 2002. Energetics and the evolution of the genus *Homo*. *Annu. Rev. Anthropol.* 31, 323–338.

Arsuaga, J. L., Martinez, I., García, A., Carretero, J. M., Lorenzo, C., García, N., and Ortega, A. I. 1997. Sima de los Huesos (Sierra de Atapuerca, Spain). The Site. *J. Hum. Evol.* 33, 109–127.

Barbetti, M. 1986. Traces of fire in the archaeological record before one million years ago. *J. Hum. Evol.* 15, 771–781.

Basabose, A. K. 2002. Diet composition of chimpanzees inhabiting the montane forest of Kahuzi, Democratic Republic of Congo. *Am. J. Primatol.* 58, 1–21.

Bellomo, R. V. 1991. Identifying traces of natural and humanly-controlled fire in the archaeological record: The role of actualistic studies. *Archaeol. Mont. Butte* 32, 75–93.

Bjorck, I., Liljeberg, H., and Ostman, E. 2000. Low glycaemic-index foods. *Br. J. Nutr.* 83, S149–S155.

Boag, P. T., and Grant, P. R. 1981. Intense natural selection in a population of Darwin's finches (*Geospizinae*) in the Galápagos. *Science* 214, 82–85.

Boswell, J. 1773. *Journal of a Tour to the Hebrides with Samuel Johnson, LL. D.* London: Oxford University Press.

Brace, C. L. 1995. *The Stages of Human Evolution*. Englewood Cliffs, NJ: Prentice-Hall.

Brain, C. K. 1993. The occurrence of burnt bones at Swartkrans and their implications for the control of fire by early hominids. In: Brain, C. K. (Ed.), *Swartkrans. A Cave's Chronicle of Early Man*. Transvaal Museum Monograph No. 8, Transvaal, pp. 229–242.

Brand, J. C., Nicholson, P. L., Thorburn, A. W., and Truswell, A. S. 1985. Food processing and the glycemic index. *Am. J. Clin. Nutr.* 42, 1192–1196.

Brewer, S. 1978. *The Forest Dwellers*. London: Collins.

Carbonell, E. 1999. "Comment" on Wrangham et al. (1999). *Curr. Anthropol.* 40, 580–581.

Chivers, D. J., and Hladik, C. M. 1980. Morphology of the gastrointestinal tract in primates: Comparison with other mammals in relation to diet. *J. Morphol.* 166, 337–386.

Clark, J. D., and Harris, J. W. K. 1985. Fire and its role in early hominid lifeways. *Afr. Archaeol. Rev.* 3, 3–27.

Clark, J. D., and Kurashina, H. 1980. New Plio–Pleistocene archaeological occurrences from the Plain of Gadeb, Upper Webi Schebele basin, Ethiopia, and a statistical comparison of the Gadeb sites with other Early Stone Age assemblages. *L'Anthropologie* 18, 161–187.

Conklin-Brittain, N. L., Wrangham, R. W., and Hunt, K. D. 1998. Dietary response of chimpanzees and cercopithecines to seasonal variation in fruit abundance. II. Macronutrients. *Int. J. Primatol.* 19, 971–998.

Conklin-Brittain, N. L., Wrangham, R. W., and Smith, C. C., 2002. A two-stage model of increased dietary quality in early hominid evolution: The role of fiber. In: Ungar, P., and Teaford, M. (Eds.), *Human Diet: Its Origin and Evolution.* Westport, CT: Bergin & Garvey, pp. 61–76.

Coon, C. S. 1954. *The Story of Man: From the First Human to Primitive Culture and Beyond.* New York: Knopf.

Darwin, C. 1871. *The Descent of Man and Selection in Relation to Sex.* Chicago: Encyclopaedia Britannica.

de Castro, J. M. B., Arsuaga, J. L., Carbonell, E., Rosas, A., Martinez, I., and Mosquera, M. 1997. A hominid from the Lower Pleistocene of Atapuerca, Spain: Possible ancestor to Neanderthals and modern humans. *Science* 276, 1392–1395.

Donaldson, M. S. 2001. Food and nutrient intake of Hallelujah vegetarians. *Nutr. Food Sci.* 31, 293–303.

Doran, D. M., and McNeilage, A. 1998. Gorilla ecology and behavior. *Evol. Anthropol.* 6, 120–131.

Doran, D. M., McNeilage, A., Greer, D., Bocian, C., Mehlman, P., and Shah, N. 2002. Western lowland gorilla diet and resource availability: New evidence, cross-site comparisons, and reflections on indirect sampling methods. *Am. J. Primatol.* 58, 91–116.

Eaton, S. B., and Konner, M. 1985. Paleolithic nutrition: A consideration of its nature and current implications. *New Engl. J. Med.* 312, 283–289.

Fernández-Armesto, F. 2002. *Near a Thousand Tables: A History of Food.* New York: Free Press.

Foley, R. 2002. Adaptive radiations and dispersals in hominin evolutionary ecology. *Evol. Anthropol.* 11, 32–37.

Frazer, J. G. 1930. *Myths of the Origins of Fire.* New York: Hacker Art Books.

Gamble, C. S. 1993. *Timewalkers: The Prehistory of Global Civilization.* Cambridge, MA: Harvard University Press.

Goldsmith, M. L. 1999. Ecological constraints on the foraging effort of western gorillas (*Gorilla gorilla gorilla*) at Bai Hokou, Central African Republic. *Int. J. Primatol.* 20, 1–23.

Goodall, J. 1986. *The Chimpanzees of Gombe: Patterns of Behavior.* Cambridge, MA: Harvard University Press.

Goren-Inbar, N., Alperson, N., Kislev, M. E., Simchoni, O., Melamed, Y., Ben-Nun, A., and Werker, E. 2004. Evidence of hominid control of fire at Gesher Benot Ya'aqov, Israel. *Science* 304, 725–727.

Gott, B. 2002. Fire-making in Tasmania: Absence of evidence is not evidence of absence. *Curr. Anthropol.* 43, 649–656.

Gould, S. J. 2002. *The Structure of Evolutionary Theory*. Cambridge, MA: Harvard University Press.

Gowlett, J. A. J. 1999. Lower and Middle Pleistocene archaeology of the Baringo Basin. In: Andrews, P., and Banham, P. (Eds.), *Late Cenozoic Environments and Hominid Evolution: A tribute to Bill Bishop*. London: Geological Society, pp. 123–141.

Gowlett, J. A. J., Harris, J. W. K., Walton, D. A., and Wood, B. A. 1981. Early archaeological sites, further hominid remains, and traces of fire from Chesowanja Kenya. *Nature* 294, 125–129.

Grant, P. R., and Grant, B. R. 2002. Unpredictable evolution in a 30-year study of Darwin's finches. *Science* 296, 707–711.

James, S. R. 1989. Hominid use of fire in the Lower and Middle Pleistocene: a review of the evidence. *Curr. Anthropol.* 30, 1–26.

Janson, C. H., and van Schaik, C. P. 1993. Ecological risk aversion in juvenile primates: Slow and steady wins the race. In: Pereira, M., and Fairbanks, L. (Eds.), *Juvenile Primates: Life History, Development and Behavior*. New York: Oxford University Press, pp. 57–76.

Kaplan, H., Hill, K., Lancaster, J., and Hurtado, A. M. 2000. A theory of human life history evolution: Diet, intelligence, and longevity. *Evol. Anthropol.* 9, 156–185.

Knott, C. 2001. Female reproductive ecology of the apes: Implications for human evolution. In: Ellison, P. (Ed.), *Reproductive Ecology and Human Evolution*. New York: Aldine, pp. 429–463.

Koebnick, C., Strassner, C., Hoffmann, I., and Leitzmann, C. 1999. Consequences of a long-term raw food diet on body weight and menstruation: Results of a questionnaire survey. *Ann. Nutr. Metab.* 43, 69–79.

Lambert, J. 2002. Digestive retention times in forest guenons (*Cercopithecus spp.*) with reference to chimpanzees (*Pan troglodytes*). *Int. J. Primatol.* 23, 1169–1185.

Leigh, S. R. 1994. Ontogenetic correlates of diet in anthropoid primates. *Am. J. Phys. Anthropol.* 94, 499–522.

Lévi-Strauss, C. 1969 . *The Raw and the Cooked. Introduction to a Science of Mytholog*. New York: Harper & Row.

Lieberman, D. E., Krovitz, G. E., Yates, F. W., Devlin, M., and St. Claire, M. 2004. Effects of food processing on masticatory strain and craniofacial growth in a retrognathic face. *J. Hum. Evol.* 46, 655–677.

Lucas, P. 2004. *How Teeth Work*. Cambridge, MA: Cambridge University Press.

Ludwig, B. 2000. New evidence for the possible use of controlled fire from ESA sites in the Olduvai and Turkana basins. *J. Hum. Evol.* 38, A17.

MacLarnon, A. M. D., Martin, R. D., Chivers, D. J., and Hladik, C. M. 1986. Some aspects of gastro-intestinal allometry in primates and other mammals. In: Sakka. M. (Ed.), *Definition et Origines de L'Homme*. Paris: CNRS, pp. 293–302.

Milton, K. 1987. Primate diets and gut morphology: Implications for hominid evolution. In: Harris, M., and Ross, E. B. (Eds.), *Food and Evolution: Towards a Theory of Human Food Habits*. Philadelphia, PA: Temple University Press, pp. 93–115.

Milton, K. 1999. A hypothesis to explain the role of meat-eating in human evolution. *Evol. Anthropol.* 8, 11–21.

Milton, K. 2002. Hunter-gatherer diets: Wild foods signal relief from diseases of affluence. In: Ungar, P. S., and Teaford, M. F. (Eds.), *Human Diet: Its Origin and Evolution*. Westport, CT: Bergin & Garvey, pp. 111–122.

Monnier, J. L., Hallegoue, B., Hinguant, S., Laurent, M., Auguste, P., Bahain, J. J., Falgueres, C., Geebhardt, A., Mergueria, D., Molines, N., Morzadec, H., and Yokoama, Y. 1994. A new regional group of the Lower Paleolithic in Brittany (France), recently dated by electron spin resonance. *C. R. Acad. Sci.* 319, 155–160.

Oka, K., Sakuarae, A., Fujise, T., Yoshimatsu, H., Sakata, T., and Nakata, M. 2003. Food texture differences affect energy metabolism in rats. *J. Dent. Res.* 82, 491–494.

Pera, P., Bucca, C., Borro, P., Bernocco, C., De Lillo, A., and Carossa, S. 2002. Influence of mastication on gastric emptying. *J. Dent. Res.* 81, 179–181.

Petring, O. U., and Blake, D. W. 1993. Gastric emptying in adults: an overview related to anaesthesia. *Anaesth. Intensive Care* 21, 774–781.

Ragir, S., Rosenberg, M., and Tierno, P. 2000. Gut morphology and the avoidance of carrion among chimpanzees, baboons, and early hominids. *J. Anthropol. Res.* 56, 477–512.

Remis, M. 1997. Western lowland gorillas (*Gorilla gorilla gorilla*) as seasonal frugivores; use of variable resources. *Am. J. Primatol.* 43, 87–109.

Remis, M., Dierenfeld, E. S., Mowry, C. B., and Carroll, R. W. 2001. Nutritional aspects of western lowland gorilla (*Gorilla gorilla gorilla*) diet during seasons of fruit scarcity at Bai Hokou, Central African Republic. *Int. J. Primatol.* 22, 807–836.

Remis, M. J., and Dierenfeld, E. S. 2004. Digesta passage, digestibility and behavior in captive gorillas under two dietary regimes. *Int. J. Primatol.* 25, 825–846.

Robbins, M., Sicotte, P., and Stewart, K. J. 2001. *Mountain Gorillas: Three Decades of Research at Karisoke*. New York: Cambridge University Press.

Rowlett, R. M. 1999. "Comment" on Wrangham et al. (1999). *Curr. Anthropol.* 40, 584–585.

Rowlett, R. M. 2000. Fire control by *Homo erectus* in East Africa and Asia. *Acta Anthropol. Sin.* 19, 198–208.

Secor, S. M., and Faulkner, A. C. 2002. Effects of meal size, meal type, body temperature, and body size on the specific dynamic action of the marine toad, *Bufo marinus. Physiol. Biochem. Zool.* 75, 557–571.

Speth, J., and Spielmann, K. A. 1983. Energy source, protein metabolism, and hunter-gatherer subsistence strategies. *J. Anthropol. Archaeol.* 2, 1–31.

Stahl, A. B. 1984. Hominid diet before fire. *Curr. Anthropol.* 25, 151–168.

Straus, L. G. 1989. On early hominid use of fire. *Curr. Anthropol.* 30, 488–491.

Tutin, C. E. G. 1994. Reproductive success story: variability among chimpanzees and comparison with gorillas. In: Wrangham, R. W., McGrew, W. C., de Waal, F. B. M., and Heltne, P. G (Eds.), *Chimpanzee Cultures.* Cambridge, MA: Harvard University Press, pp. 181–193.

Tutin, C. E. G., and Fernandez, M. 1985. Foods consumed by sympatric populations of *Gorilla g. gorilla* and *Pan t. troglodytes* in Gabon: Some preliminary data. *Int. J. Primatol.* 6, 27–43.

Tylor, E. B. 1878. *Researches into the Early History of Mankind.* London. PUB?

Ulijaszek, S. J. 2002. Human eating behaviour in an evolutionary ecological context. *Proc. Nutr. Soc.* 61, 517–526.

Ungar, P. 2004. Dental topography and diets of Australopithecus afarensis and early Homo. *J. Hum. Evol.* 46, 605–622.

Ungar, P. S., and Teaford, M. F. 2002. *Human Diet: Its Origin and Evolution.* Westport, CT: Bergin & Garvey.

Valero, H., and Biocca, E. 1970. *Yanoáma: The Narrative of a White Girl Kidnapped by Amazonian Indians.* New York: E. P. Dutton.

Westerterp, K. R. 2004. Diet induced thermogenesis. *Nutr. Metabol.* 1, 5.

Westerterp-Plantenga, M. S., Rolland, V., Wilson, S. A., and Westerterp, K. R. 1999. Satiety related to 24 h diet-induced thermogenesis during high protein/carbohydrate vs high fat diets measured in a respiration chamber. *Eur. J. Clin. Nutr.* 53, 495–502.

Wrangham, R. W. 1979. On the evolution of ape social systems. *Soc. Sci. Inf.* 18, 335–368.

Wrangham, R. W. 2000. Why are male chimpanzees more gregarious than mothers? A scramble competition hypothesis. In: Kappeler, P. M. (Ed.), *Primate Males.* Cambridge, MA: Cambridge University Press, pp. 248–258.

Wrangham, R. W. 2005. The delta hypothesis: Hominoid ecology and hominin origins. In: Lieberman, D. E., Smith, R. J., and Kelley, J. (Eds.), *Interpreting the Past: Essays on Human, Primate and Mammal Evolution in Honor of David Pilbeam.* Boston: Brill.

Wrangham, R. W. 2006. Food-softening and the problem of Middle Paleolithic cooking. *J. Anthropol. Archaeol.*, in press.

Wrangham, R. W., and Conklin-Brittain, N. L. 2003. The biological significance of cooking in human evolution. *Comp. Biochem. Physiol* A 136, 35–46.

Wrangham, R. W., Conklin-Brittain, N. L., and Hunt, K. D. 1998. Dietary response of chimpanzees and cercopithecines to seasonal variation in fruit abundance. I. Antifeedants. *Int. J. Primatol.* 19, 949–970.

Wrangham, R. W., Jones, J. H., Laden, G., Pilbeam, D., and Conklin-Brittain, N. L. 1999. The raw and the stolen: Cooking and the ecology of human origins. *Curr. Anthropol.* 40, 567–594.

Yamagiwa, J. 1999. Socioecological factors influencing population structure of gorillas and chimpanzees. *Primates* 40, 87–104.

Yamagiwa, J., Maruhashi, T., Yumoto, T., and Mwanza, N. 1996. Dietary and ranging overlap in sympatric gorillas and chimpanzees in Kahuzi-Biega National Park, Zaire. In: McGrew, W. C., Marchant, L. F., and Nishida, T. (Eds.), *Great Ape Societies*. Cambridge: Cambridge University Press, pp. 82–98.

Index